D1739195

THE ANCIENT ORACLES

THE

ANCIENT
ORACLES

MAKING THE GODS SPEAK

RICHARD STONEMAN

YALE UNIVERSITY PRESS
NEW HAVEN AND LONDON

For information about this and other Yale University Press publications, please contact:
U.S. Office: sales.press@yale.edu   www.yalebooks.com
Europe Office: sales @yaleup.co.uk   www.yalebooks.co.uk

Set in Minion Pro by IDSUK (DataConnection) Ltd
Printed in Great Britain by TJ International, Padstow, Cornwall

Library of Congress Cataloging-in-Publication Data

Stoneman, Richard.
   Making the gods speak: the ancient oracles/Richard Stoneman.
      p. cm.
ISBN 978–0–300–14042–2 (cl:alk. paper)
1.   Oracles, Greek.   2.   Divination — Greece.   3.   Greece —
Religion.   I.   Title.   II.   Title: Ancient oracles.
   BF1765.S76 2011
292.3′2 – dc22

                                                                    2010034993

A catalogue record for this book is available from the British Library.

10 9 8 7 6 5 4 3 2 1

Thee, the son of God most high,
Famed for harping song, will I
Proclaim, and the deathless oracular word
From the snow-topped rock that we gaze on heard,
Counsels of thy glorious giving
Manifest for all men living,
How thou madest the tripod of prophecy thine
Which the wrath of the dragon kept guard on, a shrine
Voiceless till thy shafts could smite
All his live coiled glittering might.

Ye that hold of right alone
All deep woods on Helicon
Fair daughters of thunder-girt God, with your bright
White arms uplift as to lighten the light
Come to chant your brother's praise,
Golden Phoebus, loud in lays.

A.C. Swinburne, 'Delphic Hymn to Apollo' (a free translation of the
Delphic Paean I, *Collectanea Alexandrina,* ed. J.U. Powell
(Oxford 1925), 141)

Contents

Illustrations and Maps

ILLUSTRATIONS

MAPS

Preface

The idea for this book arose from a series of visits to the western coast of Turkey from the mid-1990s, lecturing about classical sites on gület holidays with Westminster Classic Tours. A theme for a tour is always attractive, and as we visited at various times the sites of Pergamon, Erythrae, Didyma, Labranda, Claros, Cnidus, Telmessos, Olympos, Limyra, Patara and Sura, the importance of oracles as a strand running through the lives of the ancient inhabitants of the region insistently presented itself. What began as a light-hearted exposition of some remarkable phenomena deepened itself, as it began to take the form of a book, into an exploration of some intriguing and, perhaps, perennial features of the human psyche. Early listeners to these talks raised many pertinent questions and I am grateful to all the guests on those tours as well as to the Anglo-Turkish Society for inviting me to give an illustrated talk on the subject in December 2003. The receptiveness of Heather McCallum at Yale University Press to the idea gave me the impetus to produce the present book.

I am grateful, as always, to the libraries that have been indispensable to my research: the London Library and the Institute of Classical Studies. Since moving to Exeter in 2006 I have been able to make full use of the privileges afforded to Honorary Fellows of the University of Exeter, including its library and office facilities.

I am particularly grateful to the two anonymous readers for the Press, as well as to Rachael Lonsdale, for their acute and systematic reviews of an earlier version of the text. All faults that remain, as those who consult oracles know well, are mine and not those of the advisers.

Richard Stoneman
University of Exeter, 2010

Abbreviations

Note: The normal conventions for classical authors are followed: see Liddell-Scott-Jones' *Greek–English Lexicon* and the *Oxford Classical Dictionary*. I have expanded some of the more telegraphic ones for the sake of clarity. Works in Plutarch's *Moralia* are cited by their individual titles.

Standard abbreviations for classical journals may be found in the *Oxford Classical Dictionary* and *L'Année Philologique*. Note especially the following abbreviations of journals and other works.

ANRW	*Aufstieg und Niedergang der römischen Welt*
Ant Class	*Antiquité Classique*
AP	*Anthologia Palatina*
APF	J.K. Davies, *Athenian Propertied Families* (Oxford 1971)
BMC	*British Museum Coins*
CIG	*Corpus Inscriptionum Graecarum*
CJ	*Classical Journal*
Coll. Alex.	*Collectanea Alexandrina*, ed. J.U. Powell (Oxford 1925)
CRAI	*Comptes rendues de l'Académie des Inscriptions et Belles Lettres*
Delt Ch AE	*Deltion tes Christianikes Arkhaiologikes Etaireias*
DK	*Die Fragmente der Vorsokratiker*, ed. H. Diels and W. Kranz
GRBS	*Greek Roman and Byzantine Studies*
HSCP	*Harvard Studies in Classical Philology*
HThR	*Harvard Theological Review*
IG	*Inscriptiones Graecae*
IGRRP	*Inscriptiones Graecae ad res Romanas pertinentes*
JANES	*Journal of the Ancient Near Eastern Society*
JAOS	*Journal of the American Oriental Society*
JHS	*Journal of Hellenic Studies*
JRA	*Journal of Roman Archaeology*
JRS	*Journal of Roman Studies*
LdÄ	*Lexikon der Ägyptologie*
LSCG	*Lois sacrées des cites grecques*
Mus. Helv.	*Museum Helveticum*
P	*Papyrus*

PDM	*Papyri Demoticae Magicae*
PG	*Patrologia Graeca,* ed. J.P. Migne
PGM	*Papyri Graecae Magicae*
POxy	*Oxyrhynchus Papyri*
PSI	*Papiri della Società Italiana*
REA	*Revue des Etudes Antiques*
RFIC	*Rivista di Filologia ed Istruzione Classica*
Rh Mus	*Rheinisches Museum*
SEG	*Supplementum Epigraphicum Graecum*
SIG	*Sylloge Inscriptionum Graecarum*
Syll[3]	Ibid.: 3rd edition
Symb Osl	*Symbolae Osloenses*
TAM	*Tituli Asiae Minoris*
TAPA	*Transactions of the American Philological Association*
UPZ	*Urkunden der Ptolemäerzeit*
ZPE	*Zeitschrift für Papyrologie und Epigraphik*

Map 1 Mainland Greece.

Map 2 Western Asia Minor.

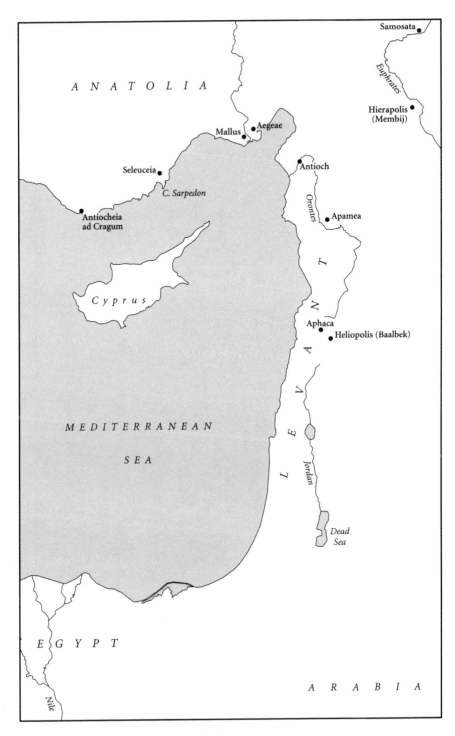

Map 3 South-eastern Asia Minor and the Levant.

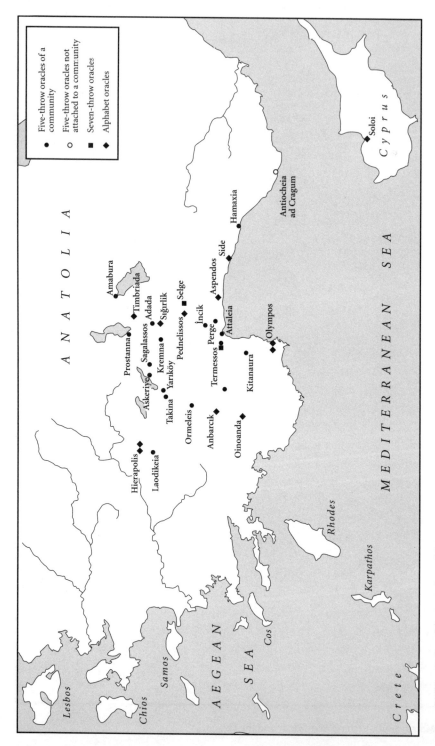

Map 4 Dice oracles of Lycia and neighbouring regions.

Introduction

Apollo will never fail me, so his tremendous power, his oracle charges me to see this trial through.

Aeschylus, *Libation-Bearers* ll.269–70 (tr. Robert Fagles)

Phoebus says clearly, 'Wait, friend'.

Dice oracle at Olympus, Lycia

In sickness and in fear, in distress and despair, before important life decisions and puzzling quandaries, people seek answers that introspection alone cannot give. The advice of friends may fail, or be no more reliable than one's own reflections. Even professional advisers may be suspect,[1] and sages, from the Hebrew prophets and the Arab *kahins* to Greek *mages* like Empedocles,[2] often concerned themselves with revelations rather than practical advice. One seeks an independent assessment of one's situation and chances. A higher power is required. But in most cultures, from antiquity to the present, people have had recourse to the distant gods for assistance, whether by prayer or by visiting, for example, healing sanctuaries like Lourdes in southern France. Such recourse to the gods is a form of divination (though divination need not involve gods at all).[3] In these cases, the afflicted seek to divine the opinion of the gods in the hope that a god's words will also offer guidance. This book is about the distinctive ways in which the ancient Greeks and their neighbours sought to ascertain the opinions of the gods, how they set about making the gods speak.

Over more than a thousand years, Greeks consulted oracles for guidance. Oracles and sacrifice formed the twin pillars of Greek civic religion, and both came to an end only with the abolition of all forms of pagan observance by Theodosius I in AD 395. But even then the oracles continued, sometimes attached to Christian or Muslim shrines, but more often in different forms. The consultation of random passages of sacred books (*sortes*) or of dream books is not unknown even now and the many methods of fortune-telling are another of divination, of the search for advice or for foreknowledge. The monotheistic religions in particular frown on divination and on any form of contact with the divine world that does not go through channels approved by the hierarchy, but that does not stop people from reading tea leaves, consulting Tarot cards, or seeking contact with the dead through mediums. The difference is that the gods are not imagined as speaking directly to the enquirer. Greek gods communicated in words.

It may seem remarkable that through all the centuries preceding the imposition of the Christian religion, the validity of oracles was rarely questioned. They were an integral part of the structure of religious beliefs and it was very hard to live in an ancient society without becoming involved with its religious practices. The numerous stories about oracles, which tend to make higher claims for the powers of the oracles than is attributed to them in the observable practices, are comparable to the tales that support belief in other religions – the hadiths about Mohammed, say, or the stories about Christ, Mary and the apostles in the apocryphal Gospels and Acts. But the narratives were not relegated to a separate category like hadith and apocrypha, which are not part of the doctrinal requirements of their respective religions; the Greek stories remained part of the belief system. In stories, oracles were often riddles: it was a test of human ingenuity to understand them, and failure was not the fault of the gods even if the outcome seemed different from what had been predicted. Direct attack on oracles as false is surprisingly rare in the classical world. It was not until the second century AD that sceptical discussions began to gather momentum – at just the same time as there is evidence of a renewed recourse to oracles throughout the Roman empire. The development of philosophical thought in the Hellenistic period led to increased debate about the truth-status of oracles. The problems of fate, foreknowledge and determinism began to be clarified in this period; the ways in which philosophers engaged with the generally accepted validity of oracles form an important theme of this book.

Christian writers, anxious to discredit every aspect of pagan religion, worked hard to prove that oracles were either fraudulent or the work of evil demons or 'false gods', a dilemma which was still not resolved when the French author Bernard de Fontenelle discussed the oracles in the seventeenth century. Nineteenth-century scholars likewise tended to assume that there was something 'false' about a religion that so little resembled the Christianity in which they were rooted, and often made clear their belief that the oracles were mere trickery.[4] All those who wrote about oracles (and who did not accept them as the words of the gods)[5] expressed their scepticism in one of three ways. From Aeschylus to Eusebius, and in the first modern writers to write on oracles, Anton van Dale and Bernard de Fontenelle, the criticisms take one of the following forms. (1) The promises and predictions of the gods are false, the gods are deceivers (Jocasta in Sophocles' *Oedipus Tyrannus*). (2) The utterances of the oracles are nothing but the result of trickery by human officials (Oedipus' attack on Creon in the same play; W.G. Forrest 1982). (3) The oracles are the work of false gods, evil demons (Eusebius, Fontenelle). (2) and (3) should be mutually exclusive, but in practice any sceptical writer may be found holding any or all of these views simultaneously, as do Eusebius and van Dale. Fontenelle states that the oracles are frauds, but 'it may be that God has sometimes permitted the demons to animate the idols'.[6] As Michael Wood writes, 'Just as Milton is not about to question the general possibility of oracling, Fontenelle can't quite get rid of the demons who didn't give the oracles, and is thereby robbed of the one argument that would close the case: that the demons didn't give oracles because there are no demons.'[7]

This book tries to go beyond these categories to assess the oracles not as revelations or misguided foolishness, but as ways of dealing with a problem. Michael Wood's book perhaps attempts a similar analysis of oracles but its ultimate message seems to be no more than 'Life is uncertain, so people need oracles.'[8] Can we do better than that?

Modern anthropological theory is more ready to accept the possibility of genuine 'belief' in beings whom no modern would accept as real. Increasingly it becomes clear that religious ideas are a result of the ways in which the human mind has evolved through natural selection.[9] In this respect, all religions have a similar intellectual status, and one need not concur with any of them (as I do not) to accept that all have been equally valid and 'true' for their practitioners. The study of ancient oracles, and their modern analogues, will tell us something about the human mind at its present stage of evolution.

Evolution of religious ideas in general, and of consultation of the gods in particular, is indeed perceptible even in the three thousand years or so of human history on which we can look back – from the Hebrew patriarch or Assyrian king whose god speaks to him in dreams or face to face, to the Greek gods who speak through intermediaries, and often in riddles, to the gods of the Neo-Platonists who utter cult instructions for achieving union with the divine. The trajectory concludes with the Christian declaration that all the pagan gods are evil demons, and the prompt migration of the oracular powers to Christian and, later, Muslim settings such as the shrines

of saints. This book tries to say something about the thousand years of the
Greek experience, and the new ways in which oracles were interpreted and
reinterpreted from the sixth century BC to the end of the fourth century AD.

SOURCES

Many of the oracles of the ancient Greeks have survived, but rounding
them up is a complex business and ascertaining their status is a challenge.
First, there are the oracles known to us from literature: the oracles to
Oedipus in Sophocles, and to Croesus in Herodotus, for example. These
come embedded in stories and there is always a question, even in the case
of those presented as history, whether these oracles were ever actually
uttered by a real-life prophet. Fictional oracles may not behave in the same
way as real-life ones. Secondly, many oracles are known to us because they
were famous in antiquity and formed the subject of discussion by philosophical writers – for example, those discussed in Cicero's *On Divination*
or in Plutarch's essays about the Delphic oracle. Like the first category,
these cannot be shown ever to have been uttered by a prophet, but the fact
that they were often discussed shows that they were the kinds of things
people believed oracles said. Thirdly, many oracles were inscribed on
stone, at Delphi, Didyma and elsewhere, or on lead, as at Dodona; many
oracles from Claros were also inscribed, however not at the site itself but
in the cities who sent the consulters. These at least we can be sure were
actual utterances. Fourthly, scholars from the fourth century BC onwards
made collections of oracles. Extant collections include Book XIV of the
Palatine Anthology, the fragmentary *Philosophy from Oracles* of Porphyry
(chapter 11) and the *Tübingen Theosophy* (chapter 13). One cannot be
absolutely sure that all the oracles cited in these collections were really
uttered, but there is a presumption that they were. These scholars were
followed in the modern world by E.D. Cougny, whose pioneering collection of three hundred-odd oracles culled from ancient sources appeared as
chapter VI of the third volume of the edition of the *Palatine Anthology* by
F. Dübner (Paris 1864–90). Modern collections of oracles from particular
sites have been made by Parke and Wormell (Delphi), Fontenrose
(Delphi, Didyma), Eidinow (Dodona), Merkelbach and Stauber (Claros)
and Oesterheld (Claros): for details see the bibliography. But a scholar who
wished to state that he had read every extant oracle produced by an ancient
Greek could still hardly do so with confidence. The gods remain elusive.

CHAPTER 1

Why Did the Greeks Consult Oracles?

THE SORT OF STORIES THEY TOLD: (1) OEDIPUS

One of the most famous of Greek dramas opens with a mission to the Delphic oracle to learn what is causing the mass sickness, or plague, afflicting legendary Thebes.[1] The chorus in Sophocles' *Oedipus the King* expresses the terror and hope of the suffering citizens:

> *Sweet-speaking utterance of Zeus,*
> *What have you brought from golden Delphi to dazzling Thebes?*
> *My trembling guts are racked with fear*
> *– hail Healer of Delos –*
> *as I abase myself before you.*
> *What new or ancient demand are you exacting with the turning years? . . .*
>
> *Lord of the light, I pray you to shoot your undefeated shafts*
> *From your twisting golden bow*
> *To help us in our need.*
> (151–7, 204–6)

The imagery of the racking pain of the sufferer recurs in the tension of Apollo's bow: the god is both the bringer of disease and its release, and it is also his words that will tell the citizens what to do to be freed from the plague. Later, in dialogue with Oedipus, the chorus leader states clearly: 'it is for Phoebus Apollo to tell us who we should be looking for, the person who has caused the plague' (277–9).[2]

The plot of the play, as is well known, revolves around an oracle given to Laius, king of Thebes, that his son would grow up to murder his father and marry his mother.[3] No choice is offered, no 'if' to let Laius off the hook.[4] Despite all the king's efforts to prevent his son reaching maturity, the word of the god was fulfilled, and brought about Oedipus' horrible fate. His end was the fulfilment of a decree of Fate – a conundrum that was to puzzle thinkers about divine prophecy throughout antiquity, for if it was predetermined, was the warning just a nasty trick by the god to shift the responsibility onto help-less humans? Oedipus' first inkling of what is happening comes in his words, 'Zeus, what have you decided to do to me?' (738).[5] The puzzle of the Oedipus legend, this perfect 'tragedy of Fate', will reappear many times in this explo-ration of the Greeks' relationships with their oracles.

The date of *Oedipus the King* is not known, but it will not have been many years removed from the plague that afflicted Athens in the early years of the Peloponnesian War (429 BC). At this time of distress people naturally recalled old oracles, and among them was a verse which the old men claimed had been delivered in the past and which said: *War with the Dorians comes, and a death will come at the same time.* There had been a controversy as to whether the word in this ancient verse was 'dearth' [*limos*] rather than 'death' [*loimos*]; but in the present state of affairs the view that the word was 'death' naturally prevailed; it was a case of people adapting their memories to suit their sufferings:

1 Oedipus consults the Delphic oracle. Still from Pier Paolo Pasolini, *Edipo Re*, 1967.

Then also the oracle that was given to the Spartans was remembered by those who knew of it: that when they inquired from the god whether they should go to war, they received the reply that, if they fought with all their might, victory would be theirs and that the god himself would be on their side. (Thucydides II.54, tr. Rex Warner)

As in Sophocles' fictional situation, here too those suffering the distress of disease turn to oracles: this time, not for an utterance that will bring an end to suffering, but, more fatalistically, for an explanation of that suffering. There is psychological truth here: to name one's affliction is, to some extent, to control it. Sigmund Freud's psychoanalysis was based on the presumption that to understand is to heal.[6] The oracle itself may be open to interpretation: the 'solution' of the oracle may be the solution of the problem, as Simon Goldhill points out in a subtle paper.[7] There is a continuum leading from prediction to explanation to warning to advice: if one could truly understand what the god was conveying, one's situation would be righted. So at least people might believe, although the idea that a thing is fated should preclude its being averted.

A further step, allowed for by most divinatory systems, is that what is fated can be averted if the sufferer knows what to do. The analogy is, in Babylon for example, a medical one: a symptom may portend a certain disease, but correct treatment can cure it. Omens are just warnings and can be averted by ritual:[8] they take an 'if' form. But an oracle is more solemn than an omen and harder to avert. One reaction may be to cast doubt on the truthfulness of oracles, as Jocasta does in *Oedipus*: 'pay no heed to such hoaxes. When a god wants something to happen, he has no need of dark doings. It will all come into the light.' The youthful Voltaire's Jocasta, in his *Oedipus* (which ran for forty-five nights in 1718), goes even further: she has the last word in the play, showing the radical scepticism you would expect from that author:

Priests, and you Thebans, who were once my subjects,
Honour my ashes, and remember ever,
That midst the horrors which oppressed me, still,
I could reproach the gods; for heaven alone
Was guilty of the crime, and not Jocasta. (tr. Tobias Smollett)

Scepticism like Jocasta's is rare in Greek literature, but a pregnant example is Thetis' anguished rage at Apollo's deception of her in a lost play of Aeschylus: 'I believed that Phoebus' mouth divine, filled with the breath of prophecy, could not lie. But he himself, the singer . . . is now the slayer of my son' (tr. Paul Shorey).[9]

The people of Thebes or of Athens could not, surely, be to blame for their own misfortune: easier to lay the blame on a supernatural power that had deserted them or in some way had it in for them. How could they get the god on their side, or at least get him to tell the truth?

This complex mixture of uncertainty, fear and apprehension of possible guilt may be among the basic impulses to religious belief, and the latter can easily shade into an impulse to deny the gods or to accuse them of plain malice. All these things are evinced in the practice of oracle consultation to a greater or lesser extent throughout world history. Yet, as Pascal Boyer writes in *Religion Explained*: 'Religion does not explain misfortune, it is the way people explain misfortune that makes religion easier to acquire (197).' One of the methods of explanation is to create a cause and effect story, and the agent, obviously not visible to us, is predicated as being an outsider but also a person – a god.

The Sort of Stories they Told (ii): Alexander

Asking the gods what to do is not a long step from asking a god to foretell the future, and this fortune-telling aspect of oracles is evident in many stories – especially, as it happens, ones about kings and rulers. Many of the best-known focus around one of the most famous persons of antiquity, Alexander the Great. Instead of questions of civic or general import, Alexander poses an intensely personal one. When he was founding Alexandria (332/1BC), according to the *Alexander Romance*, one of the first questions the Macedonian king put to his newly discovered god, Sarapis, was 'Lord, show me also, when and how I am going to die.' The god replied:

> *It is better for a mortal man, and more honourable,*
> *And less painful, not to know in advance*
> *The time appointed for his life to end.*
> *Men, being mortal, do not understand*
> *That this rich, varied life is endless, as long*
> *As they have no knowledge of its misfortunes.*

Seneca could not have put it better.[10] Perhaps Marcus Aurelius was thinking of Alexander's desire for immortality[11] when he wrote, loftily, 'Go to now and talk to me of Alexander, Philip and Demetrius of Phalerum. If

2 Alexander the Great prays to Sarapis before the founding of Alexandria, fourteenth century, from MS D of the *Alexander Romance*.

they saw what Universal Nature willed and went to school with her, I will follow; but if they were mere grandiose performers, no one has condemned me to imitate them.' Still, Alexander's request was one that has preoccupied many before and since; and scenes of this kind occur so frequently in classical writings that he might even be thought to have set a kind of fashion. Certainly he was not the first, though the only historical characters of an earlier date than Alexander to be recorded are the historical pharaoh Mycerinus and the legendary one Thulis.

The story pattern perhaps originated in Egypt.[12] Herodotus (2.133) writes of Mycerinus (Menka'ure, fourth Dynasty, *c*.2600 BC):

He received an oracle from the city of Buto [the most reliable of Egyptian oracles according to Herodotus, 2.152.3] that he had only six more years to live and would die sometime within the seventh year. He thought that this was dreadful, and he sent emissaries to the oracles with an indignant reproach for the god. He protested the fact that his father and uncle, both of whom had closed the sanctuaries, ignored the gods, and ruined men's lives, had lived a good many years, while a god-fearing man like himself was going to die so soon. A second message came from the oracles, explaining that it was precisely because he was a god-fearing man that his life was being cut short – that he had not behaved as he should. Egypt was supposed to suffer for a hundred and fifty years, and his two predecessors had understood that, while he had not. When Mycerinus received this message and realized that his fate had already been sealed, he had plenty of lamps made, so that he could light them at nightfall, and drink and carouse without stopping all day and all night; he also used to roam through the marshes and groves, and anywhere else that he heard was a particularly good place to take pleasure. His plan was to prove the oracle wrong: by turning his nights into days, he hoped to convert his six years into twelve.

The Byzantine encyclopaedia Suda tells us a story of Thulis (s.v.), who approached the oracles with similar high expectations of the god's favour, and received a similar comeuppance:

> This man was ruler of all Egypt even as far as Ocean and he called one of the islands therein Thule after his own name. Elevated by his successes, he repaired to the oracles of Sarapis and, after making sacrifice, asked the following question. 'Tell us, O mighty with fire, O undeceiving, O blessed one, who directs the paths of the air, who before I ever became king ever ruled so widely? And will there ever be the like after me?' An oracle was given to him as follows: 'first God, then the Word and the Spirit with them; everything is born along with them and tends to unity in Him [?]. His power is eternal. Go with swift feet, O mortal, treading out the unknown course of your life.' As he left the oracle, Thulis was murdered by his own people in the land of the Africans.[13]

The same story is told by the Byzantine chronicler John Malalas (2.3), who also informs us that Thulis was successor to Horus as king of Egypt. Though set in the legendary past, the story betrays its late and Christian origins by the identity of the god consulted, and the theology he puts forth. Still, the core of the story is no doubt old. Alexander seems to have learnt his longing for immortality from the endless afterlives of the Pharaohs to whose company he arrogated himself. Alexander's mother, Olympias, made dedications at the oracular shrines of Dodona[14] and Delphi,[15] and her marriage may have followed consultation of the oracles at Samothrace where she and Philip of Macedon met, but no sources mention any questions that she put, or suggest the kind of angst that her son exhibits in this fictional episode.[16]

Even Alexander's own best-known oracle consultation, at the shrine of Ammon at Siwa, did not seek an answer to this question: he was interested to know whether the murderers of his father had all been punished, whether he was really the son of Zeus (or Ammon) and would conquer the whole world.[17] He did not in this case emulate the conduct of his admired queen Semiramis, who 'went to the oracle of Ammon to enquire of the god regarding her own end. And the account runs that the answer was given her that she would disappear from among men and receive undying honour among some of the peoples of Asia, and that this would take place when her son Ninyas should conspire against her.'[18] So we may assume that such stories belong to the realm of fiction, but reflect the kind of concerns that interested people in the Hellenistic age.

Like oracles of civic import, these can also turn riddling, as the story about Alexander's successor Seleucus shows. He consulted the oracle at Didyma 'to enquire about his return to Macedonia' and received the reply, 'Do not hurry back to Europe; Asia will be much better for you.'[19] Other similar stories and omens probably come from a lost *Seleucus Romance.* At some undetermined time, presumably later, Seleucus once 'specially consulted an oracle about his death' and received the answer, 'If you keep away from Argos you will reach your allotted year, but if you approach that place you will die before your time.' This of course turns out to be an oracle with an unexpected outcome, since who would have guessed that there was a place called Argos in the neighbourhood of Lysimacheia, where an altar had been constructed by the Argonauts? 'As he was still listening to this story, he was killed by Ptolemy, who stabbed him in the back.'[20]

Alexander the Molossian was caught out in the same way: 'He was deceived by the oracle at Dodona, which bade him be on his guard against Acheron and Pandosia; for places which bore these names were pointed out to him in Thesprotia, but he came to his end here in Brettium.'[21] Compare also puzzling prophecies like Shakespeare's famous 'No man of woman born shall slay Macbeth'; at Sophocles, *Trachiniae* 1159ff., Heracles knows of a prophecy that no man living shall slay him. (It is the blood of the dead centaur that destroys him.)[22]

Such oracles were important elements in forming a popular idea of what oracles do. Though real oracles generally gave instructions in response to straightforward enquiries, the idea persisted that they could be the source of predictions which could change your life if you knew how to handle them.

ORACLES IN STORIES ALWAYS COME TRUE[23]

This book will focus on the way in which the Greeks consulted oracles and the ways they thought about them, interpreted them and argued about them. It will be as far as possible a historical and philosophical enquiry. But a great deal of the evidence we have comes from literature and takes the form of stories. It is certainly worth the effort to disentangle 'historical' from 'legendary' responses of the Delphic oracle, as Fontenrose (1978) does; but from the point of view of understanding the attitude to oracles, it matters relatively little. The importance of 'story' may be illustrated, again, by that of Oedipus. We have seen how and why the people of Thebes turned to the oracle; but what does the oracle do in the story? It turns the series of events into a plot, with its successive revelations and dramatic irony.[24]

Sophocles' *Oedipus* is not the only tragedy to revolve around the fulfilment of fate,[25] though it is the classic presentation of the theme. It combines several story patterns, such as the son who does not know his father, like Sohrab and Rustam or the story of Merope (Euripides' *Periboea*); the exposure of the 'dangerous' child, like Cyrus, Astyages (Herodotus 1.107–8); and the hero's dispatch of a monster (cf. Perseus), in Oedipus' case (uniquely) by his *cleverness*. What is unique in the Greek version of the story, as Propp (1975) points out, is the *prophecy*. The prophecy, he says, takes the form of a conditional sentence: if Laius' son grows up, he will kill his father; if Oenomaus' daughter marries, his son-in-law will kill him; if Cyrus grows to manhood, he will kill Astyages; if Danae has a son, he will kill Acrisius. To give a Roman example, 'When a dog speaks, Tarquin will be expelled'.[26] The conditional form, as has been remarked above, is of the same form as medical diagnosis,[27] and astrology. But for Oedipus, the prophecy cannot be averted. The oracle as devised by the author of the hypothesis to Euripides' *Phoenissae* contains no if-clause.[28] Laius asks for a son and is told what will happen when his prayer is granted. By the time Oedipus was born, there was no choice. But, although Oedipus knew the oracle, he misunderstood it. The audience knows better, and is in the position of the gods.[29]

The plot of Euripides' *Ion* is a kind of mirror-image of *Oedipus*. The orphan Ion discovers who his parents are, but the discovery leads to a happy family reunion. Oracles play an important role in the story. First, Ion's father Xuthus (not yet identified as his father), who is seeking a cure for his and his wife Creusa's childlessness, is told by the oracle of Trophonius that 'neither you nor I will return home from the oracle [of Delphi] without children' (406). Another story pattern is employed when Ion is told by Apollo that the first person he meets on leaving the *adyton* will be his son: it is of course Ion.[30] Ion is sceptical and tells Xuthus he has misinterpreted the god's 'riddle' (533); the chorus, too, thinks it may be a lie (685). It sets Ion at daggers drawn with Creusa, whom he supposes to be his stepmother, and she is enraged that this alleged by-blow of her husband's is to be brought into her household. The tension is resolved by a third revelation, this time by the Pythia herself (named *prophetis* in the text), who brings on the basket and tokens with which Ion was exposed. Creusa recognizes them, realizes that Ion is her son, the result of one of Apollo's rapes. In a striking phrase, Ion cries out (1422), 'O Zeus, what is this fate that hunts me down?' – an expression that might have seemed more suitable to the disaster that overwhelmed Oedipus. But the story ends happily, and every crucial turn in it has been generated by an utterance of the god or his mouthpiece.

Oracles always work in stories, because that is what it is to be a story. As Henry James wrote, we don't scruple to invent portents after the event, because that is how we make stories of the series of events that constitute our lives.[31]

The fact that characters in the tragedy of Oedipus rail against seers and oracles does not undermine the seers and oracles because the audience knows they are right, and Oedipus and Jocasta are wrong, as their fates will show. Sophocles' vision is not Voltaire's. The attacks on seers by Oedipus and Creon in these plays in fact reinforce the audience's faith because they know that the oracles' falsity is only apparent. Though to mistrust an oracle is a very Greek thing to do, apparent falsity may in fact strengthen belief by indicating to the believer that his judgement may be fallible.[32]

Stories are also an important buttress of religious ideas.[33] Stories have a mnemonic value, they help you to fix certain patterns (such as gods) in your mind. So stories about oracles are a way of emphasizing the power of the gods and ensuring that, in real life, people find it worthwhile to turn to them.

ORACULAR PRACTICE: SOME DEFINITIONS

The word 'oracle' is from the Latin *oraculum*, a thing spoken, which represents two distinct Greek words, both *chresmos* and *chresterion*. *Chresmos* is from the active verb *chrao*, 'to proclaim' or 'to warn' (always in an oracular context), and the middle form of the verb, *chraomai*, means 'to enquire of an oracle, to seek a response'. (It is distinguished from another common verb, *chraomai*, 'to use', which has a different root.) *Chresmos* is 'an oracular response'; *chresterion* is the place where the utterance takes place. The ambiguity of the English word, which can mean both, derives from that of the Latin, which is neatly summed up by Isidore of Seville in his *Etymologies* (15.4.3), *oracula dicta ab eo quod inde responsa redduntur; et oracula ab ore*: 'They are called oracles because responses are given from them; and "oracle" is from *os*, mouth.' In this book I shall perforce use the word 'oracle' in both meanings, but without losing sight of the Greek term in each case.

The word 'oracle' is also used to mean other things in anthropological and related literature. When reference is made to a Japanese 'oracle', for example, it is a person that is meant.[34] And there are many oracles, as we shall see, that do not involve speech in the way that Greek ones do. For these latter, 'forms of divination' might be a better term, but 'oracle' has become entrenched in such titles as E.E. Evans-Pritchard's *Witchcraft, Oracles and Magic among the Azande* (Oxford 1976), even though the poisoned chickens utter no word at all.

There are many other Greek words with a similar frame of reference. A *mantis* is a prophet or seer, one who knows the future (like Tiresias), and the thinking of the gods (Calchas in *Iliad* I), as well as other facts that are hidden from normal perception; but in historical times he is a member of a professional class of diviners, who were retained on every important civic and military occasion.[35]

A *prophetes* seems to be defined by a line of Pindar: *manteueo, Moisa, kai prophateuso s' ego*: 'prophesy, Muse, and I will interpret your utterances [in verse]'. Thus the *prophetes* at Delphi has been taken to have the job of recasting the Pythia's ravings as verses. But this was certainly not the role of the *prophetes* at Didyma, and the inference regarding Delphi cannot stand. It may be a rather loose word, like 'priest'.

Oracles are not the only means of penetrating the minds of the gods, though they were singled out by the Christian commentator Eusebius (*Praeparatio Evangelica* 4.1) as one of the twin pillars, with sacrifice, of the civic religion it was the Christians' mission to destroy. The Babylonians in particular developed a complex art of interpreting omens and portents, though a common response to such an omen may be to consult an oracle to see what it means.[36]

Dreams, too, often prompt the dreamer to seek an explanation for their puzzling and sometimes disturbing contents. Plato makes dreams a third way of contacting the gods.[37] A particular form of consulting the god in classical Greece was the deliberate seeking of a dream by *incubation*, sleeping in the god's sanctuary (see chapter 7). In Babylon, and in Greece and Egypt from the fourth century BC onwards, astrology became a complex art of prognostication of the future by the position of the stars, first at particular moments in history, and later at the birth (or conception) of individuals. This vast subject can only be referred to incidentally in a study of oracles, though its purposes and methods sometimes coincide.

Oracles need to be distinguished from omens. Omens can take over your life. Everything becomes a hidden message. The gods leave hidden clues all over the world.[38] It is one thing to be amazed at the sight of flames blazing up on Servius Tullius' head and to seek its meaning,[39] quite another to be alarmed because a black cat wanders by, or, in Theophrastus, because a mouse has gnawed a hole in a flour sack. Theophrastus defines 'superstition' as 'a desponding fear of divinities', and his superstitious man sees omens in everything. Ancient seers would have insisted that omens should be sought, not found everywhere. The same is true, *a fortiori*, of oracles: even cledonomancy (divination by utterances) requires the seeker to consult the god properly before listening out for the first utterance he hears on leaving the shrine.[40]

Oracles are one form of divination. An oracle is an answer to a question (though plenty of such answers were written down and circulated in collections which could be consulted at need). In many recorded oracles the question is unstated, unknown, or difficult to presuppose: for example a poem in the *Palatine Anthology* (14.113) is a prediction to Telesicles that his son (Archilochus) will become a great poet.[41] What did Telesicles ask the god? The oracle addresses him by name, so it must be a response, but the question is difficult to reconstruct.

Questions could be put to sources of wisdom other than oracles, but the answer would not be verbal. Diviners in Greece and Rome, as well as in the ancient Near East, and China, practised their arts on many public occasions, and their techniques took many forms: from the priests who interpreted the conformation of the livers of sacrificed animals (extispicy) and Roman augurs (who drew prognostications from the flight of birds) to more arcane practices such as lecanomancy (the use of a bowl of water to obtain visions of the future) and necromancy (summoning the spirits of the dead, who are for some reason supposed to be more knowledgeable about the future than the living).[42] What is distinctive about Greek oracles (and some Babylonian and Egyptian ones) is that the answer to the question is given as words of the god. The ideal is the direct epiphany of the god (as at Vergil, *Aeneid* 6.84–99, but this rarely happens outside fiction).[43] Extispicy may ascertain the will of the gods, and you can put your question to a pile of entrails, but the answer will not be expressed in words,[44] let alone in hexameter verses. Conversely, remarkable utterances may act as omens or predictions: one thinks of Balaam's Ass, or the moment when Achilles' horse speaks in the *Iliad*; but these animals are not gods and their behaviour is rather a miraculous omen than an oracle. The distinctiveness of Greek oracles can be thrown into relief by a fuller consideration of other forms of divination.

DIVINATION AND LOT

At the basis of divination lies the idea of the lot. As chance determines the fall of the lot, so the outcome is predicted. Plato, in discussing the rules for appointment of priests in his hypothetical state (*Laws* 6.759) makes the principle explicit: 'In all these cases the appointments should be made partly by election and partly by lot . . . . In electing priests, one should leave it to the god himself to express his wishes, and allow him to guide the luck of the draw.'[45] So the practice at Athens, where many important civic offices were in fact allotted in this way, was not just an extreme of democracy but a way of ensuring that the god's will was done. Chance is not chance but the work of a hidden mover. No wonder Chance came to be a deity in her own right in the Hellenistic age, and the subject of a treatise by the philosopher Demetrius of Phaleron. Chance is by its nature unpredictable,[46] but nonetheless what occurs by chance may look as if it forms a pattern.[47]

A cryptic utterance of the Presocratic philosopher Thales held that 'Everything is full of gods'. This is probably not a pantheist statement, though he may have meant that everything has seeds of 'motion' in it, the potential for transformation; but could he also have been thinking that every apparently inanimate object could be pressed into service to speak to us if we only knew how? Babylonians believed that everything in the universe was somehow interconnected.[48] Certainly something like this lies behind the theory of the Oracle Bones of ancient China.[49] These were carefully selected scapulae of oxen (an alternative method used the plastra of turtles, which had to have been washed up on the shore, not deliberately caught), which were poked in selected places with red-hot skewers until they cracked. The cracks were then read, either as a pre-literate kind of 'character' or their positioning was held to determine answers to a yes-or-no question. For example, 'Should the king attack Hsia Wei?' A crack on the left indicated No, a crack on the right Yes.

The famous *I Ching* of Chinese tradition works on a similar principle. The materials used are stalks of yarrow, of either full length or broken into two halves. Three throws of a die, or coin, are used, on the heads-or-tails principle, to choose each stalk, whole or broken, in turn. The inscribed side counts as yin, value 2, and the blank side as yang, value 3. Three yangs give 9, 3 yins 6, and other combinations in between are also designated yin or yang.[50] Yang gives a long line ———, yin a broken line – –. Then the throws were multiplied to give hexagrams consisting of six lines, either whole or broken, the total possible number of hexagrams being 64, like these: ☶ ☶, ☵ ☶, etcetera. The patterns into which these fall (with six rows

3 A late Ching representation of the legendary Emperor Shun and his ministers consulting the oracles of the tortoiseshell and the milfoil, 1644–c.1900.

of stalks, many thousands of combinations are possible) are then classified according to their meanings, so that a great many oracular utterances could be drawn from the throws. A notable feature of the system is its extreme complexity, necessitating the employment of experts to understand and interpret the patterns for the enquirer. Joseph Needham writes: 'The need for at least *classing* phenomena, and placing them in some sort of relation with one another, in order to conquer the ever-recurring fear and dread which must have weighed so terribly on early men. Any hypothesis would be better than none, but hypotheses which would take some of the terror out of disease and calamity there must at all costs be.' He also calls the method 'a cosmic filing system'.[51] The key feature is that at its heart is a Boolean algebra of yes-and-no, heads-and-tails. The *I Ching* is in effect a kind of computer, its operation an exercise in extracting the maximum complexity from a binary opposition. The procedure of oracles is sometimes described as 'rational'[52] or a precursor of scientific method:[53] that may be so, but it is definitely no more than an evolutionary stage towards scientific method.

Even an apparently simple procedure like the Zande poison oracle, mentioned above, is susceptible of considerable complexity. It seems simple enough that you go to the expert with your question, feed the chicken poison and if it lives the answer is Yes, if it dies it is No; but Evans-Pritchard describes how both the procedures have to be properly adhered to, and the answer has to be checked by posing more questions to further unfortunate chickens. (A Babylonian example involves getting a pig to 'choose' between two figurines: choosing the one tells you that your lover is diseased, the other that he/she is under an enchantment.)[54]

It is easy to multiply examples of this kind of binary divination. Schenke (1963) describes an oracle of Apis where the answers depend on whether the deity takes food or not; and the oracle of Aphrodite at Aphaca responded according to whether a sacred pool accepted or rejected the offerings of clothing that were thrown into it. (Some similar examples will confront us in Asia Minor in chapter 6.) Tacitus (*Germania* 10) describes a method among the ancient Germans in which two prisoners are set to fight to the death – a rather brutal form of 'heads or tails?'[55] – and Herodotus describes how the Getae, instead of tossing a coin to decide an answer, toss one of their countrymen onto a mass of upturned javelins.[56]

At its simplest this kind of divination seems like fortune-telling by tea leaves. At its most complex a modern analogy is the Tarot, where the frame of mind of both questioner and reader, the rules for the various patterns of laying out the cards, and the variable meanings to be extracted from the cards drawn, all require the elaboration of an expert.[57] The Babylonian diviner, for example, is a professional: unlike the ecstatic, he does not involve the gods in his procedure, but, like Apollonius of Tyana (*Life of Apollonius* 8.7), he is an expert at classification and interpretation.[58] For Plato (*Timaeus* 70d–72c) the god has written the message on the liver of the animal: an expert is required to read it, for it is not verbal.

Now the well-known oracles of Greece were not like this: or were they? All the famous stories of the Greek oracles tell of elaborate and sometimes riddling verse responses from the priestess, and foster the view of ancient Greece as an exceptionally verbal society. This is no doubt true, but in fact the Pythia at Delphi only prophesied on certain days; on other days the oracles could be given by lot. One envisages something perhaps as simple as the paper from a fortune cookie, with its banal and scarcely falsifiable message; but the questioner did at least have to pose a question first before drawing whatever the lot provided. At Dodona, too, a lot was used. An interpreter was required but the response was given by random means. A prophet(ess) spoke the god's words at Didyma and Claros, but fish gave the answers at Labranda and Sura (chapter 6), and dice could do the job in second-century AD Asia Minor (chapter 8). Nonetheless, at all these oracular sites a god presided, usually Apollo.[59] The inspired priestess was not the only vehicle of the god's words, but the god's words they always were. And furthermore they were answers to a question or request.[60]

THE VOICES OF THE GODS

The question then arises, why did (and do) people feel the need to seek instruction in this way in moments of crisis? Why is ratiocination not enough? Why do they think there are supernatural beings who can and want to give them guidance in this strange way? And why are the oracles so often hard to understand, or easy to misunderstand? One solution has been sought in evolutionary psychology, and presented in detail in the classic book by Julian Jaynes, *The Origin of Consciousness in the Breakdown of the Bicameral Mind*.[61] This begins from the phenomenon, common in schizophrenia, of hearing imperious voices telling the sufferer what to do. Having established that these 'voices' are located in a specific area of the right hemisphere of the brain which otherwise has little function in modern humans, Jaynes argues that this region is a vestige of an earlier stage of evolution when voices on the right side of the brain fulfilled the function in 'pre-conscious' man[62] which at present is carried out by the reasoning and verbal faculties of the corresponding area on the left side. Jaynes identifies the moment in human evolution, between about 3000 and 2000 BC in Mesopotamia, when the gods stopped speaking clearly to men, and finds it symbolized in the transition from the depiction of Hammurabi talking face to face to his god to that of a later Assyrian king kneeling in abasement before an empty throne. The gods had withdrawn, their voices had become unclear, and techniques were evolved to try to resuscitate their direct communication. In a vivid passage Jaynes explains the conquest of the Inca by the Spanish as the fate of a 'pre-conscious' people 'paralyzed by indecision' as their gods failed to tell them what to do in the face of the strangers.

4 'Hammurabi hallucinating judgements from his god Marduk' and 'Tukulti stands and then kneels before the empty throne of his god', c.1750 BC.

I do not know how one would ever prove this hypothesis, and the model does not seem to have survived intact, but Steven Mithen (1996) presents a somewhat comparable picture of 'the multiple intelligences of the early mind' as a 'cathedral' in which doorways are gradually opened up between the different 'chapels'.[63] Nonetheless, the suggestive value of Jaynes' hypothesis is considerable, just like Bruno Snell's earlier (1948) theory that Homeric man had no sense of himself as an individual but only as an assemblage of body parts. Like Snell's Homeric man, Jaynes' 'pre-conscious' man is aware of his internal organs which react in different ways in moments of crisis, and finds himself a field of play for, not just the adrenaline that fear produces, but the voices that doubt and anxiety call forth.

Can the oracles, then, be the voices of the gods, speaking or singing in verse (song is also located on the right side of the brain, whereas speech is on the left), which can be accessed by those with particular psychic dispositions? Socrates' *daimonion* is a striking candidate for a Greek manifestation. It would explain the recourse to shamans in certain part of the world, as well as the surprising reverence accorded by early Christians to apparently schizophrenic persons like St Antony and the Holy Fools of Russia (Ivanov 2006). Again, we should clarify some terms before proceeding.

Shamanism is defined by Mircea Eliade (1964) as a set of 'techniques of ecstasy'. 'By entering into trance states through communally recognized rituals, the shaman is able to communicate with spirits, travel the cosmos in search of errant or recalcitrant souls, and minister to the particular needs of clients.'[64] The commonly used term 'ecstatic possession' is in fact an oxymoron, for the implication of being a shaman is that the shaman's spirit leaves his body and goes wandering elsewhere to meet the gods and bring back their wisdom; while possession is the entry of the god into the priestess (or medium), who then speaks the god's words. The term 'shaman' properly belongs to the cultures of Siberia and North America, though Eliade sought to extend it to the whole world. In practice the distinction between ecstasy and possession can be blurred. As Du Bois (88) says, speaking of Korea, the act of inviting gods to speak through the shaman's body is conceptualized as a type of possession. Black Elk speaks of 'power from the outer world' that operates 'through me'.[65]

Speaking of the *Chaldaean Oracles*, Polymnia Athanassiadi writes:

> After years of spiritual training, an individual born with the gift of prophecy may become 'transparent to God' and, falling into a state of trance, utter verse in the language of the cultural tradition to which he or she belongs. The 'revelation' that will thus ensue may comprise one or many lines. . . . once the link with the supernatural becomes established, those around the 'prophet' begin to anticipate the utterances and are ready to take them down. Such was the practice in Babylonian temples . . . . It was also the case with Muhammad, and, nearer to home, with Ismail Emre (1900–70), an illiterate Turkish welder from Adana, to whom we owe more than two thousand songs of a distinctly theological content.[66]

Burkert (1962) argues that *goes* is the Greek for 'shaman', a medicine-man who can conjure the dead – but, like other forms of direct access to the divine it becomes suppressed as such access is institutionalized in the oracles. So it may be legitimate to regard the possession evinced by the Pythia at Delphi as one of a kind with the shaman's ecstasy, a leftover from an earlier age. Techniques are certainly involved, as many of our sources make clear: they include fasting from food and abstention from wine, as well as spiritual preparation – practices that can easily be paralleled among Native Americans, for example.[67] The use of mind-altering substances or 'entheogens' is regular in some cultures but controversial in the case of Delphi (see next chapter). However, ecstatic possession (as distinct from divine inspiration) does not seem to be the norm in Greek oracles, even though it was thought to lie at the root of Delphic practice.

WHY ORACLES WORK

What cannot be doubted, in the case of ancient Greece and Babylon, any more than in these modern examples, is that the voices were there, the gods were believed to be speaking. As Jaynes says, the Delphic and other oracles survived and functioned effectively for more than a thousand years. They can't have been simply trickery and mumbo-jumbo (though oracular practice certainly gave scope for fraud, and for accusations of fraud: see chapter 10). In practice living your life in accordance with external 'commands' is quite practicable and saves many anxieties. From this point of view it matters little whether the command comes from the draw of a lot or from the expert interpretation of a shaman's ravings: in either case responsibility is removed from the protagonist and the latter may thus be relieved of anxiety. A clear statement of this position is in Evans-Pritchard, who writes 'I found that . . . the best way of gaining confidence was to enact the same procedure as Azande and to take oracular verdicts as seriously as they take them. I always kept a supply of poison for the use of my household and neighbours and we regulated our affairs in accordance with the oracles' decisions. I may remark that I found this as satisfactory a way of running my home and affairs as any other I know of.'[68]

A modern fictional exploration of a similar approach to life, Luke Rhinehart's *The Dice Man*, presents a less sanguine view of life lived according to throws of the dice. (It is particularly pertinent in view of the dice oracles that will be discussed in chapter 8.) The book is an existentialist parable whose hero proposes that to be a Random Man kills all pride in self (107, 118, 187, 253, 330):

> 'Were a man to develop a consistent pattern of impulse control he would have no definable personality; he would be unpredictable and anarchic, one might even say, *free*.' 'He would be insane,' came Dr. Peerman's high-pitched voice from the end of the table. (251)

The Die, the narrator argues, is God (189), taking the extreme view that divine determination absolves the human actor of responsibility. (This is a position that most ancient theorists worked hard to combat.) The flaw in the narrator's scheme is that all the options given to the dice are devised by the actors themselves. If you decide that one of the options you give yourself on a throw of the dice is to rape your next-door neighbour (59, 186), that choice remains your responsibility. Another character, Dr Budweir,

> cured what seemed to be a hopeless case of death anxiety by every morning taking out a revolver loaded with one live cartridge, spinning the cylinder, placing the barrel at his temple and casting two dice. If they

came up snake eyes, he pulled the trigger. The odds each morning were thus two hundred and sixteen to one against his death. From the moment he discovered the dice exercise Dr Budweir's death anxiety disappeared: he felt a lightness such as he hadn't experienced since his earliest child-hood. His sudden death last week at the age of twenty-nine is a tragic loss. (260–1)

Trusting in oracles (or dice) as a way of deciding action raises large philosophical questions, to which we shall return repeatedly in this book. First, if the god commends a certain course of action as leading to a predictable result, does this mean that the future is foreordained? Or is there scope for changing it, for example by mending one's ways? In classical times, Stoic philosophers were proponents of hard determinism, and their arguments caused difficulties for those who wished to preserve moral choice, as well as raising the question of why it was worth consulting the god at all. It might be better not to know what horrors fate has in store for you.[69] A response given by many oracle experts is that 'fate' *can* be averted, and many people believe it without examining their belief: a clear state-ment is that of Lu Yun in his essay 'Fate' (1934):

> To my mind it is a good thing that the Chinese who believe in fate also believe that fate can be averted. Only so far, we have used superstition to counteract some other superstition, so that the final result is the same. If in the future we use rational ideas and behaviour – science in place of superstition – the Chinese will discard their fatalistic outlook.[70]

The belief that fate can be averted is not rational, for it is a contradiction in terms. However, the Babylonians saw the oracle (or omen) more like a medical symptom, which clarifies your situation and prompts appropriate action.[71] Ishtar can change fate, at least in stories.[72] Jewish Apocalyptic and the *Sibylline Oracles* share a view of announced fate as a kind of call to action: Jane Lightfoot writes (2007, 145):

> Throughout the Sibylline oracles there is a tension between what one might call conditionality and assured or preordained futurity. In the first, God's anger can be averted if a sinner repents, but is assured if he does not. . . . In the second, however, what will happen will happen anyway.

She cites John Collins: 'the fact that the end is determined adds intensity to the call for decision, but the individual's choice is not determined'.

Eusebius was to try to develop an argument for freedom of choice within God's omniscience (chapter 13): I don't think it works. 'Repentance' is a Jewish-Christian concept not appropriate to classical religion, but freedom of choice is. The case of Oedipus is still telling: could Laius (as Oenomaus of Gadara argued) have chosen not to have a son at all? Or was he simply bound by fate to suffer? Was the oracle that foretold Oedipus' doom conditional on Laius' choice, or did he have no choice?

A modern interpreter of the Tarot develops a similar argument:

> If one can successfully avert the prophesied disaster, that fact alone implies that the prophecy or divination was inaccurate. And if the event does not happen because of the evasive action, what exactly was it that was divined? . . . To account for the future's mutability, what we must discard is belief in a single fate and envisage a universe full of many potential branching futures. Which one becomes real . . . would then depend on whether a particular intervention does or doesn't take place.[73]

Secondly, even if the god foreknows what is to happen as a result of a particular course of action, is it in his or her power to change it or are they powerless in the face of a greater power, Fate? God's power to change the future is an essential article of belief if prayer is to be effective (Plato, *Laws* 10.885 argues that no one who believes in gods ever commits a bad act, unless he believes that the gods can be subsequently squared by sacrifices and supplications), and it further implies the possibility, in extreme cases, of miracles. Unlike the ancient people of Israel, and the Romans, Greeks did not countenance the existence of miracles. Wondrous events might take place, perhaps through a god's power, but they were consonant with the laws of nature. Indeed, one philosopher used the impossibility of miracles as an argument against the idea that gods had limitless power (Alexander of Aphrodisias, *On Fate* 30).

Thirdly, is the giving of advice tantamount to prediction? Many Christian writers later attacked the oracles on the grounds that they made false predictions: but it is not clear that giving predictions was what oracles (unlike Old Testament prophets) generally did. Their predictions were almost always conditional, and it was up to humans to interpret the conditions correctly. The humans who were let down might rail against the god, like Croesus or like Oedipus, but they had only themselves to blame. Oracles do not take away moral responsibility, they intensify and focus it. The moral problem becomes an intellectual one – always an attractive step for the intellectualizing Greeks.

These complex issues were explored in the kinds of stories the Greeks told about oracles, and thus the stories are of equal value with the known facts of practice in interpreting oracles as a religious phenomenon. The Greeks, as well as being great intellectuals, were great storytellers. The word *logos*, indeed, means both 'account, explanation' and 'story'.

People want their lives to become stories, not to be random and uncontrollable. Oracles, they believe, are there to help them: they are 'a sign of the gods' care for us'.[74] The chorus in Sophocles' *Oedipus the King* is terrified by the nihilistic vision of a world where the god's oracles do not work:

> *Never again will I go reverent to Delphi,*
> *The inviolate heart of Earth*
> *Or Apollo's ancient oracle at Abae*
> *Or Olympia of the fires –*
> *Unless these prophecies all come true*
> *For all mankind to point toward in wonder.*
> *King of kings, if you deserve your titles*
> *Zeus, remember, never forget!*
> *You and your deathless, everlasting reign*
> *They are dying, the old oracles sent to Laius,*
> *Now our masters strike them off the rolls.*
> *Nowhere Apollo's golden glory now –*
> *The gods, the gods go down.*
>
> (*Oedipus Tyrannus* 897–910, tr. Robert Fagles)

Jocasta's scepticism is not to be borne. The oracles are guarantors that the future will turn out as it ought: 'What was going to happen, will happen.' The phrase conveys a sense of inevitability along with the terror that in making any decision you may be simply advancing disaster. Humans cannot know. They hope that gods can and do, and will share their knowledge. A much later writer, Pausanias, sums up the idea, though he uses a Stoic term, 'Fate' (*Pepromene*), that would not have been known to Herodotus or Sophocles: 'the affairs of men, and not least those that they pursue with most enthusiasm, are concealed by Fate in the same way as pebbles are carried along in the mud of a river' (Paus. 4.9.6). Getting the god to speak to you is a way of poking your head out of the mud for a few moments.

CHAPTER 2

Possession or Policy: The Case of Delphi

*The maiden did not unleash the varied voice of her oracles calmly, as before,
but poured out an inarticulate cry in a multitude of voices, speaking Phoebus'
words from her bay-chewing jaws, imitating the utterance of the dark Sphinx.*
Lycophron, *Alexandra* 3–7

*I hear a voice and I am aware that it is speaking through my mouth, but it
is not my voice and the words are not my thoughts[1] . . . I remain seated and
feel the light touch of the veil of Apollo on my face. A warmth, like the touch
of a tender and experienced lover, rising within me.*
Bolina Oceanus cited in D'Este 2008, 192

It is inevitable that we should treat Delphi first, since it was the pre-
eminent oracle of ancient Greece and, perhaps, the reason for the reverence
accorded to oracles in general. But, as we shall see, it was strongly atypical
in its method of divination. Of the hundreds of oracles in ancient Greece,[2]
Delphi is the only one explicitly associated with spirit-possession, a
method of divination known in shamanistic cultures the world over, and
which seems also to have been prevalent in ancient Babylonia and pre-
modern China.[3] The voice of the god may have spoken more directly at
Delphi than elsewhere, but his methods were different from the norm.
Along with this unique style of divining, Delphi had a reputation for a
particular style of presentation: its oracles were obscure, riddling and
ambiguous (chapter 3). Many stories, especially in Herodotus, revolve
around the problems created by human failure to interpret the oracles
correctly. It should be said, too, in advance, that the oracles we know from
stories are of a different kind from those that are recorded on stone, where
the responses are generally clear and could be achieved through a binary
method. So, in the latter case we are dealing here with what people believed
about the way the oracle worked, not necessarily with its actual practice.

5 The Pythia seated on the tripod and giving responses; from Van Dale 1700.

A Consultation of the Oracle

It is surprising that no ancient writer gives us a straightforward account of what happened at a consultation of the Delphic oracle. Originally, consultation took place on only one day per year, Apollo's birthday (Bysios 7, in late February); but in Plutarch's day business was so heavy that two Pythias were in constant operation, with a spare one in reserve. Furthermore, consultation occurred all year round (except the three months Apollo was absent with the Hyperboreans), but access to the Pythia was on a few days only, and on other days the oracles were given by lots.

A series of rites was enjoined on the enquirer.[4] He should purify himself in holy water, offer a sacred cake and then sacrifice a sheep or goat, which constituted a fee, or part of one. The order of consultation came to be fixed by lot. Three types of attendant are mentioned: *hosios* (holy), *hiereus* (priest) and *prophetes* (interpreter is perhaps the best translation: Pl., *Tim.* 72a). From here on we are left to guess what actually happened. Roberto Calasso's account has the merit of being evocative.

6 Delphi. Temple of Apollo.

On entering the temple, bewildered by the throng of metallic objects
leaning from the walls and sparkling in the shadows you could sometimes
make out, in the background, the bust of a woman (and for many years
it would have been a young woman) who seemed to grow right out of
the floor. . . . Squatting on her tripod, as though on a stool in a bar, she
watched the new arrivals as they came into the megaron. The Pythia's
chamber, the adyton, was smaller than the main hall of the temple, and a
little over a yard lower. Beside it was a small booth with a bench where
those who came to consult the oracle would sit, unable to see the Pythia
as she prophesied among her sacred objects:[5] the tall tripod anchored to
the floor above a crevice in the ground, the umbilical stone wrapped in
the cords of a double net, the base of the tomb of Dionysus, a golden
statue of Apollo, a laurel tree that got a little light from above, a trickle of
water that ran behind her.[6]

Perhaps Pausanias' brief account of what went on at the oracle of Apollo at
Larissa is a good guide to the routines:

On the way up the acropolis is . . . a shrine of Apollo. . . . The statue there
now is a standing bronze called Apollo of the Ridge, because the place is

7 Aegeus consults Themis, who sits on a tripod in the posture of the Pythia. Attic red figure cup by the Codrus painter, fifth-century BC, reproduced from Eduard Gerhard, *Auserlesene griechische Vasenbilder.*

called the Ridge. He still prophesies today, and this is how his oracle works: there is a woman kept from the beds of men, who speaks for him; once in each moon a ewe-lamb is slaughtered at night, she tastes its blood, and the god possesses her. (2.24.1)

This sounds rather like the sexual union of priestess and god that also took place at Patara (Hdt. 1.182). John Chrysostom certainly thought that the Pythia had sex with the god;[7] but we should not perhaps place absolute reliance on Christian prurience and special pleading.

Two inscriptions discovered in 1903 and 1909 add considerably to our knowledge of the procedure at the shrine in Larissa. The first gives the names of two *promanties* and two secretaries who were responsible for substantial refurbishment of the shrine: they placed the navel-stone in obedience to an oracle, they moved the altar, added an offering box, improved the access road and rearranged the dedicatory statues, levelled the terrace, strengthened the temple doors and installed a silver couch. The second refers, besides the officials named above, to a *pyrophoros* (fire-bearer) and a female *promantis*. (On the analogy of Didyma, the *promantis* is the prophetic priestess herself; spares were kept in reserve as at Plutarch's Delphi.) One pictures a thriving sanctuary with substantial architectural features and a busy staff – a local parish church to the great cathedral of Delphi.

THE CASE OF KOROPI

Another oracular shrine whose procedures may be reconstructed in some detail is that at Koropi in Thessaly.[8] A decree was inscribed on stone in AD 117 regarding the adornment of the shrine:

> It is right and proper, since the *manteion* is old and was honoured by our ancestors, and because many strangers come to the manteion, for the city to take some additional care over proper order (*eukosmia*) in the sanctuary. The Council and people decided: When the *manteion* is being consulted, the priest of Apollo chosen by the city, and one each of the generals, and the *nomophylakes* (guardians of the law), and one *prytanis*, one treasurer, one secretary of the god and the prophet shall process; and if one of the appointed officials is sick or away, let another one be sent; and the generals and *nomophylakes* are to appoint three citizens of thirty or over as truncheon bearers with authority to apprehend trouble-makers . . . .

> When the aforesaid arrive at the *manteion* and have carried out the sacrifice according to the ancestral customs and have obtained good omens, the secretary of the god shall receive the memoranda (*apographas*) of those who wish to consult, and, writing down their names on a white board, shall immediately post the white board in front of the temple and shall call out and lead each in turn, unless there are any who have the right of precedence. If the one called is not present, he shall lead in the next, until the one called appears. Those appointed shall sit in the sanctuary decorously, in white clothes and ritually pure and sober, and receive the tablets (*pinakia*) of the consultants. When the *manteion* [i.e. the session] has finished (*sunteletai*), they shall put them in an urn and seal it with the seal of the generals and *nomophylakes* and with that of the priest, and shall leave it in the sanctuary. At daybreak the secretary

of the god shall bring forth the urn, show to the aforesaid the seals, open it, and calling out each person on the list shall give back the *pinakia*.

The examiners then swear an oath by Zeus Akraios, Zeus Koropaios and Artemis Iolkia that all has been done correctly.

What is most remarkable about this detailed description is what it does not say. What happened to the urn while it was in the temple? What did the god do? How were the answers revealed? It is easy to suppose that the urn was secretly opened without breaking the seals (as Lucian said of Alexander of Abonuteichos: chapter 7), but can we imagine that the priests just made up the answers? No one can have believed that that was the case. Yet the inscription tells us nothing of the mantic procedure within the temple. Was there an inspired prophet? Or a dice box? Like the rites of Eleusis, the inscription remains a mystery. Nor is it unusual in being hidden from us.[9] It is as much a riddle as the riddles of Delphi.

THE PYTHIA'S TRANCE

Delphic procedure was, as far as we know, unique. The priestess at Delphi, the Pythia, delivered her responses to enquirers by mounting a tripod (in which incense would normally be burnt) inside the innermost shrine of the temple of Apollo at Delphi,[10] going into an ecstatic trance (or, in other terms, becoming possessed by the god) and pronouncing her oracles. The common belief in antiquity about the sanctity of the place in which the oracles were pronounced is given by Diodorus Siculus, writing late in the first century BC, in his *Library of History* XVI.26:

It is said that in ancient times goats discovered the oracular shrine, on which account even to this day the Delphians use goats preferably when they consult the oracle. They say that the manner of its discovery was the following. There is a chasm at this place where now is situated what is known as the 'forbidden' sanctuary [the *adyton*], and as goats had been wont to feed about this because Delphi had not as yet been settled, invariably any goat that approached the chasm and peered into it would leap about in an extraordinary fashion and utter a sound quite different from what it was formerly wont to emit. The herdsman in charge of the goats marveled at the strange phenomenon and having approached the chasm and peeped down it to discover what it was, had the same experience as the goats, for the goats had begun to act like beings possessed and the goatherd also began to foretell future events. After this as the report was

8 John Collier, *Priestess of Delphi*, 1891.

bruited among the people of the vicinity concerning the experience of those who approached the chasm, an increasing number of persons visited the place and, as they all tested it because of its miraculous character, whosoever approached the spot became inspired. For these reasons the oracles came to be regarded as a marvel and to be considered the prophecy-giving shrine of Earth. For some time all who wished to obtain a prophecy approached the chasm and made their prophetic replies to one another; but later, since many were leaping down into the chasm under the influence of their frenzy and all disappeared, it seemed best to the dwellers in that region, in order to eliminate the risk, to station one woman there as a single prophetess for all and to have the oracles told through her. And for her a contrivance was devised which she could safely mount, then become inspired and give prophecies to those who so desired. . . . It is said that in ancient times virgins delivered the oracles because virgins have their natural innocence intact . . . [but, as a result of the rape of one of these virgins] the Delphians passed a law that in future a virgin should no longer prophesy but that an elderly woman of fifty should declare the oracles and that she should be dressed in the costume of a virgin, as a sort of reminder of the prophetess of olden time.

This story, which Diodorus probably drew from the fourth-century BC historian Ephorus,[11] became generally accepted in antiquity and is alluded to as standard by Plutarch in his *Decline of the Oracles* (42): as Plutarch was a priest of Delphi, we may presume the tale had considerable authority. But it raises a number of interesting questions. First, the reference to foretelling: as we have seen, oracles do not generally 'foretell', and the responses we shall look at shortly do not do so; but we may allow that Diodorus is speaking casually. Secondly, Diodorus speaks of the shrine as being one of Earth, though he does not mention the canonical legend which told how Apollo had displaced the ancient earth-goddess and instituted a new oracle of light and reason.[12]

Thirdly, the oracles are said to be delivered in a trance induced by gases from the earth. It is common for prophets worldwide to go into a trance, as we saw in chapter 1, and many entheogens have been used to induce the dissociated state: these 'culturally recognized tools for spiritual enlightenment'[13] include magic mushrooms, soma, datura, belladonna, peyote and ayahuasca, but never, it seems, gases from the earth. Furthermore, modern investigators could find no evidence of any kind of gaseous deposits under the Temple of Apollo at Delphi. This is not to say they did not exist in the past, for the famous toxic fumes of a certain cave at Hierapolis/Pamukkale, which guides demonstrated to nineteenth-century travellers with the sacrifice of unfortunate dogs, are also a thing of the past. In fact recent researches have found traces of ethylene, a narcotic gas, seeping through faults in the rock, which is prone to earthquakes.[14] So it is possible that the story was true, though the use of gases would remain unique.[15] If this is so, the fallback view of certain scholars, that the Pythia achieved her trances by chewing large quantities of Apollo's sacred bay, can be discounted. It would not have worked in any case, as has been proved more than once: Professor Oesterreich chewed a large quantity of laurel leaves 'and found himself no more inspired than usual',[16] and Jaynes repeated the experiment to equally little effect. Scholars remain divided as to whether the inspiration of the Pythia was simply a psychological state,[17] perhaps helped along by a solemn drink of holy water from the Castalian spring,[18] while Maurizio holds to an interpretation that brings the Pythia much closer to shamanic practitioners from other cultures.[19]

The trance state of the Pythia, what might be called spirit-possession, seems to be a given. The Pythia's ecstatic state is in effect a randomizing device, which generates various cryptic forms of utterance from gibberish to riddles and allusions.[20] Maurizio envisages utterances that are obscure but not gibberish, more like the prophecies of Cassandra in Aeschylus' *Agamemnon* (1214ff.). In Jaynes' terms (340), possession now replaces bicameralism as a means of accessing the divine will. As Plato writes (*Phdr.* 244b.), in the prophetic frenzy one's normal consciousness is suppressed. Prophecy by 'raving women' is found in other parts of the ancient world too, notably at Babylon, where the woman bears the title *muahhu*, 'raving', or *apilu*, 'answerer'.[21]

The god's position in the procedure must not be denied. It was the word of Apollo that the Pythia spoke. Nevertheless, if Diodorus' story is to be believed, or if it reflects common perceptions, the role of the god was secondary to that of the trance procedure. According to the myth, Apollo was a late arrival at Delphi, where he displaced a former oracle of Earth by killing Python in the mountain sanctuary. The Pythia appears on stage at the beginning of Aeschylus' *Eumenides* to outline the sequence of events, which is recounted in greater detail by the chorus of Euripides' *Iphigeneia in Tauris* (1244–82):

Where the wine-faced, bronze-scaled serpent,
His back sparkling in the dark leafy laurels,
The monstrous beast of earth, crawled
Around the oracle of the Gods of Earth.
Still a child you were, O Phoebus, still resting

In your mother's embrace, when you
Dealt with it and imposed yourself on the holy oracle;
Now you sit on the golden tripod
On the undeceiving throne, issuing prophecies to mortals
From the sacred adyton below the earth,
Neighbour to the stream of Castalia,
Reigning in your place at the centre of the earth.
When he displaced Themis the child of earth from the holy oracle-halls
   of Pytho,
Earth gave birth to nocturnal dream phantasms,
Which uttered to the cities the ancient dreams of men
And later ones, and those that were to come,
As they slept on the dark earth.

Christiane Sourvinou-Inwood[22] has shown how this story expresses in chronological terms a hierarchical structure: it is not history, but an expression of the superiority of the divine rational law of Apollo to the primitive rule of vengeance; dark prophecy, and reliance on dream-visions, gives way to divine guidance. Apollo's songs are a step away from phantasms towards reason. The riddles of Delphi are not signs of the dangerous malevolence of the gods, but aspects of Apollo's, and his father Zeus', concern for men and desire to help them. Legend held (Paus. 10.5.9) that a series of eight temples had been built for Apollo at Delphi: the first was made of laurel branches from Tempe, the second was made by bees out of wax and feathers; the third temple was of bronze, destroyed by a thunderbolt as Pindar's eighth *Paean* tells us. A fourth temple was built by the heroes Trophonius and Agamedes (whom we shall meet again), and the temple that stood in Pindar's day (and that stands now) was the eighth in the series. The long succession emphasizes how far in the distant past (or depths of the psyche) lay the ancient and terrifying oracle of Earth.

Was The Pythia Possessed?

Plato is our closest witness for the divine madness of the Pythia.[23] He identifies three types of madness (to which he later adds a fourth, the madness of love) (*Phaedrus* 244c). The first is *mantike*, divination, which he notes is etymologically connected to *mania*, madness; it is superior to omen-taking because it is heaven-sent, 'a valuable gift when due to divine dispensation'. The second is the 'telestic' madness of the rites of Dionysus, and the third is that of poetic inspiration, which is possession by the Muses. Omen-taking he calls *oionistike*, and often evinces a disparaging attitude to it. But divinely inspired oracular prophets are to be admired: they utter many truths under divine inspiration, but have no knowledge of what they are saying.[24] Plato accepts the validity of the oracles of Apollo at Delphi (*Rep.* 427bc), as well as those of Ammon and Dodona (*Laws* 787bd and 759de).[25] Robert Burton expressed a similar view with characteristic eloquence:[26]

> Of this fury there be divers kinds: ecstasy, which is familiar with some persons, as Camden saith of himself, he could be in one when he list; in which the Indian priests deliver their oracles, and the witches in Lapland, as Olaus Magnus writeth (lib.3 cap. 18) ecstasi omnia praedicere, answer all questions in an ecstasy you will ask, as what your friends do, where they are, how they fare, etc. The other species of this fury are enthusiasms, revelations, and visions, so often mentioned by Gregory and Beda in their works; obsession or possession of devils, Sibylline prophets, and poetical furies.

Blindness is common in shamans.[27] It is more than symbolic that Tiresias is blind; Oedipus' abuse of his blindness foreshadows his own. Who is really blind?

Some modern instances may be helpful, beyond that of Genghis Khan, who used to deliver his own oracles after entering into a trance.[28] A recent book collects the experiences of some modern self-styled oracular priestesses:[29]

> While you are possessed, you are blacked out. Almost like when you have a dream and you don't remember anything. Sometimes you have a 'dream' while you are possessed and it will be as if you were dreaming. I was first possessed at the age of six, and it was a dead ancestor who possessed me. (118: Sophia Fisher, referring to the Haitian Vodou (i.e. voodoo) tradition)

> The thing about oracular work that always sticks in my mind and often surprises me is how physical the experience is. . . . One very feminine and lovely high priestess that I know speaks always in a ladylike way, but she can deliver some deep and booming oracles at times! . . . I now know that there is a very physical sensation when I am giving an oracle, I can feel the energy of the deity entering my physical body (133, 134, 138: Kay Gillard)

> A word of advice is that it can be a good idea to practice this technique sitting down until you are more assured – for one thing this ensures that you will not fall over when the Deity arrives or leaves! (168: Emily Ounsted)

One thing that becomes clear from these testimonies of oracular possession, the voices of others speaking through the women, is that the oracles
are not 'responses' in the Greek sense. 'Oracular material can just be
gibberish or be so filtered by the subconscious mind of the man or woman
acting as a channel to be almost useless' (106: Vivienne O'Regan). It may
take the form of 'speaking in languages which were not understood by the
Seeress' (87: Janet Farrar).[30] When any kind of content is specified it seems
to be a revelation rather than a response: 'I have ended an Oracular trance
by mentally fighting my way back to consciousness by choosing to use my
own words to end the Oracle, and I have had the experience ended for me
as the Deity in question left rather abruptly causing me to fall over (fortu-
nately I was caught by the quick reflexes of the people present!)' (172:
Emily Ounsted).

It will perhaps help to keep the experiences of these women in mind
when considering what the Pythia underwent in her trances. It is also more
than tempting to regard such testimony as parallel to the recorded data
from anthropological investigations, and to account it an example of the
kind of splitting of the brain that Jaynes described. Such incoherent
mouthings will have had need of an interpreter, then as now, unless we
are to imagine, with Jaynes, that the compartmentalization of the brain,
becoming more marked over evolutionary time, has resulted in greater
unintelligibility of the divine voices.

Was the *Prophetes* a Crook?

Those who cannot accept that the Pythia was divinely inspired – or even
that, as a woman, she can have played any significant part at all – tend to
assume that the whole Delphi procedure was a sham – as Calasso says,
'some kind of collaboration between a team of Madame Sosostris and cold
Parnassian priests who polished up the metrics of the Pythia's groans, and
of course decided her meaning to suit their own dark designs.'[31] But did the
prophetes at Delphi have a central role in the transmission of the oracles?
Hugh Bowden proposes that the consultant took his question direct to
the Pythia, made what he could of her reply and wrote it down, and went
away to act accordingly. He dismisses the common view that the Pythia's
utterances were reformulated by the *prophetes* in hexameter verse.[32] In
Plutarch's discussion (402 B), it is taken for granted that the Pythia speaks
the oracles herself. The fact that several stories tell of bribery of the Pythia
(herself)[33] tends to support the view that her part was central. Also, the
story of Alexander the Great marching into the *adyton* and forcing the

Pythia to speak to him[34] implies a model where her direct utterance constituted the oracle to the enquirer. A similar story about one Philomelos[35] also
implies that the consultant has direct access to the Pythia, and it is her
unmediated word that constitutes the prophecy.

For Lisa Maurizio (1995, 86), the role of the *prophetes* was to help the
consultant formulate his question and to interpret the response as received:
that is, the consultant heard and took down the Pythia's words, and the
prophetes helped him understand what it meant. A problem with this view
has been that people are reluctant to imagine the Pythia speaking in hexameter verse. Bowden (2005, 34) regards it as impossible that an unlettered
peasant woman should speak extemporaneously in verse; but studies of
oral poetry have shown that this is just the kind of person who *does* easily
compose oral verses. Furthermore, Arab *kahin*s, who may sometimes have
prophesied in trances or epileptic seizures, uttered 'oracles' distinguished
by elaborate rhyme and recherché vocabulary.[36] The naming of the Pythia
as *prophetis* in *Ion* (42, 321) suggests no sharp distinction between the
woman and the prophet. At Didyma the oracle-speaker was called the
promantis and was probably a man before 334 BC, certainly a woman thereafter;[37] *prophetes* at Didyma was the title of the chief priest. The model may
be applicable to Delphi also. (At Claros the *mantis* was apparently a man:
Iamblichus *On the Mysteries* III.11.)

Herodotus (8.135) is explicit about the presence of transcribers at Ptoon,
and Plutarch (407B) refers to the *chresmologoi* who hang around the shrine
at Delphi and put the Pythia's pronouncements into eloquent verse.[38] If
Plutarch's observation is to be trusted, it may be that the Pythia spoke in
verse, perhaps of an unmetrical nature, or even in prose, and it was not the
prophetes but the freelance oracle-collectors who were responsible for
the verse form of the oracles that went into circulation. His Theon tells us
that people like Onomacritus would sit beside the shrine 'waiting to catch the
words spoken, and then weaving about them a fabric of extempore hexameters or other verses or rhythms as "containers", so to speak, for the oracles. I
forebear to mention how much blame men like Onomacritus, Prodicus, and
Cinaethon have brought upon themselves from the oracles by foisting upon
them a tragic diction and grandiloquence of which they had no need.'

Of the views that make the *prophetes* a vital intermediary, an extreme
interpretation is that of William Golding in his posthumous novel, *The
Double Tongue*. Set in the Roman period, the novel's hero is a priest, Ionides,
who runs Delphi as a political player though the trances of the Pythia are
genuine. 'I gave the answer we had agreed on, but you were still mouthing',
he says to her at one point. And again, 'As for me, – well, I suppose I am an

old fraud – or you could say a really honest man who understands what he is doing and' – here he suddenly injected passion into the contrary argument and opinion – 'and realizes that the only thing that matters is the oracle, the oracle, the oracle! Preserve that and all is preserved'.[39]

W.G. Forrest (1982) is in no doubt about the role of the priests: referring to Delphi's prophecies concerning the Lelantine War, the political revolutions of the seventh century BC, the Sacred War and finally the Persian War, he writes (320)

> That a divinely inspired oracle should produce accurate predictions of the future over a period of two hundred years and more is a belief that would tax the credulity of the most devout; that human priests should arrive at one original and correct answer in four would seem to be just about the right score.

In other words, the oracle was a purely political institution: Forrest discounts all consideration of Delphi's role or status, and also raises in one's mind the question of why anybody paid attention to it if it was found to be simply erroneous 75 per cent of the time. The fact that all oracles could be *used* for political purposes does not entail that they were *produced* for political ends.[40]

If all the Pythia produced was incoherent screaming, her response itself would simply be interpreted as a Yes or No. But Xenophon's question before his departure to war (p. 45 below), simple though it was, was not susceptible of a Yes or No answer; it required the names of some gods, i.e. an articulate response. One must remember that the Pythia only prophesied on a few days of the year, while the oracle was available for consultation in all the months except winter when Apollo was absent with the Hyperboreans. For many purposes a simple lot oracle could be used, which would indeed give a Yes or No answer. The Pythia could be expected to give answers with more detailed content, as did the Tibetan oracle at Nechung. Her importance is undeniable. More than thirty stories in Herodotus alone show events being shaped by the word of the Pythia.[41] It would not be surprising if she also had a staff to shield her from the direct access of the consultants, but I believe she spoke the verses herself – perhaps not very perfect ones[42] – and that the role of the *prophetes* here is an ancillary one. The Pythia's riddles were her own.

CHAPTER 3

The Riddles of the Pythia

The Lord whose oracle is in Delphi neither speaks out nor conceals, but gives a sign.

Heraclitus fr. 14 Marcovich

Hide these from me, as more unutterable than the unutterable: for the gods did not prophesy about them plainly, but through riddles.

Porphyry, *Philosophy from Oracles*, fr. 305 Smith

THE ORACLE AS RIDDLE

I turn now from what happened at the oracle to the stories that enshrined what people believed about the powers of the oracle. Herodotus' story of King Croesus of Lydia constitutes a virtually independent 'oracular romance',[1] and raises most of the questions that bedevilled Greek thinking about oracles for the next millennium. Croesus was the most successful of kings and regarded himself as not only the wealthiest but the happiest of men. He was distinguished also for his piety to the gods, and notably for his generosity to the shrine of Apollo at Delphi. He adorned it with many gifts and regarded Apollo as his special protector. Yet all this did not save him from defeat, and almost execution, at the hands of King Cyrus of Pessia. Following this disaster, Croesus sent envoys to Delphi to remonstrate with the god,

> enjoining them to lay his fetters upon the threshold of the temple, and ask the god, 'If he were not ashamed of having encouraged him, as the destined destroyer of the empire of Cyrus, to begin a war with Persia, of which such were the first-fruits?' As they said this they were to point to the fetters; and further they were to inquire, 'if it was the wont of the Greek gods to be ungrateful?'

9 Preparation for rendering and receiving responses at Delphi. From Van Dale 1700.

The Lydians went to Delphi and delivered their message, on which the Pythia is said to have replied – 'It is not possible even for a god to escape the decree of destiny. Croesus has been punished for the sin of his fifth ancestor [Gyges] who, when he was one of the bodyguard of the Heraclidae, joined in a woman's fraud and, slaying his master, wrongfully seized the throne. Apollo was anxious that the fall of Sardis should not happen in the lifetime of Croesus, but be delayed to his son's days; he could not, however, persuade the Fates. All that they were willing to allow he took and gave to Croesus. Let Croesus know that Apollo delayed the taking of Sardis three full years, and that he is thus a prisoner three years later than was his destiny. Moreover it was Apollo who saved him from the burning pyre. Nor has Croesus any right to complain with respect to the oracular answer which he received. For when the god told him that, if he attacked the Persians, he would destroy a mighty empire, he ought, if he had been wise, to have sent again and enquired which empire was meant, that of Cyrus or his own; but if he neither understood what was said, nor took the trouble to seek enlightenment, he has only himself to blame for the result. Besides, he had misunderstood the last answer which had been given him about the mule. Cyrus was that mule . . . his mother a Median princess, and his father a Persian and a subject . . . .

Such was the answer of the Pythia. The Lydians returned to Sardis and communicated it to Croesus, who confessed, on hearing it, that the fault was not the god's. Such was the way in which Ionia was first conquered, and so was the empire of Croesus brought to a close.

Herodotus' vivid narrative encapsulates many of the concerns and anxieties that presented themselves to a Greek in face of the treatment of men at the hands of the gods. At first blush, it seems that the gods have it in for men: reversal of fortune is the result of divine *phthonos* or envy/malice.[2] Humans are not to get above themselves, lest they put themselves on a level with the happy gods. The Pythia's reply here shows that the position is much more complicated.

Herodotus is no philosopher and does not lay out a theory of divine power: his unexamined but deeply rooted assumption is that human life is a wheel,[3] on which a man may move from fortune to misfortune without apparent cause; a cause, however, underlies his fate, even if it is only expressed as 'what was going to happen, happened' (as in the case of Polycrates, 3.40). (This is different from the belief that emerges in tragedy and later: 'what happened, [happened because it] had to happen.') You may strive to take action opposite to the action which the god tells you will lead to disaster, but through misunderstanding the oracle you do just what you were trying to avoid.

First, Croesus could not have avoided misfortune, because of the curse laid on his ancestor Gyges: there was absolutely nothing he could do, or could have done, about this, and he must just suffer (1.13.2, Fontenrose 1978, Q 96). No one can escape his fate, and even if you try to avoid the doom of which you are warned, you will find that your efforts are to no avail because the result foreseen by the god or foreordained by fate[4] comes about anyway. The oracle is always right.[5] Furthermore, this lets other participants in the action off the hook: in 6.135.2 Timo's assistance to the attacker Miltiades was not blameworthy because Miltiades was fated to do this evil thing which was in turn to lead to his undoing.

Secondly, the god is not all-powerful: he entered into negotiations with the Fates, but they would not let Apollo change what was destined, though he could modify its timing and even its manner. Croesus was rescued from the pyre on which he would, one supposes, have died, so his gifts and piety were not altogether vain. The story is thus one of what A. Moreau (1990) has characterized as 'myths of useless precautions': fate cannot be averted, and, as Herodotus often puts it, 'what was going to happen, happened'. Oracles in stories always come true.

Thirdly, Croesus had not tried hard enough to understand the oracle,[6] and made an impetuous decision. Pride and haste lead him to a single interpretation of this pronouncement, and his action leads to his doom. His impetuousness – a moral failing – is expressed as an intellectual one, in that he failed to seek clarification of an utterance he had not perhaps even seen as ambiguous. As Sir Thomas Browne expressed it: 'Croesus . . . deceived himself by an inconsiderate misconstruction of his oracle, that if he had doubted, he should not have passed it over in silence, but consulted again for an exposition of it'.[7]

Just sixteen years before Croesus' fall in 547/6 BC, on the other side of Asia, Sun Wenzi the Lord of Wei consulted the Oracle Bones and received a similarly ambiguous answer: 'There is a fellow who goes out to campaign but loses his leader'. Unlike Croesus, Sun Wenzi made a point of consulting an expert about who was meant; reassured, he went on to capture his enemy.[8]

Which leads us to the question the Pythia does not answer (nor did Croesus clearly pose it): Why would the god make his answer so difficult to understand? Why would he, in effect, cheat you? Is he simply shirking his responsibility, dumping his worshipper in it? Ambiguity is the defining feature of so many oracles, from the Pythia's pronouncements to that in Shakespeare's *The Winter's Tale* (II.ii. 134–6: 'The king shall live without an heir, if that which is lost be not found'). This is a criticism that philosophical and Christian authors levelled at the gods of the oracles on the basis of stories like this,[9] and Croesus might justifiably have felt that he deserved a clearer response for his gifts. It begs the question of whether the gods have any responsibility to humans, a question to which the answer is, to those who look with the coldest eye,[10] No.

That conclusion – malice of the gods – is the one to which writers with an existential bent like the tragedians would push the argument. Plutarch, in his treatise *Why the Oracles at Delphi are no longer given in verse* (407D), has a more subtle answer. He connects it to the much greater political importance of the Oracle in the past, and suggests that it was not prudent always to give clear-cut advice to political leaders: 'it was not to the advantage of those concerned with the oracle to vex and provoke these men by unfriendliness through their hearing many of the things they did not wish to hear'. That is, it was better to let Croesus blame himself for misunderstanding the oracle than to tell him outright that a campaign against Persia would fail. Plutarch's argument allows for considerable human intervention in the process, since he implies that it is not the god as such that is the source of the obscurity but the staff who provided the answer that the consultant took away. The ambiguity protects both the speakers and the god, as Eusebius (*PE* 5.23) was quick to point out as evidence of failure.

Plutarch elsewhere (*On the E at Delphi*, 384ff.) suggests that there are in fact two types of oracle: one offers help in distress, while the other is simply a riddle for the curious. This seems rather to evade the issue: how would you know which is which? Plutarch is undermining his own position.

A third view may regard ambiguity as an essential feature of statements about the future, which is what oracles are. Ambiguity is also inherent in Babylonian divination, as Bottéro shows (1974,182ff.), referring to the 'polyvalence of the apodosis': but he is speaking of omens rather than oracles, and the latter, being verbal, ought, one might suppose, to be clear. But the future is obscure, and the obscurity of the oracle becomes a metonym of the obscurity of the future.[11] The nature of the riddle is to be metonymic – the kenning, which expresses A through B, is another form of the riddle – and the interpreter of an oracle is matching an enigmatic text to an enigmatic situation.[12] Orpheus, in the Derveni Papyrus (c.7) 'says momentous things in riddles', and Heraclitus, according to Diogenes Laertius 9.6, shrouded his doctrines in obscure language so that people would take them more seriously. To answer a riddle correctly can be a matter of life and death, as Oedipus found when he encountered the Sphinx;[13] and the form of folktale known as the *Halsrätsel* has been explored by Johan Huizinga.[14] When the future is dark and dangerous, it is perhaps too glib to expect the god to get you out of it. To misinterpret the *world* can also be fatal. The lesson of ambiguity is that, if you keep your wits about you, and the gods on your side, you may reach a successful conclusion,

Ancient Greeks often seem to write and behave as if anything puzzling or obscure is actually a warning or guidance in disguise. Thus the body of the shaman Epimenides was preserved by the Spartans, in accordance with an oracle, because of the tattoos that covered its surface (Epimenides DK 3A2). 'The skin of Epimenides' became proverbial for something hard to understand.[15] It was assumed that the tattoos *had* a meaning, which could be elicited by the wise.

The riddling character of oracles is further emphasized by the fact that they are composed in hexameter verse. Peter Struck[16] shows how there is a continuity with a certain type of literary interpretation of hexameter poetry such as Homer's. Poetry is often identified with prophecy, for example in the Derveni Papyrus and by Plato, *Symposium* 192d: 'the soul prophesies and speaks in riddles'.[17] In *Charmides* 164e he writes that 'God, like a prophet, expresses this in a sort of riddle, for "Know thyself" and "be temperate" are the same, as I maintain.' The oracle-monger who pokes his nose in at the foundation of Cloud-Cuckoo-Land in Aristophanes' *Birds* (967 ff.) also speaks in riddles, using the common prophecy pattern, 'if x then y'.

A dream can function in the same way as an oracle. Thyamis' dream in Heliodorus 1.18 is a riddle which he interprets incorrectly: the goddess appears to him and announces, 'You will have her and have her not; you will be a wrongdoer and slay your guest; yet she will not be slain.' Only the course of events shows that the goddess was not talking – as she seemed to be – nonsense.

For everyday purposes people would turn to the oracle in the hope of guidance less fraught with potential doom than Croesus' was. Xenophon's account of his consultation of the Delphic oracle before joining Cyrus' expedition against the Persian king is the *locus classicus*:

> Socrates . . . recommended Xenophon to go to Delphi and to consult the god on the question of the expedition. Xenophon went there and asked Apollo the following question: 'To what God shall I pray and sacrifice in order that I may best and most honourably go on the journey I have in mind, and return home safe and successful?' Apollo's reply was that he should sacrifice to the appropriate gods, and when Xenophon got back to Athens he told Socrates the oracle's answer. When Socrates heard it he blamed him for not first asking whether it was better for him to go on the expedition or to stay at home; instead of that he had made his own decision that he ought to go, and then inquired how best he might make the journey. 'However,' he said, 'since this was the way you put your question, you must do what the god has told you.' (Xen. *Anab.* 3.1)

TESTING THE ORACLE

Getting the question right, and not begging the question, put the onus on the consultant to think clearly about the problem before approaching the god. It was, however, prudent to check the credentials of your oracle as well, as another story in Herodotus makes clear. Again it concerns Croesus. The king decided to test all the oracular shrines by posing them the same question in a sealed casket: Delphi was the only one (apart from that of Amphiaraus) that successfully revealed to Croesus its knowledge of what he was doing at the precise moment the question was unfolded (the synchronization involved is startling): he was boiling a tortoise and a kid together in a bronze cauldron. One might feel that the god would resent having his time wasted with obvious trick questions of this kind – he was not a performing monkey – but this problem does not seem to have arisen for Herodotus. In fact, the practice of testing the oracle is, cross-culturally, a very common one.

Another story in Herodotus (8.133–6) tells how the Persian general Mardonius sent a man called Mys to tour all the oracles of Boeotia seeking for signs relating to his forthcoming campaign in Greece; when Mys came to Ptoon, the oracle prophesied in his own language, namely Carian. Herodotus does not tell us what the prophecy was, but the implication is that this is the one Mardonius chose to follow: 'and trusting in the oracles he sent Alexander son of Amyntas to Athens [seeking an alliance].'

Croesus' procedure may be compared with that of Sennacherib, for he too consulted several diviners.[18] Mesopotamian divinations were normally double-checked, as were dreams (chapter 7). But one might also set a trick question to one's chosen oracle. For example, someone asked the Tibetan oracle at Nechung, 'Someone born in a sheep-year is very sick. What should be done with him? Please give a clear answer':

> The recipient was already an oracle-priest of some standing, and in his next trance he produced an equally enigmatic reply: 'If possible, buy new ones. If not, have them repaired and you will still be able to use them for some time.' Here both question and answer were cryptic; the sick 'somebody, who had been born in a sheep-year' turned out to be a kenning for a pair of sheepskin bellows kept in a government office and recently torn.[19]

Other such stories of testing are mentioned by Evans-Pritchard with regard to the Azande. In the Old Testament, Gideon (Judges 6:36–9) tests God by spreading a fleece on the floor; 'and if the dew be on the fleece only, and it be dry upon all the earth beside, then shall I know that thou wilt save Israel by mine hand, as thou hast said'.[20] Like Apollo in the case of Croesus, Yahweh does not resent being tested, but sends the required sign.

A nice example from Roman history is the story of the augur Attus Navius,[21] who insisted that no action should be taken on the composition of the Roman army until the birds had given their consent. Tarquin had no patience with such mummery and contemptuously berated Navius: 'Then I would ask you, holy sir, to declare by your gift of prophecy if what I am thinking of at this moment, can be done.' Navius replied that it could. 'Very well,' said Tarquin, 'I was thinking that you would cut a whetstone in half with a razor. Get them, and do what those birds of yours declare can be done.' Navius did it. And the whetstone, Livy tells us, stood next to a statue of Navius for many years thereafter; and thus the prestige of augury was established. Confounding a sceptic is a worthy use of divine powers.

Plutarch (*Obsolescence of Oracles* 434DE) tells a similar story about a ruler of Cilicia who kept company with Epicurean philosophers and did not believe in oracles; he tested the oracle of Mopsus by sending a man to sleep in the temple, carrying a sealed tablet with a question for the god; and his dream was of a handsome man who uttered the one word 'Black'. When he returned to the king, the latter broke the seal on the tablet and revealed the question: 'Shall I sacrifice to you a white bull or a black?' Result: confusion of Epicureans, conversion of the king.

Sometimes, however, posing trick questions to the oracles could lead to a comeuppance: a man called Daphitas for a joke asked the Delphic oracle where he should find his horse, even though he did not have one. The oracle replied that he would meet his death in a fall from a horse. Daphitas thought he had successfully fooled the oracle by forcing it to give an answer which could not come true. But it did, because King Attalus of Pergamum had him thrown to his death from a rock called the Horse.[22] Posidonius saw this as an example of the workings of Fate, but Cicero dismissed it as a silly tale which proved nothing, since a rock is not really a horse and never can be. We shall return to Cicero's views on divination and fate, but for the moment the story may stand as an example of a testing of the oracle that backfired, unlike the others that we hear of.

Unexpected fulfilments of oracles need not cause discomfiture to the victim. Quite the reverse, in the case of the Delphians' enquiry as to whether they should remove their belongings and their families from the city in face of the Gaulish invasion of 278 BC. The response ran (in iambics): 'I will take care of this, along with the white maidens.' In the event, the Celts were driven back by a blinding snowstorm.[23] Phalanthos, setting out to found a colony in about 710 BC, was told to acquire land where he should see rain falling from a clear sky (*aithra*); when he reached Italy, his wife, who was called Aithra, burst into tears which fell upon his head, so he knew that was the place.[24]

Socrates himself was unable to understand the oracle to Chaerephon that no one was wiser than Socrates: he was sceptical and tried to disprove it by finding a wiser man. In the end he realized that his wisdom consisted in his consciousness of his own ignorance.[25] So by profound reflection, Socrates had reached an understanding not just that, but *how* the oracle was true.

Such stories warn against a too-complacent rationalism like that into which Whittaker (1965, 44) slips when he writes that 'a favourable reply results in only a small chance of disaster'. The oracle was rarely tested empirically, he suggests, to see whether what it predicted about colonization, marriage, journeys, etcetera was fulfilled in detail. It seems more likely that colonists *would* look back at the pretext on which they were sent out; but if things did not seem to have turned out right, the let-out would be that they had misunderstood the oracle.

Tested or not, an oracle might always lead to a result less desirable than that which was anticipated by the consultant. The stories we have considered so far in this chapter all belong to the category of legend and folktale, and it is almost certain that the responses given to Croesus are not historical. But many of the stories in Herodotus' *Histories* concern oracles that, as far as we can tell, were actually given in the course of the Persian Wars. Many of them are not particularly obscure, and lead us to a consideration of the political role of Delphi.

Applying the Oracles

The Delphic oracle is all-pervading in the history of Herodotus and it has been generally assumed that it was equally all-pervading in the political life of archaic Greece and neighbouring cultures such as Lydia.[26] Its fame even reached Tarquin's Rome.[27] It is possible to categorize the oracles in Herodotus in various ways. Kirchberg[28] has five classes: cathartic (where a curse or crime is to be annulled), advisory (what to do?), to impel colonization, to establish cults, and finally 'charismatic' (religious experiences of some kind). I would be tempted to cut the cake slightly differently:

1. To find the cause of a calamity or strange event *and* to find out what to do about it[29]
2. Apodotic oracles, 'If or when x occurs, then y. . .'[30]
3. Straightforward predictions (this usually applies to rulers)[31]
4. Institution of cult or similar (the special case of the Spartan constitution)[32]
5. Colonization[33]
6. Juridical (in his account of Egypt, but never in Greece)[34]

The prominence of oracles about colonization has led to the view that the oracle played an important political role in early Greece and exercised a conscious policy of colonization. Plato's ideal vision certainly made Delphi the ultimate political authority (*Laws* 871, 921), not least in the matter of founding cities and establishing cults (738, 828), but that does not mean he was reflecting any common reality. The counter-argument is that the consultation is not the key moment in the process of decision-making. For Morgan, it is little more than a rubber stamp for decisions that have already been taken elsewhere;[35] she regards the role of the oracle as one of solving, or refocusing, issues that cannot be resolved by debate. Delphi does not have a 'policy' (38). Bowden rejects this (11) in favour of the view that the Athenians did, generally, wait until the god told them what to do before acting. Some such stories are clearly legend, like the one about the foundation of Cyrene, which shows how the Greeks constructed stories to prove that the gods were on their side in actions of the legendary past (Hdt. 4.154ff.). But others show oracles changing the course of political events.

The prominence of Delphi in the history of the Persian Wars led to a charge that was made both in antiquity and by modern scholars, that the oracle favoured the Persian attackers over the Greek states.[36] An oracle cited in Herodotus 7.220.3 shows the oracle discouraging the Spartans from resistance since the Persian foe was bound to overcome. Just imagine if it had given such a prophecy to Croesus! The difference, of course, is that in this case the oracle was proved false and the Greeks were eventually victorious. But in local instances the oracle had to be followed. When Harpagus and his army marched on Caria in the First Persian War, the people of Cnidus decided to cut through the Isthmus that led to their city (Hdt. 1.174). However, the chipping of the stone caused a very large number of injuries to their eyes and other parts of their bodies, 'so they sent emissaries to Delphi to ask what it was that was blocking them'. The reply came back:

> The isthmus is not to be fortified or dug through;
> If Zeus had wanted an island, he would have made an island.

So the Cnidians stopped digging, and surrendered to Harpagus and his army without a battle.

THE 'WOODEN WALLS' AND PURPOSIVE INTERPRETATION

One episode above all shows how oracles could be put to work in a political context. It is of particular interest because the resolution of the debate over it depends on the assumption that the oracle was ambiguous or riddling (unlike that to the Cnidians, which was plain enough). The oracle given before the battle of Thermopylae (Hdt. 7.140) could easily be seen as an incitement to surrender to the Persian foe:

Fools, why sit you here? Fly to the ends of the earth
Leave your homes and the lofty heights girded by your city . . .
Fire will bring it down,
Fire and bitter War . . .
Many are the strongholds he will destroy, not yours alone;
Many the temples of the gods he will gift with raging fire.

Depressed by this oracle, the Athenians sent a second embassy and received a second prophecy.

No, Pallas Athena cannot placate Olympian Zeus,
Though she begs him with words and many cunning arguments.
I shall tell you once more, and endue my words with adamant
While all else that lies within the borders of Cecrops' land
And the vale of holy Cithaeron is falling to the enemy,
Far-seeing Zeus gives you, Tritogeneia, a wall of wood.
. . . Blessed Salamis, you will be the death of mothers' sons
Either when the seed is scattered or when it is gathered in. (Hdt. 7.141)

This oracle became nearly as famous as the oracle to Laius, and appears repeatedly in later discussions of oracles.[37] Herodotus explains that various interpretations of this oracle were proposed, and the older citizens argued that the oracle referred to a wooden stockade of the kind that had surrounded the acropolis in the past: if such a stockade were built now, they said, this would be the secure protection promised by the god. Another view was that the god referred to a fleet. Themistocles, the leading citizen in Athens, favoured this view and explained away the apparent dire prediction of 'death of mothers' sons' in the last lines of the prophecy by drawing attention to Salamis' epithet, 'Blessed'. The dead would be, it was presumed, Persian not Greek.[38]

Themistocles' view carried the day and the silver reserves from the mines at Laurion were employed in building a substantial fleet of triremes. Robert Parker[39] has shown how this interpretation of the oracle did not succumb to the ambiguity of the riddle but brought it into the open as a focus for public debate. He quotes the use of oracles by the Tiv people of Africa, for whom the oracle is 'a distracting device that allows the principals to construct an explanation that can be handled'. It was the democratic debate in the assembly that then reached the final decision on action. The people did not simply follow the orders of a god, nor did they, like Croesus, jump to conclusions. But neither did the exercise of democratic debate render the god's advice irrelevant. It was assumed that the god meant something and that his advice should be heeded; but it was not privileged as a divine injunction. It moved the debate to a new level and allowed a new focus on an unresolvable situation.[40] Furthermore, Themistocles' role showed the importance of interpreters, though it is striking in this story that the interpreter, as befitted a democratic context, was a citizen, Themistocles, not a professional oracle-reader.

The last oracle in Herodotus (8.77 with 9.42–3) is a telling one.[41] The oracle predicts disaster for the Persians. Mardonius asked his senior commanders

if they knew of any oracle predicting the destruction of the Persian army in Greece. The assembled officers said nothing, some because they genuinely did not know of any such oracles, and others because, although they were aware of oracles to that effect, they did not consider it safe to mention them. Finally Mardonius broke the silence. 'It may be that you are unaware of any such oracles,' he said, 'or it may be that you are too afraid to speak up. In any case, I'm perfectly well aware of them and I'll tell you what I've heard. There is an oracle to the effect that the Persians are fated to come to Greece, sack the sanctuary at Delphi, and afterwards perish to a man.' (9.42)

So the Persians deliberately bypass the sanctuary of Delphi; but Herodotus goes one better (9.43):

I happen to know that the oracle which, according to Mardonius, referred to the Persians was not designed for them, but for the Illyrians and the army of the Encheleis. However, there was an oracle of Bacis which refers to the battle in question:

> On the Thermodon and the grassy banks of the Asopus
> A gathering of Greeks, and a shout of foreign babble.
> There, before their time, before their fate, many bow-bearing Medes
> Will fall, when their day of death comes upon them.

The Greeks won because they were able to interpret the oracles correctly. The Persians, who could not understand or did not know the oracles, and were frightened even to mention them (unlike democratic Greeks), were blind to the divine plan: they found themselves fighting against Destiny (Moira). The fault of the Persians was that they relied on omens and on non-verbal divination;[42] they could not make the gods speak.

The decline of the political influence of oracles began at the end of the Peloponnesian War (404 BC).[43] Thucydides makes few references to the divine and divination in his *History*, and they are rarely friendly. In Book 2.1 he mentions the prevalence of professional soothsayers in Athens at the beginning of the war; and in 8.1, after the failure of the Sicilian expedition (over which they had not consulted Delphi, perhaps fearing an adverse answer, like Didyma's: Bowden 1995, 149), he tells us:

> When the Athenians did recognize the facts, they turned against the public speakers who had been in favour of the expedition, as though they themselves had not voted for it, and also became angry with the prophets and soothsayers and all who had, at the time, by various methods of divination, encouraged them to believe that they would conquer Sicily.

Plutarch (*Life of Nicias* 13.1–2) shows how the oracles had been manipulated at the outset of the expedition:

> There is said to have been considerable opposition from the priests; but Alcibiades found other diviners and published the claim, derived from some supposedly ancient oracles, that the Athenians would win great fame in Sicily. He was also helped when some envoys returned from the shrine of Ammon with an oracle to the effect that every single Syracusan would fall into Athenian hands; but the envoys suppressed oracles with the opposite import because they did not want to jinx the expedition.

This narrative shows clearly how politicians could manipulate oracles. The oracles were put forward as items of debate in the assembly, but the people were deprived of knowledge of all the possible relevant utterances. And in fact the prophecy about 'every single Syracusan' did come true, when the Athenians laid hands on a copy of the muster-list of the Syracusan army. So hasty interpretation was added to inadequate information.

The implication of Thucydides is that this episode spelled the end of extensive consultation of oracles as part of the democratic process in Athens. Certainly we hear much less of it from now on – though we know that the Boeotians, for example, continued to consult the oracle of Apollo at Ptoon throughout the fourth century BC. Professional divination played a more prominent role in politics than oracles.

The Delphic Oracle and Cult

While the use of the oracle in politics may have declined from this point (as Plutarch laments), its use for cultic[44] and even for personal matters continued unabated. One minor cultic enquiry shows the lengths to which the Athenian consultants went to randomize the oracle's response. It is preserved on an inscription of Eleusis of 352/1 BC (*IG* II². 204 = *SIG* 204 = Fontenrose 1978, H21):

> On a tin plate they inscribed the question 'Is it better for the demos of the Athenians that the basileus let the lands now unworked within the sacred orgas for the building of a portico and repair of the goddesses' sanctuary?' On another they inscribed the question 'Is it better for the demos of the Athenians that the lands now unworked within the boundaries of the sacred *orgas* be left unworked for the goddesses?' They put one plate (taking care not to know which) into a gold hydria and the other into a silver hydria, which they sealed and which their envoys showed to the Pythia and asked: Should the Athenians act according to the words in the gold hydria or according to those in the silver hydria?

The response was: 'It is better for them that the lands be left unworked.'

Another inscribed Delphic response set up at Magnesia on the Maeander in *c*.278–250 BC concerns the importation of three maenads, devotees of Dionysus, from Thebes to establish a cult at Magnesia: the beginning is missing, but the first part is in hexameters, containing the actual instruction of the god:

> Go to the sacred plain of Thebes, to collect three maenads from the clan of Cadmean Ino. They will bring you rites and good customs, and will establish the revels of Bacchus in the city.

The inscription continues with a prose postscript:

> And Kosko organized the thiasos named after the plane tree, Baubo the thiasos outside the city, and Thettale the thiasos named after Kataibates. After their death they were buried by the Magnesians, and Kosko lies buried in the area called Hillock of Kosko, Baubo in the area called Tabarnis, and Thettale near the theatre.[45]

Or again: an inscription from Anaphe of *c*.110–100 BC records the enquiry of Timotheos: 'Is it better that he ask the city for a place of his choosing in the sanctuary of Apollo Agelatas or in the sanctuary of Asclepius on which to build a temple of Aphrodite?' The response is 'he should ask for a place in the sanctuary of Apollo, and when the temple is completed the city's decree and the oracle and the expense should be inscribed on a stone stele'.[46] Other examples include the introduction of funeral games at Agylla (Hdt. 1.167) and the decree of a share of the first fruits to the poet Pindar (Paus. 9.23.3).

Such occasions may not seem so momentous as the political involvement of Delphi in the survival of Greece, but they were the bread and butter of oracles for many centuries. Delphi, however, declined in power and influence in the fourth century BC following a major earthquake in 370 and the spoliation of the sanctuary during the third Sacred War in 346.[47] The sack by the Gauls in 279 BC was a further blow. The development of democracy in a state like Athens, too, may have sidelined the oracle in favour of public debate and professional expertise.[48] Plutarch's treatise on the obsolescence of the oracle, written in the second century AD, worries about the question why the Pythia's word is no longer sought so assiduously, why her political importance has declined, and why the oracles are no longer given in verse. He questions whether the gods can in fact die, whether the powers of Earth can with time wear out so that prophecy is no longer possible. But if Plutarch had survived for another century or so he would have found the oracle still going strong. Always the centre of Earth, always the name that sprang first to mind when an oracle was mentioned, Delphi retained its prestige if not its political centrality.

This long look at the unusual oracle at Delphi has posed many questions. How far were the oracles genuine, and accepted as telling important truths? Were they central to political operation, including those of democracy, or did they simply act as a rubber-stamp for decisions that had been taken elsewhere? Did they take sides in politics? Were they simply venal? Did they speak (and continue to speak) in verse or simply give laconic yes/no answers? These questions will remain in our minds as we consider the other types of oracle in the Greek world.

CHAPTER 4

From Egypt to Dodona

. . . as famous as Dodona's vocal grove . . .
    Nicholas Brady, from Henry Purcell's *Ode on St Cecilia's Day*, 1692

Would I do better . . . if I took a wife?
Agis asks Zeus Naios and Dione about the coverings and pillows which he
lost, whether someone from outside stole them?
    Questions to the oracle at Dodona, Eidinow 2007, p. 84.3, 117.4

DODONA

The oracle of Zeus at Dodona presents a very different image from that
of Delphi. Situated on the fringe of the Hellenic world in Epirus (Delphi,
by contrast, was officially the centre of the world), it had for Greeks an
air of remoteness and strangeness, for all its busy importance in daily life.
The site is first mentioned in Homer's *Odyssey* (14.327 = 19.296) where
mention is made of the oak of Zeus, while in *Iliad* 16.235 the poet
mentions the priests, the Selloi, 'who sleep upon the ground and never
wash their feet'.[1] Already these references contain several unexpected
items: the prophetic god is Zeus, not his son Apollo; it is a tree that gives
the oracles; and the behaviour of the priests is unexplained. It is far from
unique that the prophetic god should be other than Apollo, as we shall see
later in this chapter, but the phenomenon of a prophetic tree seems to be
unique in the Greek world before the episode in the *Alexander Romance*
where the hero consults the Trees of the Sun and Moon in India.[2] The
unwashed priests are an exotic detail, though H.W. Parke[3] gathered some
parallels from other cultures: the Flamen Dialis in Rome had to sleep on a
bed with muddy feet; and according to Frazer's *Golden Bough* (II[3] 248)
priests in pagan Prussia had to sleep in contact with the earth, as did

10 The temple of Zeus at Dodona. The oak tree is modern.

Brahman fire-priests in India; and similar behaviour is attributed to the alytarch of Antioch by Malalas (12.6) in the reign of Commodus.

Finally, how did the tree give oracles? Most sources indicate that it was, at least in legendary times, by the rustling of its leaves: so Ovid *Metamorphoses* 629, *intremuit ramisque sonum sine flamine motis alta dedit*.[4] (Such a method would not be unique, for in II Samuel 5:24 the Lord tells David to wait for the Philistines in a grove of mulberry trees: 'and let it be, when thou hearest the sound of a going in the tops of the mulberry trees,[5] that then thou shalt bestir thyself: for then shall the Lord go out before thee, to smite the host of the Philistines.')[6] Dodona scarcely appears in the narratives of Greek mythology, though the ship *Argo* contained a timber from the oak of Dodona, which spoke to give advice to the Argonauts in times of need (Aeschylus fr. 20 N, Philo, *Quod omnis probus liber sit* 143).

In historical times, the role of the male priests was taken over by priestesses, as happened also at Didyma,[7] perhaps under the influence of practice at Delphi. (We may, of course, be looking in the case of Dodona at a story about the development of the shrine comparable to that about the replacement of the oracle of Earth by Apollo's intervention at Delphi. In such a case, the normal arrangement of an inspired prophetess is contrasted with some uncouth archaic past arrangement.) Strabo in his *Geography* (6.7.10–12) describes the change:

This oracle, according to Ephorus, was founded by the Pelasgi. Homer makes it perfectly clear from their mode of life, when he calls them 'men with feet unwashen, men who sleep upon the ground', that they were barbarians. . . . At the outset those who uttered the prophecies were men . . . but later on three old women were designated as prophets, after Dione also had been designated as temple-associate of Zeus.

The three, Strabo later tells us (9.2.4), rotated their duties.

But Herodotus has a different story, and this leads to two interesting questions: Why for Greeks, is it always a god who issues the oracles; and where did this tradition come from? In Book II, 53–5, Herodotus is discussing the Egyptian origins of Greek religious practices, and he recounts an Egyptian tale about the origins of the oracles of Dodona and of Ammon at Siwa: they had been founded by two priestesses of Theban Zeus who had been abducted by Phoenicians. But the prophetesses at Dodona told Herodotus a different story:

They say that two black doves took off from Thebes in Egypt, one of which flew to Libya, while the other came to them in Dodona. It perched on an oak-tree and spoke in a human voice, telling the people of Dodona that there ought to be an oracle of Zeus there. (2.55; cf. Pindar fr. 58)

Herodotus has a rationalizing explanation, that

the women were called doves by the people of Dodona because they were foreigners and when they spoke they sounded like birds. . . . After all, how could a dove speak in a human voice? . . . It is in fact the case that the divinatory methods used in Egyptian Thebes and in Dodona are very similar to one another and that the art of divination from entrails did reach Greece from Egypt. (2.57)

Pausanias 10.12.2 also regards the name of doves as a term for the priest-esses – 'the guild of Rock-Pigeons', in Peter Levi's translation. A fragment of Hesiod (240 MW) describes how '(something) lived in the trunk of the tree, and mortals fetched oracles from that spot'. The missing line may have said that the doves lived in the tree, thus indicating that it was the cooing that originally provided the oracles (like the woodpecker at the Roman Oracle of Mars described by Dionysius of Halicarnassus 1.1.4–5).[8] But all the later sources indicate that it was priestesses, called doves, who gave the proph-ecies. Parke[9] suggests the rationalizing explanation that the tree collapsed in the late archaic period, after six hundred years of activity, and the role of the birds was taken over by the human priestesses on the model of rival Delphi.

Herodotus has a tendency to find an Egyptian origin for many Greek practices, while modern scholarship tends to find closer connections with the Near East. But there is a notable dissonance between what Herodotus tells us of Dodona and what Homer says of its legendary origins. The priests Homer mentions have been replaced by priestesses. It is not the leaves that rustle, but the doves that speak. And when we come to look at the historical operation of the oracle we find that it functions by lot, without any miraculous elements.

THE EGYPTIAN CONNECTION

But Herodotus is accurate in drawing the parallel with Egypt insofar as Egyptian oracles involved a consultation of a named god, who would give a yes-or-no answer to the question posed. The method of consultation of Egyptian oracles is described in a classic article by J. Černy.[10] The god, usually Amun-Re, gives his oracles when he emerges from his sanctuary; that is, his image is brought forth by the priests. The question is put, perhaps in a very public way. For example, in sixth-century BC Napata, as described in the stele of King Aspelta, the new king was chosen by bringing all the royal brothers before the god: 'They laid down the royal brothers before the god, but he did not select any of them. . . . They laid down again the royal brother. . . . Aspelta and this god Amun-Re' said "it is he who shall be your king". The way in which the oracles were given is vividly described by Diodorus (17.50) in his account of Alexander's visit to the oracle of Ammon at Siwa:

> The image of the god is encrusted with emeralds and other precious stones, and answers those who consult the oracle in a quite peculiar fashion. It is carried about upon a golden boat by eighty priests, and these, with the god on their shoulders, go without their own volition wherever the god directs their path. A multitude of girls and women follows them singing paeans as they go and praising the god in a traditional hymn.

This kind of giant Ouija-board is described by Egyptian sources as well, and many reliefs depict the god being carried in his boat. The oracular replies were given by the nodding or jerking of the image as the priests moved; thus, one may imagine the statue lurching deeply towards Aspelta as he lay prostrate before the god. In inscriptions, the oracular answers are

11 Ammon is borne on the shoulders of priests in order to give oracular responses.

marked by the determinatives for head or arm, indicating the part of the statue that would incline to the chosen answer.

Such oracles were not unique to Egypt though they are best attested there.[11] Lucian (*On the Syrian Goddess* 36) describes the operation of the oracle of Apollo[12] at Hierapolis in Syria:

There are many oracles among the Greeks and many among the Egyptians. . . . But these do not pronounce without priests or prophet, whereas this one moves of its own volition and itself brings its soothsaying to fruition. It works like this. When it wants to prophesy, it first moves on its base, and the priests lift it up; if they do not lift it up it sweats and moves even more. When they lift it on to their backs and carry it, it drives them twisting and turning this way and that, leaping from one to another. Finally the chief priest approaches it and inquires about all manner of things: if it does not want something to be done, it retreats; if it approves, it drives its bearers forward like a charioteer. . . . I shall also mention something it did in my presence. The priests lifted up and were carrying it, but it left them on the ground below and was borne round unsupported in the air.

The last sentence sounds like one of Lucian's tall stories, but the rest of the account fits with what else we know – though Lucian's assertion that priests were not involved is belied by his own description.[13] It sounds just like the operation of an Egyptian oracle of Ammon.

There were many Ammons, and sometimes it could be beneficial to consult several. So in British Museum papyrus 10335 (Černy 1962, 39) a servant appeals for help to Amun of Pakhenty regarding some garments that have been stolen from a storehouse under his guard. He reads out the names of the villagers, and the god moves at the name of the farmer Pethauemdiamun. The latter of course denies the charge, so the servant takes his question to the Amun of Tashenyt, taking care to bring a gift of some loaves. This Amun confirms the verdict of the first, as does a third, Amun-Bukentef. The case is then referred back to Amun of Pakhenty, and the thief is forced to confess and duly punished.[14]

This procedure is known from an early date in Egypt, though the earliest instances refer specifically to appointments of kings (Tuthmosis III, 1490–1436 BC) or of the succession of high priests. Originally centred on Thebes, it spread as we have seen to many sites in Egypt, and many other gods besides Amun began to adopt oracular functions: one of the most popular was the deified Pharaoh Amenhotep I.[15] By the sixth century BC it was common to consult the oracle in judicial cases such as that of the stolen garments, or other personal questions, like that of Stotoete from Tebtunis in the Ptolemaic period:

> O my great lord Soknebtynis the great god: it is thy servant Stotoete, son of Imhutep, who says: 'if it is a good thing for me to live with Tanwe, daughter of Hape, she being my wife, send out to me this petition in writing'.

Apparently, the consultant submitted two slips with alternative questions (like the Athenians with the tin plates),[16] the god chose, perhaps by nodding to left or right, and the priest handed back the chosen slip. A Greek example from the same archive makes this clear by using the expression 'bring out [sc. the slip]':

> To Soknopaios and Sokonpieios, the very great gods, from Stotoes, son of Apnychis and Tesenuphis. 'Shall I recover from this illness which is in me? Bring this out for me.'[17]

ENQUIRIES AT DODONA

The method of consultation at Dodona also involved writing alternative questions, not on slips of papyrus, but on strips of lead. These were folded and submitted to the oracle. The answer was certainly not given by a nodding statue, but the answers came, it seems, as a yes-or-no choice, though occasionally a response replies to the question 'Which god should I sacrifice to . . .?' Many of the questions are of the same kind as those we have seen in Egypt, but the way in which the answers were given is obscure.

The lead tablets from Dodona were excavated more than a century ago but have not been fully published.[18] Almost all of them represent personal enquiries, mostly from the fourth century BC though there are also many from the fifth. There are no grand questions of state of the kind we encountered at Delphi. They are much more like the humdrum questions that Plutarch describes as being characteristic of Delphi in his own day. In most cases we have only the question, not the response. Enquiries about thefts were so familiar that a scholiast on the *Odyssey* tells a story about a sheep thief who was caught when the oak delivered a direct accusation.[19]

The questions inscribed on the lead tablets at Dodona can be divided into a number of categories. A couple of dozen concern travel, especially by sea (Eidinow 2007, 75.1, '. . . a journey by trade to Epidamnus'; 111.4, 'will the ship be safe?'); a similar number concern marriage and children (84.6, 'if I shall do better by taking a wife . . .'), and work (99.17, 'Porinos of Kymae asks the god if he would do well if he served the Satrap and Hyparch'). A dozen enquiries by slaves focus on the prospect of freedom (102.6, 'Will Kittos get the freedom from Dionysius that Dionysius promised him?'). One even asks 'Should we hire a necromancer?' – for what purpose is unexplained (112–13). Fewer than one might expect (a mere ten) relate to disease and health: perhaps most enquirers on these matters went in preference to one of the healing sanctuaries (chapter 7). A typical example is 105.2, 'Nikokrateia asks by sacrificing to which of the gods would she do better and be relieved of her disease?' One unusual question asks 'Whether it is because of the impurity of some man that the god sends the storm?', which recalls the situation in Sophocles' *Oedipus Tyrannus*.[20] Others refer to ritual activity (113.3, 'whether to make the triple sacrifice?'); to military campaigns (two only; one is 'X asks Zeus Naios and Dione whether it is advantageous to set off on campaign against Antiochos?'); and to city affairs and thefts. It is notable that the latter involve such questions as 'Should I go to court?' (115.2), and even 'Did Thopion steal the silver?' (117.3), but the oracle does not operate as in

Egypt, as a judge in a court context. The oracle is used to place the problem back in the domain of human decision-making.

The questions, thus, are reasonably plentiful; but the responses are not. One or two of the lead tablets have what appears to be a response written on the bottom – a 'rescript' in the manner of the oracle at Koropi, and elsewhere. According to Lucian in the second century AD, the fraudulent oracle-monger Alexander of Abonuteichos received questions on rolled and sealed pieces of papyrus; when they were returned to the questioners, the answers were found to be written on the bottom part of the papyrus, even though the seals had not been broken. Something similar apparently occurred at Koropi (pp. 30–1, above). But the question remains: how were the responses produced at Dodona?

A cloud of mystery hangs over this question. In historical times the twittering birds and rustling leaves were no longer the modus operandi. Instead we have various puzzling and perhaps incompatible hints at the procedure. Heracles in Sophocles' *Trachiniae* 1167–9 says that he 'wrote down the oracle beside the ancestral, many-tongued oak' – which reveals nothing. But Strabo (7 fr.1a), writing in about 10 BC, says that Zeus 'gave out the oracle, not through words, but through certain symbols, as was the case at the oracle of Zeus Ammon in Libya'. This reference, however, is to some undefined legendary time after the establishment of the oracle, and refers again to the involvement of the 'three pigeons from which the priestesses were wont to make observations and to prophesy'. Another reference in the same book of Strabo is to 'the bronze vessel of Dodona'.[21] This is probably not the same as the wall of bronze tripods that surrounded the sanctuary, which when struck might reverberate, it seems, all day. Strabo writes of a vessel within the temple, 'with a statue of a man situated above it and holding a copper scourge, dedicated by the Corcyraeans; the scourge was three-fold and wrought in chain fashion, with knucklebones strung from it; and these bones, striking the copper vessel continuously when they were swung by the winds, would produce tones so long that anyone who measured the time from the beginning of the tone to the end could count to four hundred'. The Christian writers Clement[22] and Eusebius[23] extravagantly tell how the demons caused the statue to whip the priestess into an oracular frenzy. This is clearly fantasy, and one cannot imagine how the sounding of a bronze vessel for four hundred beats could provide a response to a question. But, as Eidinow points out, the knuckle bones in the Corcyraeans' strange dedication may provide the answer; for knuckle bones were used as the ancient equivalent of dice and very commonly for choosing answers to questions (see chapter 8 on dice oracles).

However, a difficulty with this interpretation is raised by a story from the fourth-century BC historian Callisthenes about the Spartan embassy to Dodona just before their disastrous defeat at Leuctra in 271 BC. 'After their messengers had duly set up the vessel in which were the lots, an ape, kept by the king of Molossia for his amusement, disarranged the lots and everything else used in consulting the oracle, and scattered them in all directions. Then, so we are told, the priestess who was on duty at the oracle said that the Spartans must think of safety and not of victory.'[24] Two things need to be noted here. First, the use of lots in a vessel is incompatible with the use of dice/knuckle bones to give an answer: you cannot draw out a knuckle bone as you can a short straw, for knuckle bones require to be thrown (unless they were special knuckle bones with individual unique markings). The story makes clear that lots were drawn in some form. This throws us back, then, on a model much more like the Delphic one, when the god was asked to choose between the two tin plates of the Athenians and the priestess uttered her response in words. Perhaps, as Johnston (2008, 70) suggests, there were two urns, one with questions, and one with yes-or-no lots, from each of which one item was drawn at a time.

Secondly, the whole event is regarded as an omen and the response is given by the priestess on the basis of her interpretation of it. Bad omens could easily arise in an oracular consultation.[25] The priestess' interpretation of the ill-omened intervention of the ape is an example of 'last resort' prophecy. Many tales tell of responses being wrung willy-nilly from the priestess, like the Pythia's pronouncement to Alexander (pp. 37–8, above). Timoleon was consulting the Delphic oracle when a ribbon fell on his head, which was accounted an omen of success.[26] The pattern is known from the Old Testament too: In I Kings 2:28ff. 'Joab fled into the tabernacle of the Lord, and caught hold of the horns of the altar. . . . And Benaiah came to the tabernacle of the Lord, and said unto him, Thus saith the king, Come forth. And he said, Nay, but I will die here.' That was an unfortunate way of expressing his determination, for when the king heard his answer, he said to Benaiah, 'Do as he hath said, and fall upon him, and bury him. . . . And the Lord shall return his blood upon his own head.'

The direct involvement of the priestess at Dodona is supported by a story cited by Strabo (9.2.4) from Ephorus[27] about an oracle given to the Boeotians when they were at war with the Pelasgians:

the prophetess replied to the Boeotians that they would prosper if they committed sacrilege; and the messengers who were sent to consult the oracle, suspecting that the prophetess responded thus out of favour to the

Pelasgians ... seized the woman and threw her on a burning pyre, for they considered that, whether she had acted falsely or had not, they were right in either case, since if she uttered a false oracle, she had her punishment, whereas, if she did not act falsely, they had only obeyed the order of the oracle.

The murderers were then brought on trial before the two remaining priestesses, 'who were also the prophetesses'.

Dodona increased in international importance during the fourth century BC. Following Philip of Macedon's capture of Delphi in 346 BC, Athens cultivated relations instead with Dodona, until they were warned off by Philip's wife Olympias who ordered them to stay away from what was her property (as a Molossian princess): Zeus had instructed the Athenians to adorn the sanctuary of Dione at Dodona, but a letter came from the queen of Macedon 'that the land where the sanctuary stood was in Molossia, and therefore hers; and that it was inappropriate for them even to touch a single thing in it'.[28]

Dodona seems to have become inactive soon after this date, for reasons that are unclear. In 167 BC it was sacked by the Romans and joined the silent chorus of oracles that uttered no more (Strabo 7.7.3), even though the cult of Naia was still being celebrated there in AD 243–4.[29]

CHAPTER 5

The Gods, the Heroes and the Dead

Wherever you went in ancient Greece you were likely to run across an oracular site. Pausanias in his travels encountered dozens, and there are others he does not mention. Their distribution is rather uneven: for example, there were fifteen oracles in Boeotia (including the ancient one of Tiresias at Orchomenos, visited in legend by Pelops), but only three in Arcadia.[1] The useful tabulation in Trevor Curnow's book[2] is sometimes rather optimistic, but draws attention to the prevalence of oracular possibilities even at quite small and obscure shrines. Many of these are associated with Apollo, the pre-eminent oracular god: Abai,[3] Hysiae in Boeotia, where anybody can drink from a well and utter oracles,[4] Koropi,[5] Ptoon,[6] Tegyra[7] and Thebes, where the oracle of Amphiaraus was consulted by Croesus[8] while the oracle of Apollo of the Ashes operated by cledonomancy.[9] Other gods also appear: Demeter at Patrae, where a mirror was lowered into a well and showed an image of the sick person alive or dead – 'the oracle is as truthful as that',[10] Hera at Perachora where Strabo (8.2.2) refers in passing to 'an ancient oracle', Hermes at Pharai (chance utterances again),[11] Dionysus at Pangaeum in Thrace,[12] Night at Megara,[13] Zeus at Skotoussa,[14] Pan at Troizen (with Asclepius)[15] and at Akakesion.[16] The last named no longer functioned in Pausanias' time, though an ever-burning fire was tended before the god's image; but in the past the god had used the nymph Erato as his mouthpiece for his responses.

A possible oracle of Poseidon at Onchestos has been deduced from an obscure passage of the Homeric *Hymn to Apollo* (230–8), which describes how 'the newly-tamed colt takes respite, burdened as it is from hauling the beautiful wagons, and the driver, good as he is, leaps to the ground and proceeds on foot. The colts meanwhile shake their harness as they are released from his mastery. If they go on to wreck the chariot in the wooded grove, they look after the horses but leave the chariot where it is. That is how it first becomes holy; they pray to the lord, while fate keeps the chariot for the god.' It has been thought that this describes an oracular procedure with the response given according to the movements of the horses freed from human control.[17] But it seems much more likely that it is in fact a 'rule of the road' (as Allen and Sikes in their commentary (1904) caustically term it): Poseidon's sacred animal was left to his control within his sanctuary, to do what he liked with, and men could only resume control after they had passed over the holy ground. No oracle comes into question.

Pausanias was keen on such manifestations and eagerly recounts when oracular practices are still current in his day, as for example at Apollo's oracle at Larissa (2.24.1).[18] In discussing the hero Amphilochus' altar at Athens, he mentions his cult at Mallos and refers to it as 'the best oracular shrine of these times' (on what grounds is, unfortunately, not stated).

On the fringes of the Greek world, in Illyria, there was an oracular sanctuary of the Nymphs at Apollonia,[19] whose operation is described by Dio Cassius:[20]

What I have marvelled at above all else is that a huge fire issues from the ground near the Aous river and neither spreads to any extent over the surrounding land nor sets on fire even the place where it abides nor makes it at all dry, but has grass and trees flourishing near it. In pouring rains it increases and towers aloft. For this reason it is called Nymphaeum, and in fact it furnishes an oracle, of this kind. You take incense and after making whatever prayer you wish cast it in the fire as the vehicle of the prayer. At this the fire, if your wish is to be fulfilled, receives it very readily, and even if the incense falls somewhere outside, darts forward, snatches it up and consumes it. But if the wish is not to be fulfilled, the fire not only does not go to it, but, even if it falls into the very flames, recedes and flees before it. It acts in these two ways in all matters save those of death and marriage; for concerning these two one may not make any enquiry of it at all.

ORACLES OF THE DEAD

Besides this prevalence of oracular gods throughout the Greek landscape known to the writers of the early centuries AD, there is a preponderance of two particular types: oracles of the dead, and of the heroes. The heroes are a particular class of the dead, and we may look at the oracular dead first of all.[21]

The custom of consulting the dead for an oracle was familiar to Greeks from the beginning of their literature. In *Odyssey* XI, Odysseus goes to the edges of the world, by the River of Ocean, to sacrifice by the River Acheron and call up the dead. The Acheron of legend, like the Styx, shared its name with a river of the real world, so that the episode became localized by the Acheron in Thesprotia (north-western Greece), which also became the supposed site of the descent of Theseus and Pirithous to the Underworld. In this episode, though the hero is seeking information, he also gives it, answering the questions of the shades about the present state of the upper world. Ergo, the dead are not omniscient, here.

In the classical period, a great scene of Aeschylus' *Persians* presents the evocation of the dead King Darius by his wife Atossa, and the same playwright's *Psychagogoi* probably had a similar theme. Plenty of later stories concern encounters with ghosts or their deliberate evocation. Many of the magic papyri are concerned with spells to call up spirits of the dead and consult them.[22] Some epitaphs even invite the passer-by to call up the dead person's ghost, like the priestess Ammias at Thyateira in the second century AD,[23] and Athanatos Epitynchanos in fourth-century AD Phrygia.[24] The Ayia Triadha sarcophagus from Minoan Crete shows a group of celebrants before the tomb of a dead man, who has emerged and is standing before them in his shroud, perhaps to speak. Such necromancy was commonly frowned on, though no doubt widely practised.[25] Saul's consultation of the Witch of En-Dor is a case in point.[26] One can add examples from Hebrew tradition here.

TALKING HEADS

It may be that this association of the oracular voice with the dead ancestor speaking within your head has something to do with the rather frequent occurrence of the preservation of skulls as sources of oracles. In Jewish tradition the Teraphim, commonly translated as idols or 'household gods', seem to have had an oracular function: 'for the idols have spoken vanity, and the diviners have seen a lie, and have told false dreams' (Zechariah 10:2). A legend in the Tanhuma, *Va-yetze* 12,[27] asks: 'What is teraphim? A man, a first-born, is slaughtered. His head is plucked off and pickled in salt and spices. Then the name of the spirit of uncleanness, written on a plate of gold, is placed under his tongue. The head is affixed to a wall, lamps are lit in front of it, and people prostrate themselves before it.'[28] Several of the prophets have both ephod and teraphim to consult. (Micah: Judges 17:5–18:6; at 18.20ff. the Danites steal his 'gods which I made for myself'; the king of Babylon consults livers, teraphim and arrows: Ezekiel 21:21.) In the Greek world, both Orpheus and Trophonius took on oracular status only after their heads were removed; Cleomenes of Sparta pickled a friend's head and

12 Ayia Triadha sarcophagus, *c*.1400 BC.

used to discuss his plans with it;[29] and in Nizami's *Iskandarnameh*[30] the hero Iskandar visits a land of skull worshippers: murdered men provide the skulls, which foretell the future (including the weather forecast). Iskandar, excoriating this as the 'work of demons', has the skulls destroyed. Hippolytus (*Refutation of all Heresies* 4.41) explains how easy it is to make a skull speak by inserting a speaking tube.

13 J.W. Waterhouse, *Consulting the Oracle*.

Physical heads may be replaced by ghosts: Diogenes Laertius (I.7) says that the Persian magi were skilled at divination because they were able to perceive ghosts. The *daimones* who are said by Plutarch to be instrumental in running the oracles are souls of the dead and are taking this role already in the Derveni Papyrus of the late fifth century BC (col. 6).[31]

Perhaps the ghost was thought to come with bad intentions, unlike an oracle. But the practice is based on the presumption that the dead have special access to wisdom.[32] Phlegon tells a story of a boy who was eaten by a ghost, except his head, after which the head began spontaneously to produce oracles.[33] The idea that the dead have special knowledge lends support to Julian Jaynes' euhemeristic theory that the dead are 'early gods' and that it is their voices that the no-longer-bicameral mind seeks to hear again.[34]

The common mode of consulting the dead seems to be by incubation.[35] The altered perspicacity of the sleeping soul is alluded to by Cicero (*div.* 1.63–5) and Iamblichus (*de myst.* 3.3), and it may be that death, as an extreme case of sleep, was thought to provide even more perfect knowledge.[36] Ghosts commonly appeared in dreams, as Patroclus' did to Achilles in the *Iliad*.

Pausanias refers to a necromantic shrine at Phigaleia (3.17.9) – 'an impressive and snake-haunted spot'[37] – which is operated by priests, so not a den of skullduggery, despite Frazer's comment (ad loc.) 'Sometimes, perhaps, the credulous were deluded by phantoms raised by the jugglery of the necromancers. Hippolytus has described in detail the tricks by which the ancient magicians raised spectral apparitions in the dark.'[38] At Hermione,[39] Pausanias identifies an entrance to Hades but without specifying that oracles could be obtained there. At Tainaron[40] there was a visionary pool. A brief passage in Sophocles (fr. 832 Radt) refers to an oracle of the dead at Tyrrhenia, while Hadrian is supposed to have written oracles to be delivered by the dead Antinous.[41] The Sibyl's claim that the god of the dead gave oracles at Dodona is certainly false, and is probably a Christian jibe, a way of expressing the inferiority of the pagan gods by implying that they are Underworld demons.[42]

There was also an entrance to Hades via the cave of the Nymphs at Heracleia in Pontus[43] – home of Heraclides Ponticus, who wrote several books about oracles and about apparitions of the dead – and Plutarch (*Cimon* 6) describes how the Spartan king Pausanias visited the *nekyomanteion* here to appease the ghost of a girl, Cleonice, whom he had tried to seduce and then stabbed by accident. No other reference to this place occurs, so we do not know how its oracular reputation was achieved.

A special case is the place where Orpheus' skull was washed up at Antissa on the island of Lesbos. Philostratus in his *Life of Apollonius of Tyana* (4.14) says that Apollonius visited this shrine of Orpheus. 'People were no longer going to Gryneion for oracles, nor to Claros, nor to any place where the tripod of Apollo stands, but Orpheus alone was giving oracles, his head having lately arrived from Thrace. So the god appeared to him as he was prophesying and said "Stop doing my business, since I put up with you long enough when you were a singer". This story is probably fiction, though Lucian also attests to the presence of the head beneath the temple of Dionysus there.[44]

The most significant site associated with the cult of the dead is the *nekyomanteion* at Ephyra.[45] It is first mentioned (if we discount the Odyssean reference) in Herodotus (5.92) as the place where Periander of Corinth sent to enquire about some missing money. What happened was that the ghost of a girl he had wronged, Melissa, appeared and refused to tell him where the money was, because she was cold and naked: 'the clothes Periander had buried her in were no use, the ghost explained, unless they were burnt'. So Periander assembled the finest clothing of all the women of Corinth and burnt it in a pit, after which Melissa gave him his answer. Like so many oracles, it did not come about in quite the way he had expected.

14 Landscape of the mouth of the Acheron, seen from the 'Oracle of the Dead'.

If we turn to historical evidence for the *manteion* at Ephyra, there is little to be had. Pausanias tells us that it had ceased to operate by his time (AD 150), though Clement describes it as active[46] and mentions the use of bowls. However, there is no epigraphy for this site nor for any other of the *nekyomanteia* (with three exceptions).[47] Excavations at a building thought to be the *nekyomanteion* turned up various winches and windlasses, which were interpreted by the excavators as the remains of machinery for creating ghostly apparitions;[48] but they are now given a more prosaic explanation as the accoutrements of a working farm: the building is not a sacred one at all (though the numerous votive figures of Persephone require some explanation). The excavators also interpreted the vessels full of beans as intended for inducing strange dreams; but it seems that beans were in fact excluded from the diet of those who consulted the oracle (a common ritual prohibition).

Menippus in Lucian's dialogue of that name describes the rites by which he was brought into contact with the dead at Babylon, rites which Dakaris surmised were based on those that took place at the Acheron; but the description probably owes as much to the practice of the Chaldaean theurgists familiar in Lucian's time as to the known rituals of the Acheron, and displays Lucian's gift for humorous exaggeration of familiar behaviour. Notable is the literary quality of the sheep-sacrifice, which is taken from the *Odyssey*,[49] and the extremely long period of purification (twenty-nine days). Menippus is

15 The so-called Oracle of the Dead, Nekyomanteion, on the Acheron.

not, of course, seeking an oracle; he is visiting the Underworld as a tourist, and the place where he emerges is the oracle of Trophonius at Lebadeia.

HERO ORACLES: THE CASE OF TROPHONIUS[50]

This brings us very neatly to the topic of hero oracles, of which Trophonius' was pre-eminent in Greece, largely as a result of Pausanias' lengthy description of the manner of consultation. Here for once there is no doubt about the procedures involved.

Trophonius and his brother Agamedes were dishonest heroes: architectural geniuses, they built a number of temples including the fourth (legendary) temple of Apollo at Delphi. They cunningly devised a treasury, also at Delphi, with a stone that could be secretly removed, and used this to slip in and help themselves to the deposits whenever they wanted. The king of Hyria, who entered the treasure-house, set a trap for the thieves. Agamedes was caught in it, so Trophonius cut his head off to prevent him being identified, or giving Trophonius away. The earth promptly opened and swallowed Trophonius up 'in the sacred wood at Lebadeia at what they call the pool of Agamedes' (Paus. 9.37.3).

Despite his shoddy behaviour, Trophonius was revered as a hero (many heroes were less than admirable in their habits), and in due course acquired a temple and a statue at the site of the oracle (Paus. 9.39.3). Pausanias' long and detailed description, which is based on his own consultation, is one of the most vivid accounts of religious practice from antiquity.[51] He tells how the man who 'decides to go down to Trophonius' spends several days purifying himself in 'a building which is consecrated to Good Fortune and the Good Spirit'. He makes a series of sacrifices, at each of which a seer observes the entrails of the victim to see whether the consultant will be received kindly. On the night of the descent they slaughter a ram at a pit, calling to Agamedes. 'It makes no difference that all the earlier sacrifices have given good omens unless the entrails of this ram carry the same meaning.' (So what were the other ones for?) Then the consultant is washed in the river Hercyna and oiled; proceeding to two springs, which are very close together, he must drink 'the water of Forgetfulness, to forget everything in his mind until then, and then the water of Memory, by which he remembers the sights seen in his descent'. Special dress is required for the consultation: a linen tunic and heavy local boots.

> The oracle is on the mountainside above the sacred wood. It is surrounded by a circular platform of white stone, of the same circumference as a very small threshing floor, and something less than five feet in height. There are bronze posts standing on the platform linked together with bronze chains: there are doors to pass through. Inside the circle is a chasm in the earth, not natural but most carefully constructed with skill and architectural sense. It is shaped like a kiln with a diameter of about ten feet, I would say, and hardly more than twenty feet deep. There is no way down, but when a man is going to Trophonius they bring him a light, narrow ladder. When you get down you can see an opening between wall and floor about two feet wide and a foot high. The man going down lies on the ground with honey-cakes in his hands and pushes his feet into the opening and then tries to get his knees in. The rest of his body immediately gets dragged after his knees, as if some extraordinarily deep, fast river was catching a man in a current and sucking him down. From here on, inside the second place, people are not always taught the future in one and the same way: one man hears, another sees as well. Those who go down return feet first through the same mouth.

On emerging, the consultant is quizzed by the priests about his experiences; still shaking with terror, he is carried back to the building in which he was purified. 'Later he comes to his senses no worse than before, and can laugh again.' (Fontenelle in 1687 [1971.23] was sarcastically surprised that he had not laughed out loud during the actual 'consultation.') He concludes the experience by dedicating an account of whatever he has seen or heard, written out on a wooden tablet.

Another visitor who consulted Trophonius, according to the life written by Philostratus about the same time as Pausanias, was Apollonius of Tyana (8.19.1–2). Philostratus describes the cave 'enclosed by a circular palisade of iron stakes [Pausanias said bronze], and you enter it as it were by sitting down and being drawn in. People go in processions dressed in white clothing and carrying honey cakes in their hands to mollify the serpents that bite people as they descend.' Apollonius went down with a question couched in the best and purest philosophy, which apparently so pleased the hero that he kept Apollonius for seven days, and when he emerged it was at Aulis more than forty miles away, carrying a copy of Pythagoras.

Although one cannot regard Philostratus' story as the literal truth (especially the hero's underground lending library), Pausanias' detailed account reflects personal experience. The period of purification will have been important, though there seems to be no sign of a special diet, but it is important that no artificial stimulants are mentioned: piety and concentration were relied on to induce the religious experience. Water is part of the ritual, as seems to be commonly the case with oracular sites, but also in many others, notably healing shrines (see chapter 7).[52] It is notable that Pausanias (unlike Apollonius in the story) makes no mention of what he learnt from the oracle, or how the response was given, or even what his question was. This is in keeping with the practice of silence, observable also in the Eleusinian Mysteries, in which Pausanias had likewise been initiated.[53] All he leaves us with is the description of the outward trappings of the ritual; the religious core remains unexpressed.

Pausanias also tells a cautionary tale about one of King Demetrius' men who demanded admission without proper rites, and was cast out dead. For van Dale (1700, 196), who provides a wonderful engraving to illustrate the whole underground complex, this was a prime piece of evidence for the fraudulence of the oracles. His underground suite includes a special chamber where priests bludgeon impious enquirers to death.

A few inscriptions fill out the picture.[54] There was, for example, a (variable) fee to be paid:

> It seemed good to the city of the Lebadeians that whoever goes down into the cave should dedicate to Trophonius in his treasury a silver coin and ten cakes worth ten drachmas each. And whoever goes down and deposits ten

16 The interior of the cavern of Trophonius with its chambers and vaults. From Van Dale 1700 and labelled by Van Dale, 'Suspicious consulters, or those who have broken into the shrine, are murdered by the priests and thrown out by the non-sacred opening'.

cakes of ten drachmas, he shall be liable for three talents. Amyntas the son of Perdiccas the king of the Macedonians[55] went down into the cave on his own behalf and dedicated ... twenty ... Archemanidas [?] son of Dameas of Pellana went down and dedicated three minas. Telemachos son of Polemarchos a Dorian from Kytenion [placed] 2 darics and 115 drachmas in the treasury for Trophonius ... Pythonikos son of Philokrates from Tanagra, ten staters. Hecataeus son of Hecatodoros of Cos, 5 staters.[56]

In later times a chapel of St Christopher was built on the spot, according to a scholiast on Lucian.[57]

Some other hero oracles of mainland Greece continued to thrive in Pausanias' day, including the dice oracle of Heracles at Bura (chapter 8) and the oracle of Ino at Sparta (chapter 7). An alleged oracle of the seer Tiresias at Orchomenos is mentioned only by Plutarch, as having expired as a result of a plague in the neighbourhood.[58] Odysseus' grandfather, the equally cunning Autolycus, had an oracle at Sinope in Asia Minor (Strabo 12.3.11:

he does not specify the mode of operation), and there was one of Tiresias at Thebes. This thin gleaning of hero oracles only emphasizes by contrast the unusual nature of Trophonius, and the far greater importance of Apollo (and some other gods). In most cases it was the gods, not the dead, whom the Greeks wanted to speak to them in oracles, even though the heroes were prepared to speak to them directly, in dreams, whereas the gods required an intermediary.[59]

CHAPTER 6

The Oracle Coast: Sibyls and Prophets of Asia Minor

THE SIBYLS

Asia Minor is home to some of the oldest oracles in the Greek world. It has a claim to be the heartland of Greek prophetic speech, for this was where the legendary Sibyls originated. According to Pausanias (10.12.1–4), the Sibyl Herophile had been born long enough ago to foretell the Trojan War. 'She wrote all this while raving and possessed by the god; elsewhere in the oracles she said her mother was an immortal, one of the nymphs on Ida, but her father was a man.' He quotes lines in which she claims her home town as Marpessus in the Troad; nonetheless, the people of Erythrae laid vigorous claim to her and pointed out the cave where she was born: their edition of her oracles contained no reference to Marpessus. According to Pausanias, Herophile was a great traveller, and visited not only Claros and Delos but even Delphi (where in his time there was a statue of her). Some dedications survive from third-century BC visitors to her cave at Erythrae; it was restored in 162 BC and in the 160s AD. An elegiac inscription[1] commemorating the visit of Lucius Verus at this time repeats the genealogy from a nymph and a man called Theodoros, but insists that Herophile's birthplace was Erythrae: 'sitting on this rock, I sang to mortals prophecies of the sufferings that would come upon them later; I lived as a pure virgin for three times three hundred years upon the earth.'

Pausanias knew of many later prophetesses called Sibyls, some of them from Asia Minor (including one from the island of Samos), but for Heraclitus around 500 BC there was only one 'Sibylla', who 'with raving mouth uttering things without laughter and without charm of sight or scent, reaches a thousand years by her voice on account of the god'.[2] No source explains the cause of her 'raving': no chasm of fumes is invoked to account for her foreknowledge, but only possession by the god. The position is somewhat parallel to that of the Trojan prophetess Cassandra, a mortal woman but rewarded by Apollo for an amour by being given the gift

17 The Sibyl. Coin of L. Torquatus 58 BC.

of prophecy (but because she did not want a long-term relationship after her rape, he laid on her the curse that no one would believe her oracles). Sibylla somehow managed not to be possessed by the god while remaining virgin, an unusual achievement in mythology, but one that made her a model for the Pythia at Delphi and some other prophetesses.

The question has arisen whether the origins of the idea of the 'raving prophetess' came from Assyria.[3] Parke is sceptical, but the argument of Burkert, who first propounded the idea, seems to have some force. Babylon and Assyria are characterized by a class of prophetesses known as 'raving women' (see further chapter 7), as well as men, who would utter a kind of automatic speech while possessed by one of several gods or goddesses.[4] Speaking in the first person, as the god, the prophet would comment on questions of cult and royal policy, rarely private affairs. Very prominent in Mari (1830–1760 BC), such prophecies are rarer in sixth-century BC Babylon, though there was a guild of *zabbu* (prophets); and in seventh-century Assyria, as we shall see, revelations were often offered to the kings. Cilicia in the Sibyl's time lay within the ambit of the Assyrian empire, so that practices known in Assyria might well make an impact in this region; and if Assyrians were established in the south-east of Asia Minor, their ships – as well as Burkert's 'wandering mages' – surely reached its western coast as well. The Hittites, too, had links with the region,[5] and divination among them was in the hands of 'old women', who, though they mostly seem to have practised divination by lot or by the observation of birds, also are regularly associated with sacred springs, such as that at Eflatun Pinar.[6] Telmessus, on the fringes of Lycia and Cilicia, was well known in classical antiquity as *urbs religiosissima*[7] and the home of great diviners, not least Alexander the Great's courtier Aristander,[8] and it may have been an important link between the Greeks and the world of the Near East. It remains, as

Parke remarks,[9] surprising that the Troad should be the location of the first recorded instance of a raving prophetess in the Greek world; but the vagaries of preservation of our information are not to be minimized.

Heraclitus around 500 BC leaves it unclear whether he regarded the Sibyl as contemporary, recent, or ancient (though the reference to her prophecies covering a thousand years suggests that he put her before the Trojan War, despite the present tense 'reaches'). But Heraclides Ponticus (fr. 131a–c Wehrli) put her 'in the time of Solon and Croesus'. If this did not derive from something in the Sibylla's oracles, it was perhaps a natural conclusion from her appearance in the account of Croesus' reign given by Xanthus of Lydia (c.mid 5 BC), who had her turn up at Croesus' pyre to berate the Persian executioners: 'Miserable men, why do you pursue what is impious? Neither Zeus nor Phoebus nor famous Amphiaraus will permit it. But obey the undeceiving oracles of my words, lest you perish by an evil fate for your folly against God.'[10] The Sibylla makes no such appearance in Herodotus: as Parke suggests, she would not fit well into the theological structure Herodotus has erected for his account of the Croesus romance.[11] Parke (1988, 53) compares her with the prophetic Mother Shipton of the English Civil War, who may have been a literary figment or may have been a real wise woman from Knaresborough.

MOPSUS

The Sibyl was far from being the only prophetic figure of legendary Asia Minor. Another story, about the foundation of the oracle at Claros, deepens the picture.[12] The prophet Calchas, returning from the Trojan War accompanied by Amphilochus the son of Amphiaraus, encountered at Claros another distinguished prophet, Mopsus, and rashly challenged him to a competition. 'I am amazed in my heart,' he said, 'at all these figs on this wild fig-tree, small though it is: can you tell me the number?' Mopsus replies 'They are ten thousand in number, and their measure is a medimnus; but there is one over, which you cannot put in the measure.'[13] The reply was checked and proved true, at which Calchas collapsed and died.[14] An alternative version of the story[15] said that the question was how many piglets were inside a pregnant sow: 'Mopsus said "Three, of which one is female", and that when Mopsus proved to have spoken the truth, Calchas died of grief.'

Amphilochus, Calchas' companion, had survived the encounter with Mopsus, but another story[16] tells how Amphilochus and Mopsus together founded the city of Mallos in Cilicia, but fell out about who was to be the ruler. They fought a duel and both were killed and buried in tombs

18 Mopsus, identified as a seer by his wings and by the mirror (used as a 'crystal ball'), which he holds, on a coin of Mallos, *c.*390–385 BC.

carefully positioned to be out of sight of each other, for their hostility continued even in death, as did their oracular powers. The oracle of Amphilochus was regarded by Pausanias as 'the best' of those operating in his day: nearly five hundred years before him, Alexander the Great had performed sacrifices to Amphilochus as he marched along the coast from Soli.

Mopsus was also regarded as the founder of many cities on Turkey's southern coast, including Aspendus, Phaselis, Perge and Sillyon.[17] The legend reflects the gradual Hellenization of Lycia and Cilicia, for Mukšuš is a Luwian name, known from Hittite texts. The seer is given a Greek genealogy, as son of Tiresias' daughter Manto, by Apollo, and even appears in Linear B texts as Mo-qo-so. Mopsus is the predominant type on the coins of Mallos of the imperial period, where he is represented as wearing wings and carrying a mirror, signs of his shamanistic abilities. His rivalry with the Greek heroes may reflect prehistoric dynastic quarrels, but it also emphasizes the unusual importance of oracular sites in western and southern Asia Minor. And the Hittite connection suggests another possible link with oracular practices further to the east.

OF MICE AND FISH

Apollo himself had many oracular shrines in the region: little is known beyond their names, but enough bits of information survive to give a sense of their variety of practice. At Magnesia on the Maeander 'the statue of Apollo is extremely ancient and gives you physical powers of every kind; men consecrated to this statue leap from precipitous cliffs and high rocks, they pull up giant trees by the roots, and travel with loads on the narrowest footpaths.'[18] Though no communications from the god are mentioned, the cult is of a shamanistic kind.[19]

At Smyrna there was an oracle of 'first utterance heard', described by Pausanias 9.11.5, and Alexander was supposed to have had a prophetic dream there. At Aegae the title of the god was Apollo Chresterios, so one would suppose there must have been an oracle, but we know nothing about its operation. There are fine buildings and dedications by the gymnasiarchs but no reference to oracles. In AD 197 an envoy was sent to Apollo at Delphi; we are not told why.[20]

Gryneion had a shrine of Apollo, which Strabo called an oracle,[21] and depicted the speaking god on its beautiful coins: Virgil (*Aeneid* 4.345) mentions it but gives no details. Aelius Aristides visited the site but makes no mention of an oracle.[22] Other evidence for an oracular cult was lacking, and scholars doubted that there was one, until George Bean in 1954[23] published a response from Apollo of Gryneion to the people of Caunus, telling them which gods to propitiate in order to get good harvests. (Apollo and Zeus, the answer begins, before breaking off.) So a single fragmentary find can overturn a hundred years of sceptical discussion: a dedication by 'Philetairos the son of Attalus to Apollo Chresterios' (*CIG* 3527) was found by Cyriac of Ancona in the ruins of a temple between Myrina and Cyme, but was pronounced a fake by Buresch,[24] perhaps too brusquely. The shrine was important enough to have a book written about it by a scholar called Hermias, but we have no citations beyond a mention of the white robes worn at the festivals.[25] Philostratus (*Life of Apollonius* 4.14) says that Apollonius visited the oracle here but found it had been eclipsed by Orpheus, 'whose head had recently arrived from Thrace'.

Philostratus is also the source for the strange account of the ghost of Protesilaus at Elaious in the Troad, who gave oracles to athletes, healed the sick, and told a tale of the Trojan War that differed from that of Homer.[26] It is possible that the whole story is Philostratus' invention.

At Hierapolis there was a Charoneion, a cave of toxic vapours under the temple of Apollo, which only the eunuch priests of Cybele could enter without ill effects.[27] There was an oracle here of Apollo Kareios, but its responses[28] show no indication of ecstatic possession by anyone; rather, they are obtained by choosing a letter from a pot and reading off the corresponding 'fortune', a style of oracle widespread in south-west Asia Minor especially in the early empire (see chapter 7).

At Chryse in the Troad, Apollo was worshipped as Smintheus, 'mouse-god', because the god had destroyed a plague of mice here. Strabo (13.1.48)

19 Coin of Myrina, depicting Apollo of Gryneion. Reverse: Apollo advancing right, holding a branch of bay, second century BC.

who recounts the legend, and describes the cult-statue of Apollo with his foot on a mouse, makes no mention of an oracle, but Menander Rhetor, a rhetorician writing in the third century AD, gives detailed instructions on how to write an oration in praise of the shrine: 'the god came to us from Lycia, and occupied the Smintheum, and established an oracle in the place and set his tripods astir' (II.439.21). He describes a festival established for Apollo by Alexander, and suggests addressing the god: 'Sminthian Apollo, how should we address thee? As the sun that is the dispenser of light and source of the brilliance of heaven? Or as Mind, as the theologians say, penetrating all heavenly things and passing through the aether to this world of ours? As the creator of the universe, or as the Second Power?' The Neo-Platonic tone of these questions shows that Apollo was as ready to consider theological questions here as he was at Claros; but unfortunately we have no further information about the operation of the oracle. Alas, it seems unlikely that the mice gave the responses.

At Labranda there was a pool inhabited by fish with golden necklaces and earrings, which 'accept food gladly';[29] they may also have given oracles like the fish at Sura and perhaps Limyra (see below).[30]

Two oracles above all dominated the regions of western Asia Minor: Didyma and Claros. Claros had the reputation of being the oldest oracle in the region, tracing its foundation to Mopsus, but Didyma, whose origins also lay in legend, appears much earlier in the historical record and I shall accordingly treat it first.

20 The Smintheion.

21 Pool at Labranda, possible site of the fish oracle, fourth century BC.

22 Didyma. Temple of Apollo.

DIDYMA[31]

Didyma was the holiest shrine of the great city of Miletus, to which it was connected by a Sacred Way 16.4 kilometres long. It may have functioned as an oracle as early as 900 BC; an enclosure around an altar and the sacred spring were built as early as the seventh century BC. The temple of Apollo there was one of the first Ionic temples, only slightly post-dating that at Samos (575 BC), and it had received gifts from the pharaoh of Egypt, Necho, who reigned 609–593 BC. As usual there was a foundation legend: a shepherd named Branchus had been seduced by Apollo and his reward was the gift of divination. (The other known act of Branchus' life was to stop an epidemic by incantations.)[32] His descendants, the Branchidae, formed the hereditary guild of prophet-priests. Croesus tested the oracle at Didyma and, even though it did not solve his question, he sent it gifts.[33] The temple was destroyed in the Ionian Revolt, 494 BC, when Xerxes banished the Branchidae to Sogdia after he conquered Asia Minor, and removed all their treasures to the palace in Susa. The oracle seems to have remained silent until Alexander passed through Didyma in 334 BC and commissioned a new temple, which was only begun after his death by Seleucus I and was not completed for five hundred years. This is the temple whose remains stand today.

Its ground plan is unusual:[34] instead of a doorway leading directly from the columned pronaos into the cella, the person entering the temple faced at the back of the pronaos a high wall with two small side doors leading into sloping passages which progress to the eastern chamber, and a further central aperture or doorway at a height of 1.45 metres from the floor. The eastern chamber gives access to a flight of twenty-two steps leading down

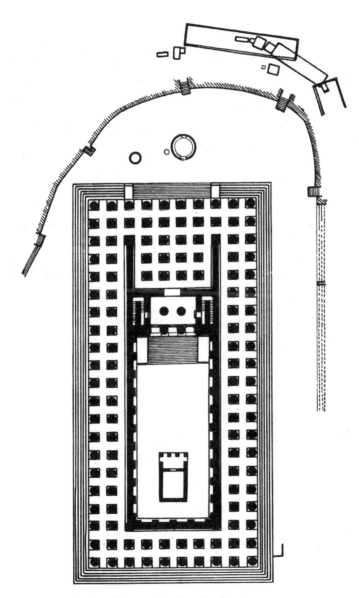

23 Didyma. Ground plan of the temple of Apollo, fourth century BC.

24 Didyma. Sloping passage from the pronaos to the interior courtyard.

into the *cella* or *adyton*, while small staircases at either side of the eastern chamber may have led up to an attic room. The enormous *adyton* (54 × 22.5 metres) was open to the sky; near its western end was a *naiskos*, or miniature temple (14.2 × 8.5 metres), in which stood the cult statue of the god. Below its floor was a *bothros*, or pit, for offerings; to the north-east of the *naiskos* was the sacred spring.

In archaic times the oracles were delivered by a priest called a *prophetes*, who was chosen by lot (Fontenrose [Hereafter F] no.47) and held office for one year. After Alexander's intervention in 334 BC, the prophet was a woman, perhaps reflecting the practice that had become canonical at Delphi and had also influenced Dodona.[35] The name *prophetes* became that of the chief priest, while the prophetess was called the *promantis* and seems to have been required to be a virgin. A long and elaborately worded response in hexameters[36] gives a positive answer to the simple question: 'Is it better that we appoint Satorneila priestess of Athena Polias, although she is a married woman?':

25 The naiskos in the courtyard of the Temple of Apollo, Didyma, fourth century BC.

> You are late, citizens, in coming to hear the mantic voice concerning a priestess of Kratogeneia, who burst through the head of her wise father and leapt in armoured dance in the house of the immortals, whence it has been her lot to govern manifold citadels . . . .

The question must have been prompted by the fact that priestesses were normally virgins:[37] at Claros, Apollo testified to the 'purity' of Claudia Prisca[38] and one wonders whether a virginity test was involved.[39]

The way in which the *promantis* received her inspiration is described, not very clearly, by Iamblichus in his book *On the Mysteries*, five hundred years after the refoundation.[40] Iamblichus' book is a reply to Porphyry's *Letter to Anebo* in which he belittled physical rituals of all kinds as a way of making contact with the gods; Iamblichus sets out to show that every kind of divination is an appropriate means of establishing such contact.[41] First Iamblichus mentions Porphyry's statement that the prophetess inhales vapours from the water of the sacred spring. He goes on:

> And as for the woman at Branchidai who gives oracles, it is either by holding the staff first given by a certain god that she is filled with the

divine radiance; or else when sitting on the axle she predicts the future; or whether dipping her feet or skirt in the water, or inhaling vapour from the water, at any rate, she receives the god: prepared and made ready by any or all of these preliminaries for his reception from without, she partakes of the god. This is what is shown by the abundance of sacrifices, the established custom of the whole ritual, and everything that is performed with due piety prior to divination: also the baths of the prophetess, her fasting for three whole days, abiding in the innermost sanctuaries, already possessed by light, and rejoicing in it for a long time.[42]

One thing that is clear is the importance of water in the ritual, as in so many oracular procedures.[43] But she does not seem to be drinking the holy water, any more than the Pythia at Delphi received her inspiration from drinking at the Castalian spring. Iamblichus has no doubt of the reality of the prophetess' inspiration, and the method of attaining it is comparable with that in other shamanistic procedures, in which prolonged fasting is generally important.[44] Native American sources are just one example among many.

'On the promantis' delivery of responses we have no information at all.'[45] Various scenarios have been proposed. The consultant may have entered the adyton and come close enough to the naiskos to see the god's image, propose his question to the promantis and receive a direct answer.[46] Alternatively,[47] the consultants all remained in the pronaos; the prophet took the consultants' written questions, obtained the responses from the *promantis*, and then ascended the steps from the adyton and crossed the east chamber to the doorway 1.45 metres above the floor of the *pronaos*: here his epiphany would have been something like that of the 'woman-at-the-window' depictions known from the Near East. Günther's reconstruction is attractive in so far as it resembles the data from Koropi, where the priests receive the questions, take them into the shrine, and in due course (at daybreak, at Koropi) bring them out with responses.

I think one could develop this scenario further. High windows are generally used for the epiphany of a priestess or goddess. One was located in the outer wall of the temple of Artemis at Ephesus, enabling a similar kind of epiphany, perhaps of the goddess herself. Is it possible that at Didyma the promantis herself appeared at the window and spoke the words that she had received from the god in her inspired state? The actual production of the responses would, as at Koropi, have been secret from the consultants.

Fontenrose exhibits the usual scepticism that the priestess could have composed long hexameter poems in a state of frenzy, and supposes that the chief priest (called the prophet) or scribes composed the responses in

advance, or transcribed her utterances into verse. This interpretation
ignores the universal indications of the ancients that the prophetess, as at
Delphi, spoke the god's words, and my answer to Fontenrose would be the
same as that to Bowden, that she could have spoken in verse in a state of
inspiration rather than frenzy. Perhaps we could add the responses from
the oracles of Delphi and Didyma to the limited canon of women's writing
from the ancient world?

Unlike Claros, Didyma kept a record in stone of its responses on site,
and we can accordingly read a large number of them, sometimes with the
question as well.[48] Most are in prose, but sixteen of the inscribed ones,
those classified by Fontenrose as 'historical', as well as all the 'quasi-historical' and 'legendary' responses, are in hexameter verses. They almost all
take the form of instructions, not predictions or riddles like those of the
legends of Croesus and Oedipus. Many of the historical ones are concerned
with the proper execution of building projects (F18, F19), such as Apollo's
temple (F13). Others prescribe cultic practices, like F14: 'The god said:
"propitiate Asphaleos Poseidon".'[49] F8 concerns collecting cash for Artemis:

> Will it be both pleasing to the goddess and advantageous to the demos
> both now and for the future to conduct the money collections for Artemis
> Boulephoros Skiris as the Skiridai interpret and propose, or as is now
> done? The envoys must report the god's response to the assembly, and the
> demos, having heard it, must deliberate how everything shall be done in
> accordance with the god's counsel.

F12 gives a positive response to the enquiry whether the Milesians should
make a treaty with the people of Heraclea under Latmos. An interesting
case is that of a poet who consulted the oracle as to whether he should
make a visit to the king of Bithynia (F16): this is not inscribed, but the
anonymous poet himself tells us of it in his address to the king:

> Hearing that of contemporary kings you alone show kingly quality, I
> wanted to have experience of it in person and to come into your presence
> and see what a king is, that I might be able to inform others in my turn.
> [This is presumably a coded appeal for generous patronage, which could
> then be the subject of an encomium of the king to spread his fame abroad.]
> Therefore I chose as adviser for my design the regulator of the kingdom's
> affairs. . . . I mean Apollo Didymeus, lawgiver and leader of the Muses, in
> accordance with whose response, to which I am entirely obedient, I have
> come; for you have offered a nearly common hearth to the learned.

An oracle, which was probably from Didyma, predicted the rule of the Emperor Trajan (r. AD 98–117).[50] As Trajan had refurbished the Sacred Way that led from Didyma to Miletus, and held the office of *prophetes* in (or before) AD 102, this was probably a prudent prediction if nothing more. But that the oracle should make a prediction at all is, as we have seen, unusual.

A couple of oracles known from literary sources relate to dilemmas in political affairs: F36, 'the god drove the oligarchs from his oracle for a long time' (how?).[51] In F38, the people of Cyme sent envoys to Branchidai to ask whether they should surrender Pactyes to the Persians. (Answer: Yes). This was worked up into a good story by Herodotus:[52] Aristodicus, mistrusting the response, removed all the birds' nests from Apollo's temple. This prompted outrage from the oracle, whereupon Aristodicus asked 'Do you, Lord, thus protect your suppliants, but bid the Cymeans surrender their suppliant?' The god replied 'Yes, I bid you do so, so that you may more quickly perish for your impiety, and that hereafter you may not consult the oracle about surrender of suppliants'. This is clearly a cautionary tale with several points, and need not be taken as historical truth except in so far as it reflects perceptions of the proper way to speak to the god.

The overall picture that emerges from the historical utterances of the prophetess is a somewhat prosaic one, of steady consultation, by individuals and communities, on matters both religious and practical. Small personal queries of the kind that predominate at Dodona are not in evidence, but that may be an accident of the sources, for why would the authorities wish to set up inscriptions about stolen bed linen and so-and-so's choice of a wife? Most of the enquiries known are from local enquirers, but the reputation of Didyma was international: it received assistance from the emperors Caligula and Trajan (though not, apparently Hadrian). Its activity continued, like that of Claros, for centuries after Delphi had gone into decline, and it, like Claros, was still receiving questioners when Christianity was making headway in the empire (chapter 8).

CLAROS

Xenophon of Ephesus' *Ephesian Tale*, written in the Roman period, opens with the hero and heroine, Anthia and Habrocomes, falling in love at first sight at a festival in Ephesus. Love-sickness sets in, and both sets of parents are at their wits' end: eventually, they send to consult the oracle of Apollo at Colophon. As it happens, both sets of messengers reach the sanctuary at the same time. Both of them receive the same response from the god:

Why do you long to learn the end of a malady, and its beginning?
One disease has both in its grasp, and from that the remedy must be
accomplished.
But for them I see terrible sufferings and toils that are endless;
Both will flee over the sea pursued by madness;
They will suffer chains at the hands of men who mingle with the waters;
And a tomb shall be the burial chamber for both, and fire the destroyer;
And beside the waters of the River Nile, to Holy Isis
The saviour you will afterwards offer rich gifts;
But still after their sufferings a better fate is in store.

(Xen. Eph. 1.5.6)

The fathers are mystified by this oracle (though it seems straightforward as literary oracles go), but decide to take the initial advice and marry the pair. After the wedding the couple set off on a tour by sea, completely failing to grasp the menace of line 4. Their departure thus sets in train the melodramatic plot of the novel. The oracle – to compare small things with great – performs a function similar to that in Sophocles' *Oedipus Tyrannus* in motivating the action of the characters and getting the plot moving.[53]

The oracle consulted by the Ephesian fathers is a real one. Apollo's oracular shrine was in fact located at Claros, a few miles away from Colophon but within its territory.[54] Probably a sacred place from earliest times, when Mopsus had established himself there (see above), it had come into its own in the Hellenistic period when a massive Doric temple was built to enclose the oracle chamber. We have a good many oracles issued by the god at Claros, from 334 BC to the third century AD, for people came from all over Asia Minor, especially in the early empire, to seek its advice.[55] However, none of the oracles (apart from being in hexameter verse) looks much like that given to the Ephesian fathers in Xenophon's novel. The literary handling of the oracle is at variance with its everyday practice. The oracles that we have are not on the whole riddling in form, though they are often pompous and obscure because of their ornate phraseology and neologisms,[56] and they are not predictive but constitute answers to requests for help or advice. (The oracle that so annoyed Oenomaus of Gadara, and induced him to write his book on *Wizards Unmasked*, is a clear exception to this pattern.) Merkelbach and Stauber (1996) make a distinction between the long hexameter responses for city delegations and the shorter 'off the peg' texts produced like fortune cookies for individual consulters. Their no. 9 is in a variety of metres that imitate the onset of prophetic frenzy (anapaests) followed by the god's response (trochaic tetrameters).

A good example is one that was inscribed at Ephesus:[57]

... Artemis of the beautiful quiver, from my family. For she is the leader of every city as midwife in childbirth, increaser of crops and giver of fruits. Bring a gold and ivory statue of her from Ephesus and place it joyfully in a temple; she will ward off pains and undo the destructive enchantments of plague, consuming with blazing faggots in torchlit nights the symbolic figures of wax made by the arts of the magicians. When you have carried out my instructions for the goddess, honour her with hymns and sacrifices as delighting in the bow, invincible, unapproachable, with unerring aim, the famous sharp-sighted maiden; in dances and in feasts let maidens and boys all over the salty lands of the Maeonian River Hermos celebrate her, crowning her with broad myrtle crowns and calling on the pure Artemis of the Ephesian land, that she shall be your uncorrupted helper for ever. But if you do not execute this instruction, you will pay the penalty of fire [i.e. disease?]. Pronounced by Apollo.

A gentler oracle for Nicomedia orders the people to honour Demeter in order to improve their crops.[58] Oracles for cities in Pamphylia and Cilicia give advice on how to protect themselves against pirate raids.[59]

Claros had the reputation of being the oldest oracle in the region. The Hellenistic temple was an imposing affair, with a facade 26 metres long, with six columns along the front; its length was eleven or twelve columns, and there were five steps up to the facade. The site was excavated by Louis Robert between 1950 and 1961; a plan to re-erect the peristyle from the fallen remains foundered as a result of the instability of the ground, and the considerable rise in the water table since antiquity. So one visits now the half-submerged altars of Apollo and Artemis, with terrapins basking on their surfaces, and admires the imposing bulk of the torsos of the statues of the gods, which were once twenty feet high. (Fibreglass replicas now stand in their original positions.)

The most exciting discovery of the excavators was the oracular chamber itself, situated directly underneath the cult statue of Apollo. To approach it, one went down a flight of steps 13 metres from the facade into a tunnel below the earth. This tunnel ran for 25 metres and changed direction seven times before ending up, via a 'dogleg' in a 'cavern' consisting of two rooms: the first contained an omphalos, or navel-stone, like that at Delphi, and

26 Claros. Altars of Apollo and Artemis.

27 The author with the cult statue of Artemis at Claros, still *in situ, c.*1985. The marble statues have now been removed from the site and replaced with standing fibreglass replicas.

28 Claros. The vaults of the underground passage to the adyton.

stone benches, the second the sacred spring at which the prophet would drink to obtain inspiration.

Tacitus (*Annals* 2.54) has a succinct description of what went on, a propos the visit of Germanicus to the shrine (he later died in suspicious circumstances before he could become Roman emperor):

> There, it is not a woman, as at Delphi, but a priest chosen from certain families, normally from Miletus, who ascertains simply the number and names of the applicants. Then descending into a cave and drinking a draught from a secret spring, the man, who is commonly ignorant of letters and of poetry, utters a response in verse answering to the thoughts conceived in the mind of any enquirer. It was said that he prophesied to Germanicus, as oracles usually do, an early doom.

Pliny the Elder (*Natural History* 2.232) adds some information which seems to suggest that anybody might drink the water of Apollo: 'in the cave of Apollo of Claros at Colophon there is a pool a draught from which causes marvellous oracular utterances to be produced, though the life of the drinkers is shortened'.[60] (One thinks of the ill effects of other oracular procedures, such as that of Trophonius which prevented the consultant from laughing again, at least for a long time.) But Iamblichus, while confirming the oracular power of the water itself, is explicit that it is the prophet only who drinks 'on certain appointed nights, after performing many preliminary ceremonies, and after drinking, he delivers his oracles, no longer seen by the spectators present'.[61] Probably those who descended into the earth had also undergone a rite of initiation (of which we also hear here), as was also the case at Samothrace where oracles could, it seems, sometimes be obtained from the gods of the Mysteries.[62] Questioners who had not been initiated waited outside.

The position is complicated by the evidence of three inscriptions from the Hadrianic period,[63] which describe three separate officials: the priest (*hiereus*), the prophet and the *thespiodos*, or singer of oracles. The respective roles of these three are uncertain: it has usually been supposed that the prophet uttered the words of the god while the *thespiodos* put them into verse. The priest would then be the administrator of the shrine, as at Koropi. But Louis Robert argued for a reversal of these roles.[64] It is notable that the normally sceptical Tacitus accepts without comment the information that the unlettered 'priest' composed the oracles in verse. However, I doubt whether Tacitus ever visited an oracle, and he may be speaking loosely. Modern scholars have been unwilling to accept composition by the unlettered priest, and besides there is the need to find a job for the *thespiodos*; Robin Lane Fox writes in his brilliant evocation of the Clarian scene: 'Was this inspired utterance immediately cast in neat iambic verse? Some of the surviving oracles are metrical tours de force and they make this notion impossible. There was, after all, a thespode [sic].'[65] Perhaps it is best to imagine a collaborative effort between the *thespiodos* who spoke the god's words and the *prophetes* who transmitted them to the consultant; but this militates against Tacitus' idea of the unmediated delivery to the consultant.

The rational and prosaic Richard Chandler,[66] visiting the site in the early nineteenth century, commented that the unlettered priest,

> after drinking of this spring ... uttered responses made on the subject on which each [consulter] had thought in his own mind; but this practice was prejudicial to his health, perhaps from the dampness of the place, and he was commonly short-lived. He got by rote, I conceive, or else carried down with him, the answers ready prepared; and the god would soon have lost his reputation, had the consulters been so cunning as to have kept every one his secret from the agents and spies employed to dive into their business.

A kinder gloss is put on this process by Lane Fox[67] who imagines informal discussions beforehand between the consultants and the staff, 'starting the

simple process by which a good counselling service works. They gave away
enough to suggest an answer before they asked the questions for which
they had come. There was no conscious fraud, no insincerity.'[68] I think it
likely that, as at Delphi and Didyma, the prophetess received (what she
believed to be) the word of the god in a state of inspiration and that this
was communicated to the questioner by an intermediary. But the evidence
is insufficient to decide the question.

The oracle was visited from far and wide, particularly in the years
following the Emperor Hadrian's visit in the course of his tour of the
empire in AD 135–8. Everyone, it seems, who came, left inscriptions
recording their visit. All the available stone surfaces – the propylaea, the
orthostats, the columns, the bases, even the steps of the temple are covered
with inscriptions, 220 in all. They include pilgrim graffiti, lists of priests,
records of embassies,[69] details of capital cases, troop levies, financial
accounts and details of festival arrangements; they provide a vivid picture
of the busy life of the sanctuary and the numerous officials involved in its
daily round.[70] Freya Stark in her description of her visit to Claros[71]
compares this plethora of writing to the personal columns of a daily news-
paper; but in fact the inscriptions comprise everything except the personal
details that would be represented by the questions to the oracle and its
responses. The numerous records of the oracle's responses that we have

29 Claros. Inscribed temple steps.

come from everywhere but Claros, for the cities that sent consultants to enquire set up the answers in their own town squares.[72] So, though the inscriptional clutter is similar to that described by Pliny the Younger (*Letters* 8.8.7) at the oracle of Clitumnus near Spoletum, the content is quite different: close to the image of the god Clitumnus, 'the written oracles lying there prove the presence and prophetic powers of his divinity . . . you can study the numerous inscriptions . . . many of them you will admire, but some will make you laugh'.

The enquirers, indeed, that we know of are in large part communities not individuals. There were personal enquiries, as at Dodona, but few records have survived: one is Tacitus' account of Germanicus' enquiry, who, on his visit to Claros received a doleful answer. 'It was conveyed to Germanicus through riddles, as is the wont of oracles, that his death was imminent.'[73] Another is the enquiry of the inveterate consulter of oracles, Aelius Aristides (early second century AD), who received the response that he would be healed at Pergamum.[74] One Stratonicus, probably a priest at Didyma (Buresch 1889, no. 24) had a dream which so frightened him that he enquired of the oracle whether it was true: he received the reply:

> One long year [or, A long time still][75] is allotted to you;
> But honour the eye of life-giving Zeus with placatory sacrifices.

Buresch attributed the oracle to Claros, assuming that Stratonicus consulted the neighbour shrine rather than his own; but Busine attributes the response rather to Didyma: in either case, the individual enquiry is unusual.[76]

The Cynic writer Oenomaus of Gadara, writing about AD 120, recorded three responses he had received from the god at Claros, which were so ridiculous that in his eyes they completely discredited the oracle: one was 'from a wildly-whirling sling a man shoots stones and slays with his throws geese fed on grass'. You can understand his irritation if he received such a reply, but of course we do not know what his question was; and the inscribed texts of Clarian oracles are not at all like this meaningless gibberish, though no. 20 comes close: 'Up, with swift hand, work hard and get on with your fishing; for it will give you a rich reward, which I apportion to you.'

In the first and early second centuries, it is communities whose enquiries and responses are recorded. The people of Antioch, perhaps in the reign of Tiberius, consulted Claros to find out more about the bones of a giant they found when the river Orontes was diverted: they were told the bones belonged to Orontes the Indian.[77] Several, of greater moment, concern the plague that swept through Asia Minor in the wake of Lucius Verus' withdrawal from Mesopotamia.[78] The city of Caesarea Troketta set up the response it received in reply to its enquiry of how to be released from the disaster:[79]

> You who inhabit Troketta beside snowy Mount Tmolus, honoured by Bromios and the most mighty son of Cronos, why indeed now in amazement do you wend your way to my threshold, desiring to approach the pavement of truth? To you in your care I shall shout a prophecy all of verity.
>
> Woe! Woe! A powerful disaster leaps on to the plain, a pestilence hard to escape from, in one hand wielding a sword of vengeance, and in the other lifting up the deeply mournful images of mortals newly stricken. In all ways it distresses the new-born ground which is given over to Death – and every generation perishes – and headlong tormenting men it ravages them.
>
> Such are the evils which are intended at once.
>
> But, Ionians who are eager to see an escape from these things in accordance with divine law, who indeed have contrived to come near to my aid, from seven fountains strive to provide pure liquid. Fumigate it from afar and draw it off eagerly and sprinkle the houses at once with nymphs who have become pleasant.
>
> In order that unstricken the men who are left behind on the plain may achieve to their fill the fair things out of the blessings which are revived again, straightway provide that you set up Phoebus in the midst of the plain, with one hand wielding (a bow) . . .

A response like this is clearly not a case where a 'priest might produce stock answers in verse';[80] the envoys from Troketta might feel that their counsellor had a rather obscure and convoluted way of expressing himself, but the essential message they had to take home was clear: 'set up a statue of Apollo'.

Apollo, besides being the god of prophecy, was also the god of plague: the strings of his lyre might sing of past and future, but the string of his bow dispatched death, and at the Smintheion north of Claros he was worshipped as Apollo Smintheus, 'mouse-god' – no doubt covering plague rats in the rubric. So it was not just self-advertisement that led the god to prescribe a statue. In fact, Apollo at Claros very commonly prescribed statues as a solution: at Callipolis (Gallipoli),[81] another enquiry about plague elicited an instruction to offer sacrifices and a statue. Other enquiries about the plague from Pergamum[82] and from Hierapolis (Pamukkale)[83] elicited orders to send, respectively, a sacrifice and a choir, and a 'proskynema' ('team of worshippers') to Claros. Such sacred embassies then had their record inscribed somewhere on the stones of Claros. Another enquiry from the region of Yelinez-Serai (Upper Tembris valley) received a response that explicitly identified Apollo with the sun:

> Set up for me in this place an altar for all to see, facing towards the rays of the far-seeing sun, and perform lawful sacrifices on it each month, in order that having become your protector, I may make things seasonable. For it is I who am the provider of fruits to mortals whomsoever I wish to preserve and to whom I know how to keep bringing good repute.[84]

At Adrianopolis (Edirne)[85] a group of Thracian ladies recorded that they had dedicated 'the ordained images of the gods in accordance with the oracles of the Lord Apollo of Colophon'.[86] At Syedra in Pamphylia the god ordered the authorities to set up

> an image of blood-stained, man-slaying Ares . . . while holding him in the iron chains of Hermes. Let Justice on the other side call him to trial and judge him. Make him like a suppliant: thus he will be peaceful towards you, after he has driven out the unholy mob far from your country, and will restore the prosperity you pray for.[87]

We do not know what enquiry it was that elicited this remarkable order; but a brilliant study by Louis Robert[88] has elucidated the statue group by reference to coins of Syedra issued in the first and second centuries AD (from Tiberius to Gallienus) depicting precisely this unusual statue group, of Justice pronouncing judgment over an Ares disarmed and bound by Hermes. The occasion of the original oracle is most probably trouble with brigands in the early empire. That it is from Claros is assured by the fact that another oracle of Claros, erected at Iconium (Konya),[89] prescribes the erection of statues of Hermes, 'slayer of Argus', and of Law (Thesmos) on either side of an image of Ares.[90] The wording of the Iconium oracle is quite different, so if the priest or *thespiodos* had 'stock responses' these did not extend to the wording of the remedy.

A more lavish dedication is made 'to the gods and goddesses in accordance with the interpretation of an oracle of the Clarian Apollo'. Inscriptions with identical wording have been found in several widely scattered locations in the western empire, including Vercovicium (Housesteads) on Hadrian's Wall, at Nora in Sardinia and Cuicul in Numidia, at Volubilis in Mauretania and at Corinium in Dalmatia.[91] The phenomenon is unparalleled. A.D. Nock (1928) assumed that all were drawn from a single corpus of Clarian oracles, which was used as a reference work by these far-flung military units. Eric Birley,[92] however, suggested that all went back to a single consultation by the Emperor Caracalla concerning, perhaps, his health or the well-being of the empire in general. Instructions were then sent empire-wide to set up such a dedication. Either explanation is certainly more likely than the assumption that all these groups sent letters all the way to Claros for advice and received identical replies.

Certainly it was not uncommon to consult Claros by letter. Ovid (*Fasti* 1.20) implies as much, and the dispatch of envoys from Troketta and those other places would be tantamount to sending a letter: a written enquiry was required, and there was no postal service other than your own emissary.

The order from an oracle to set up a cult statue is relatively uncommon (except Herodotus 5.82.1ff., Damia and Auxesia, which may be legendary). Oracles are often consulted on whether to set up a cult, or which god to sacrifice to in order to ensure success, but they do not otherwise send instructions to honour a particular god out of the blue, to solve the enquirer's problem. This seems to be a speciality of Claros, and Fritz Graf[93] asks why this should be. He compares the tendency to set up statues of healing gods after a cure (Lucian, *Philopseudes* 19), and suggests that such images constitute a resort to an imagined but reassuring ancient past. One might equally propose that such claims by the oracle to theological insider knowledge look forward to the future, when Claros became known for its theological expertise and was consulted on quite abstruse questions about the nature of the divine. There was something special about Claros, which looked beyond the specifics of the cult of Apollo and claimed access to a deeper awareness of the ways to put the world to rights. The gods you used for individual cases – the bound Ares is the prime example – were becoming mere instruments. The world of theurgy is not far away, when a Chaldaean oracle (fr 224 des Places 2003) might enjoin the making of an image as a virtually magical rite.[94]

ORACLES OF SOUTHERN ASIA MINOR

The southern coastal region of Asia Minor was at least as rich in oracles as the west, including many dice oracles (chapter 8) and healing oracles (chapter 7). An unusual group of oracles in this region is associated with the god Ares.[95] Herodotus (7.75–6) refers to one such somewhere in Pisidia, near Termessus, but Gonzales has identified twenty-nine sites of Ares oracles.[96] In some places the god is depicted, in full armour and a helmet with a double crest, feathers and cheek pieces. Probably he is in origin a local god (maybe related to a Hittite warrior-god) to whom the name Ares has become attached because of the similar iconography. A typical dedication from the second century AD comes from nearby Side:

> Having received an oracle from the god, Memnon son of Trebe[ines dedi-cate]d at his own expense the bronze statue on behalf of Trebenios son of Nesba. [He] ful[filled his vow, for] the god [w]as p[ropitious].[97]

In most cases, however, Apollo usurped the name and function of whatever god had preceded him, as at the healing oracle of Sarpedon (later Apollo Sarpedonius) in Cilicia. Major oracles of Apollo in the region are those of Apollo at Patara, Sura, Cyaneae and Sidyma. At Patara a foundation legend attributed the name either to a son of Apollo named Pataros or to the loss of a basket (*patara*) by a daughter of Ophion: it was blown into the sea and washed up at Patara.[98] The method of divination involved a tripod and cauldron,[99] and there was a *prophetes*,[100] as well as a virgin priestess who, according to Herodotus (1.182), slept in the temple as, it seems, the consort of the god;[101] it functioned in winter only.[102] Activity seems to have ceased at some time in the Hellenistic period, since Pomponius Mela in about AD 40 refers to the oracle as in decline; however, it was revived in the second century AD, under Antoninus Pius,[103] and became wealthy as a result of a benefaction of 20,000 denarii by the great euergetist Opramoas in AD 141.

At Cyaneae, Pausanias[104] tells us that consultation took place by gazing into the waters of a spring: a coin of Gordian depicts Apollo standing with a water vessel, and the legend Κυανείτων χρησμός, oracle of the Cyaneans. The site was supposed to have been founded by the hero Thyrxeus (Lycian Turaχssi), who again became assimilated to Apollo.

At Sidyma, Apollo was worshipped in a sea-cave called Loptoi, where a maiden, peering in, had once seen the god and immediately plunged in. The local historian Polycharmus recorded one of Apollo's utterances, which was inscribed on a rock nearby.[105] It prescribes in hexameters for the city, 'the kin of Phoebus Apollo', the procedure for tending the sacred para-phernalia: it is to be done by a pure virgin, as is suitable for the goddess: 'these blessings the lord the far-shooter reveals to you, and the goddess of wild country, the raiser of hounds'.

One of the most intriguing of these Lycian oracles is that at Sura, which was the oracular site belonging to Myra, as Claros was for Colophon and Didyma for Miletus.[106] The oracular temple still stands at the end of an inlet of the sea between crags, which calls to mind the location of Delphi. In antiquity it stood by the shore; now the sea is a mile away. Before the temple a spring of fresh water welled up into the sea, causing a whirlpool,

30 Sura. General view with the temple of Apollo bottom left. In front of it is a marshy area corresponding to the ancient fish pool. In antiquity the sea came within a few feet of the pool.

into which offerings were thrown. Polycharmus again[107] is the source for several ancient accounts. If the fish accepted the food (which seems to have taken the form of shish-kebabs) offered to them, the reply was favourable; but if, with a flick of their tails, they cast it back onto the land, the reverse. As Aelian describes it, 'the priest of Apollo scatters the flesh of calves that have been sacrificed to the god, and sea-perch come swimming up in shoals and eat the flesh, as though they were guests invited to the feast'.[108] The inscriptions of Sura include no oracles,[109] but on the acropolis two handsome plaques engraved on the rock record the dedication of a statue of priests of 'the most illustrious god Surius Apollo of the Myreans'.[110]

Further east, in Cilicia, there were oracles of Mopsus at Mopsoukrene near Mallos[111] and of Amphilochos at Mallos, where we are even told by Lucian (*Alexander the False Prophet* 19) the fee charged for a consultation: two obols.[112] Lucian's Eucrates was told that this oracle 'was a particularly intelligible and veracious one: I was told that any question, duly written down on a tablet and handed to the priest, would receive a plain, definite answer'.[113] Pausanias (1.3.4) also calls the oracle the most reliable of his time. A man from Soli got a verbal answer,[114] and dreams were also used.[115]

31 Honorific inscriptions of the priests of Apollo Surios.

The last Greek oracle further east in Cilicia was that of Apollo Sarpedonius at Cape Sarpedon on the Calycadnus delta south of Seleuceia (Silifke).[116] The oracle of Sarpedon is recorded as having given some obscure replies to the Hellenistic king Alexander Balas – 'beware of the place which was the birthplace of a two-formed being' – and to the Palmyrene queen Zenobia in (probably) AD 271.[117] Apollo was said to have saved the city from locusts by sending a flock of rose-coloured starlings, known as Seleuciads. But the fame of the site came with its transformation into a Christian place of pilgrimage and healing when it was appropriated by St Thecla in the fifth century AD, who transferred to it the healing powers that had previously been associated with the neighbouring shrine of Aegeae.

The Levant was also home to a few oracles that acquired fame as their world became Greek: that of Apollo at Daphne outside Antioch,[118] those of Aphrodite at Aphaca,[119] of Zeus Belus at Apamea,[120] of Apollo at Hierapolis/Membij[121] and Jupiter at Heliopolis/Baalbek. But they offer us no further information on the mode of operation of the oracles; at Antioch and Aphaca, we hear the gods speak only when the Christians come to silence them.

CHAPTER 7

Dreams and Healing

ANCIENT THEORIES OF DREAMING

All human beings dream. In dreams the mind, or soul, seems to wander beyond its bodily confines, and anything seems to be possible.[1] Such strange things happen, it is difficult to believe they do not carry a meaning; and from these it is a short step to the idea that the gods send dreams in order to speak to us. Most Greeks before the time of Xenophanes[2] will have held this view, as did the peoples of Mesopotamia.

Dreams and oracles are often considered in the same breath, by Plato for example (*Apology* 33) as well as, eight centuries later, Damascius,[3] who mentions the prophetic dreams of the sage Isidore. Plato (*Symposium* 202e–3a) explains:

(the daimones) form the medium of the prophetic arts, of the priestly rites of sacrifice, initiation and incantation, of divination and of sorcery, for the divine will not mingle directly with the human, and it is only through the mediation of the spirit world that man can have any intercourse, whether waking or sleeping, with the god.[4]

In literature dreams may perform the same function as oracles, of motivating action and keeping the plot on track, and providing dramatic irony, since the audience understands the meaning of dreams that may be obscure to the characters. Examples occur in tragedy (Hecuba's dream; Clytemnestra's dream of Orestes; Atossa's dream in *Persae*), and also in the novels: dreams and oracles reinforce each other throughout Heliodorus' *Aithiopica*.[5] In Sophocles' *Electra* (472–501 BC) the chorus asserts that there is no truth in dreams or oracles, putting them on the same predictive footing. When not rejected, dreams are found as hard to interpret as oracles:[6] God communicates in code, and we have to decipher the messages.[7]

According to the Delphic myth (pp. 34–5, above), dreams were the main form of prophecy available until Apollo established a proper oracle and organized the god's communications with mankind. A dream is clearly more hit-and-miss in its way of communicating as it is only rarely that the god addresses the dreamer directly (see below). Democritus thought that the idea of gods actually arose from dream visions[8] – perhaps reminding us of the idea that gods emerge from the experiences of the 'bicameral mind' – while Tertullian stated that humans' *knowledge* of gods came from dreams.[9] However, most Greeks would have regarded oracles as more reliable sources of information than dreams, and needing to be confirmed by other tests, such as sacrifice.[10]

From the earliest times, the interpretation of dreams was an important skill. In the Old Testament, Joseph's ascent to power at the Egyptian court was the result of his ability to interpret dreams (as well as reading his drinking cup, and other techniques).[11] In the Greek world, Prometheus' introduction of the art of divination included the skill of interpreting dreams: the ability to foresee the future reduced the gods' advantage over humans.[12]

Meaningful dreams[13] in Greco-Roman literature fall into two categories. First there are the dreams of everyday activity, or of aberrant activity that seems to become like an everyday occurrence in the dream: it may simply represent itself, or it may function as a symbol or allegory of something else; but secondly there are 'Homeric' dreams in which a person or god appears to the sleeper and gives him or her advice or information. (Harris calls these, respectively, episodic and epiphanic dreams.) The first type of dream can be further subdivided into the two types familiar to most modern dreamers: the anxiety dream – as when Achilles' pursuit of Hector around the walls of Troy is compared to a dream; and the merely 'weird' dream – Harris aptly calls them 'dream-like dreams',[14] which often repeats events of the day in jumbled relations. Several dreams dreamt by Alexander the Great are recorded:[15] they include his premonition of Clitus' death; his dream of the satyr at Tyre, which depends on wordplay for its interpretation; and his dream of a herb that would cure sickness in the army. These all seem both realistic and admonitory. Both kinds can also be either true or false, emerging from the gate of ivory or that of horn, as Homer and Virgil describe it. (Later, Plutarch[16] described an Oracle of Night and the Moon, in outer space, which is responsible for sending both true and false dreams.)

The second type of dream is famously represented by Achilles' vision of the dead Patroclus (*Iliad* 23, 75ff.). An unusual case is that of the dead priestess Ammias at Thyateira whose gravestone offers revelatory dreams (*TAM* 5.2.384 no. 1055):[17] 'to Ammias, her children and the initiates of the gods erected the altar with the socle for the priestess of the gods, in memory. If anyone wishes to learn the truth from me, let him pray at the altar: whatever he wishes he will obtain it through a vision, by day or by night.' Vivid examples from late antiquity include the dream dreamt by a paralyzed man, in which a speaker tells him to buy a catch of fish – and among the fish he finds the curse figurine that had paralyzed him;[18] and the occasion described by Augustine when a dead father appears to his son in a dream and tells him where the receipt for a certain debt is.[19] The figure who appears need not be dead, but may be just far away. In Herodotus 7.13, Xerxes has a dream in which 'a tall, handsome man stood over him' and ordered Xerxes to persist with the expedition against Greece that he was minded to call off, 'and then flew away'. The identity of the dream-figure is not explained, but it seems to be enough that he 'stands over' the king and speaks to him in an authoritative way. (Perhaps it is Xerxes' bicameral mind in action.) All dreams in Herodotus come true, and all are dreamt by barbarians;[20] barbarians in Herodotus can't handle oracles (cf. p. 51, above).

Even what seems a visionary dream may require interpretation: Hecuba[21] has a dream of her dead son but longs for the prophetess Cassandra to explain it to her. In the *Alexander Romance* the magician Nectanebo sends a 'sea-hawk'[22] to carry a dream to Philip.[23] The bird speaks to Philip, but at the same time the king sees a vision of the god Ammon making love to his wife: so this narrative combines the two types of dream in one. In Apuleius (11.27), Osiris appears to Asinius Marcellus and tells him to expect Lucius to arrive for initiation shortly.

The epiphanic dream is relatively uncommon (perhaps unknown) in our culture,[24] but it was regarded as prevalent in antiquity. Furthermore, even the first, episodic, type of dream was regarded as being of prophetic value. Philo (*c*.1 AD) in his book *On Dreams* begins by stating that a preceding, now lost, book was devoted to just this type of visionary or heaven-sent dream, while the second, extant, book is about dreams 'in which our own mind . . . seems to be possessed and god-inspired, and so capable of receiving some foretaste and foreknowledge of things to come'.[25]

Many books were devoted to the interpretation of dreams,[26] and theories became increasingly sophisticated. In the fifth century BC the Hippocratic *On Dreams*, which takes the form of a dictionary of dream symbols, uses the dreams for diagnostic purposes: the remedy to be applied is determined by the type of dream.[27] Dream-interpreters seem to have been numerous, and Plutarch[28] characterizes dream-interpreting as a good career for a poor man.

Aristotle's *On Divination in Sleep*[29] took a common-sense view that dreams have bodily causes; they may be dealing with the 'day's residue'; those that seem to refer to distant or future events may be just coincidence. But he does concede that there may be prophetic dreams, just as otherwise deranged people seem sometimes to have the gift of clairvoyance. The clarity of the message, like a reflection in water, depends on the state of the medium.[30] He cites the atomist theory of Democritus (B166 *DK*) by which dreams, like other images, are caused by the emanation of a film of particles from the surface of objects.[31] This would not exclude the emanation of such particles from gods, but Democritus' successor Epicurus absolutely denied the possibility of visions of the gods and prophetic dreams (as did Diogenes the Cynic, DL 6.43). Aristotle, too, with his physiological explanation of dreams, rejects the idea that dreams may be sent by gods, though the dreamer may be himself *daimonios* – 'godly'?

The rationalist argument had always been available, for even as early as Herodotus, the Persian king's dream (above) is dismissed by his adviser Artabanus as 'the day's residue' (7.16). A generation after Aristotle, the philosopher and (briefly) ruler of Athens, Demetrius of Phalerum, wrote a book *On Dreams*: we know nothing of it apart from its title, and the fact that all the dreams it discussed were supposed to have come true;[32] but as Demetrius also wrote a book *On Chance* (or *Fortune*), we may surmise that he was interested in the question of whether the future could be foreknown through dreams.

Stoic writers took both dreams and oracles[33] very seriously as prognostications of the future. Chrysippus (whom Cicero characterized as obsessed with dreams) in his book *On Dreams* drew on the earlier writer Antiphon, 'On the criticism of dreams',[34] as did his colleague Antipater; and we know also the names of Geminus of Tyre (Artemid. 2.46), Artemon of Miletus (Pliny, *Natural History* 27.7) and Phoebus of Antioch, who treated the same subject. More detail is known about Hermippus of Berytus, whose book was heavily used by Tertullian in his own treatment of dreams in *de anima*. Tertullian cites a list of fourteen prophetic dreams that were known as a matter of historical fact to have come true (46.3–9). They include examples from Herodotus, about Astyages the king of the Medes, whose daughter urinated so copiously that she flooded all of Asia (i.e. her son Cyrus became ruler),[35] and Polycrates' daughter who dreamt of her father being washed by the moon and anointed by the sun (i.e. he was crucified by the Persian king); Philip II's dream, recounted by Ephorus, that he saw his wife's vagina being sealed with the sign of a lion (i.e. Alexander the Great is inside); Mithridates' conquest of Pontus (from Strabo); and several Roman examples, such as Cicero's prophetic dream of the future greatness of Augustus (from Vitellius' commentaries).

Galen's *On Diagnosis from Dreams* is lost and was perhaps the most significant representative of a lost tradition of diagnosis through dreams. He apparently practised incubation to get answers to important questions, and even conducted a dangerous arteriotomy on himself as a result of dream advice,[36] as well as using a patient's dreams to read his condition. He gives a fivefold classification of dreams into daytime thoughts, repetition of the day's actions, activities of the prophetic soul, messages from the gods and imbalance of humours – but he says it is not easy to tell them apart. Cicero, in sceptical mode, proposed that the only *use* of dreams was for medical diagnosis (*div.* 2.69.142). Some doctors may have encouraged incubation as part of the patient's treatment.[37]

The best-known of ancient writings on dreams – because it is preserved in full – is Artemidorus' *Interpretation of Dreams* of the second century AD. Artemidorus prides himself on the depth of his research – he has even talked to market-place diviners – and the comprehensiveness of his coverage. Most of his book is devoted to the discussion of the symbolic meaning of things that happen in dreams. A dream, like an oracle, is a riddle: Cic. *div.* 2.70, 12.8. But, like Aristotle, he did not think that dreams were sent by the gods: the model is medical.[38] For example, 'to dream that one's forehead is made of brass, iron or stone is auspicious only for tax-collectors' (1.23). In similar mode, a Mesopotamian physiognomic treatise states: 'if a man has a bulging right eye, he will be eaten by dogs'.[39] Artemidorus makes a clear distinction between dreams of this kind, which he calls *enhypnia* ('dreams in sleep') and visionary or oracular dreams for which he uses the other regular Greek term *oneiros*, giving the word a false etymology from *on eirein*, 'to speak what is'.

Such dream books have continued into modern times. Byzantine examples include the *Christian Dream Book of Daniel*, an alphabetical work of reference.[40] J.C. Lawson writes of the Greece of a century ago: 'a new edition of some Μεγας Ονειροκριτης, or "Great Dream-Interpreter", figures constantly in the advertisements of Athenian newspapers, and the public demand for such works is undeniable. In isolated homesteads, to which the Bible has never found its way, I have several times seen a grimy tattered copy of such a book preserved among the most precious possessions of the family.'[41] In my own family a copy of *Zadkiel's Universal Dream Book* had moved from house to house over several generations: its frontispiece depicts the Dream of Joseph.

Later writers preferred a model in which dreams gave the dreamer access to the divine world and associated knowledge. Iamblichus (*c.* AD 245–335)[42] accepted dreams as prophetic; in fact, he shows no interest in any other kind of dream, given his general enthusiasm for all forms of divination. In his own time, he remarks, they are doing better than the other types of oracle.[43] Voices come to us on the verge of sleep and offer divine guidance. He also sees in such dreams the origin of medicine.

The latest 'pagan' author to write on dreams, the Christian Neo-Platonist Synesius (*c*.370–413 AD), situates prophetic dreaming in the context of a philosophical theory of the ascent of the soul to God. For a man who eventually became a bishop, he is very free with his discussion of the role of the pagan gods in dreams. Convinced of the value of divination as a method of predicting the future, he finds dreaming a particularly useful exercise at a time when all forms of pagan observance have been abolished. As he points out, no one can make laws against dreaming; and if you prepare yourself properly before sleep,[44] you will have no need to make a pilgrimage to Siwa or to Delphi to find the way to divinity. (This is precisely why Apollo seized Delphi from Gaia and her oracle of dreams:[45] she was making it too easy for the human race. Now direct access to the gods is restored, as in pre-Apollonian days.) Dreaming is cheap, there is no need to collect expensive foreign ingredients; it is democratic, philanthropic and philosophical. He even explains how images can be forerunners of events, in the way that landmarks are forerunners of destinations, so that sailors may know they are close to a certain city when they recognize a particular rock.

Like Apollo, Christian writers are opposed to the divinatory use of dreams and deny its validity. They include Antiochus (n. 44), who warns against being led astray by dreams – you might even convert to Judaism! Gregory Nazianzen,[46] who deplores their ambiguity; and the uneasy discussion of Augustine (*On the care for the dead*), who disbelieves in visions of the dead in dreams, though he believes that angels may sometimes send images that look like the dead. Their discomfiture is on a par with their approach to other forms of divination (see chapter 13).

Many of these writers – even Iamblichus – are interested in symbolic dreams rather than epiphanies. But it is epiphany that characterizes the oldest sorts of dream oracle, in the Ancient Near East. Here, as in Greece, sleeping in the shrine of a god was practised in order to seek a dream. This practice is known as incubation.[47]

THE ORACLES OF ISHTAR

When Esarhaddon of Assyria (r. 680–669 BC) was threatened by an invasion of the Ukka, a hostile people, he received the following reassuring oracle:[48]

O Asarhaddon, king of lands,
　Not shalt thou fear.
　The howl of winds which rush upon thee,
　I command it, that they shall not crush (thee).
　Thy foes like hogs of the reed-swamps in the month Siman from before thy feet shall run away. I am the great Beltis; I am Ishtar of Arbela who before thy feet destroys thy foes. What plans that I utter for thee do not prove real before me? I am Ishtar of Arbela. Thy foes the Ukai I will deliver into thy power. I am Ishtar of Arbela. Before thee and behind thee I will walk. Fear not. Thou art under protection. I in the midst of sorrows will advance and abide (with thee). From the mouth of Ishtar-Iatashijat, a man of Arbela.

The final sentence makes clear that the prophet dreams on behalf of the king. The names of thirteen Assyrian prophets are known, four male and nine female, who dreamt on behalf of their masters.[49]

A series of similar oracles is preserved on a great tablet from Babylon, and other tablets contain other recorded oracles. Another predicts Esarhaddon's suppression of a revolt in Kalah of Nineveh: 'verily the likeness of a shepherd thou art . . . given by the priestess Urkittusharrat of Kalah'. Both these oracles give the name of the prophet(ess) who spoke the words of the goddess. Another tablet, containing an oracle given to Esarhaddon's

32 Neo-Assyrian cylinder seal, seventh century BC. Ishtar, armed with quivers and swords and holding a bow and arrows faces a eunuch official.

son Ashurbanipal (r. 669–640 BC), provides the most explicit description from antiquity of the method of dream consultation:

> In the extreme darkness of that night in which I appealed to her a certain seer lay down and beheld an ominous dream. Ishtar caused him to see a vision of the night which he repeated to me saying, 'Ishtar who dwells in Arbela entered. Right and left quivers hung. In her hand she grasped a bow and drew a sharp sword for making battle. Before her thou didst stand; she even as a begetting mother spoke with thee, Ishtar exalted among gods cried unto thee, and counselled thee saying, "Look thou up for making battle". Whither thy face is set I advance, and thou didst say to her, "Where thou goest with thee I will go, queen of queens".'[50]

This description of the dream vision seen by the prophet shows that more than a Homeric dream was involved. The goddess appeared, but she was addressing not the dreamer but the king himself, who was also a character in the dream. We may presume that some rites preceded the seer's entry into the temple to sleep. The key point here is that the prophetic dream is induced, by the entry into the temple to sleep if by nothing else, and may be contrasted with the Egyptian norm when the dreamer dreams by chance, as Tuthmosis does of the Sphinx, or Zoser of Khnum.[51] In the fourth century BC Somtutefnakht expressed his gratitude to the god Harsaphes who appeared to him in his sleep and protected him through many dangers: he does not suggest that he sought the dream.[52]

Incubation had been practised since earliest times in the Near East: Gilgamesh had sought a revelation in this way.[53] The large number of dreams for Esarhaddon may be an accident of our evidence, not an indication that this king was especially insecure.[54] At Mari in the nineteenth century BC, dreams that were dreamt in the temple of a god were regarded as prophetic. Furthermore, the inspired visions and utterances of a medium in an ecstatic trance (not necessarily in a temple) could be used for divination. In both cases, a piece from the 'hair and hem' of the prophet was taken to the king for a verification test, which would consist in a further taking of omens.[55] A letter of Adad-Duri (Sasson 1983 calls her Addu) to Zimri-Lim describes how she 'entered the temple of the goddess Belet-ekallim, but Belet-ekallim was not there, neither were the statues that stand before her. . . . Then I had another dream, in which Dada, the priest of the goddess Ishtar-pishra, stood at the gate of the temple of Belet-ekallim, and his voice was strange, and he kept calling out: "Come back, Dagan, come back, Dagan." In addition to this, a female ecstatic got up in the temple of Anunitum and said: "Zimri-Lim, don't go on the expedition! Stay in Mari. . . ."'[56]

In Mari, as in Babylon, such dreams were just one form of divination, on a par with the examination of livers and entrails, of the flight of birds and so on – all practices that were familiar to the classical world also. The Hittites, too, used the same gamut of methods: 'old women' were experts on liver-reading and augury, but dream visions and visions by ecstatics were also employed.[57] Furthermore, the Assyrians also knew symbolic dreams, such as 'If he drinks the urine of his wife, he will have abundance'; kennings and puns also occur; and you might dream of travelling in the Underworld, where your experiences would carry a symbolic meaning.[58] What is distinctive about the oracular dream in all these cases is that the god's actual words form the oracle. There can, it seems, be no doubt as to the meaning of the omen. It has to be checked for reliability, of course, but it is not ambiguous. The god tells you what to do. What could be more reassuring to the anxious mortal with his limited vision?

However, as Mesopotamian divination developed, diviners came to prefer the 'deductive' methods of divination such as examination of livers, omens and the stars: these could be classified and tables of predictions worked out, rather in the way that the Chinese sages turned the *I Ching* into a vast filing system. The Mesopotamian diviners thus avoided direct recourse to gods; their approach has been regarded as a first step towards a rational, even scientific method.[59] Like the Greeks, they seem to have found dream oracles rather hit-and-miss. But their solution was a different one. Where the Mesopotamians sidelined the gods, and made divination into a guild practice,[60] Greeks formalized the procedure of making the gods speak.

THE HEBREW PROPHETS

The question arises as to whether dream visions were sought in a similar way in ancient Israel. The picture differs according to whether we look at the age of the Patriarchs, that of the Judges, or that of the Prophets. In the case of the first, God speaks directly to Jacob in a dream at Genesis 28:12–15: 'he dreamt that he saw a ladder, which rested on the ground with its top reaching to heaven, and angels of God were going up and down upon it. The Lord was standing beside him and said, "I am the Lord, the God of your father Abraham and the God of Isaac. This land on which you are lying I will give to you and your descendants". When Jacob wakes, he determines that the place is in fact 'the house of God and the gateway to heaven'. But God also appears to him elsewhere (Genesis 31:11–13): 'The angel of God said to me in my dream ... "I am the God who appeared to you at Bethel...."' Philo's *On Dreams* 1.159 refers to the first of these pronouncements explicitly as an 'oracle' (*chresmos*); and, though he does not call them so, the appearance of God to Moses in the burning bush (Exodus 3:4; *On Dreams* 1.194), and his appearance to Abraham with the order to sacrifice his son (Genesis 22:1–12; *On Dreams* 1.194–5), would fall into the same category. According to Strabo (16.2.35), Moses advocated incubation in preference to the worship of idols and accordingly moved the Jewish people to Jerusalem.

In the age of the Judges dream oracles are not prominent, though other forms of divination and necromancy are used – but the authors of the Hebrew Bible frown on them. The chief of these was not any of the methods we have seen in contemporary cultures, but rather the mysterious oracular stones, the Urim and Thummim, which seem to have functioned as some kind of lot oracle (see chapter 8).

In the age of the Prophets such methods of divination were anathema.[61] Mary Douglas has argued[62] that the Hebrew Bible represents a new, reformed religion that discards Near Eastern elements like oracles and the cult of the dead, magic and healing spells. Soothsaying was banned at least by the age of Josiah (640–609 BC), and maybe much earlier. Access to knowledge of the future would in earlier times have been obtained by necromancy, such as the famous case of Saul and the Witch of En-Dor calling up the spirit of Samuel.[63] Such a cult of the dead could lead to clan rivalries that would be divisive in a Judah split by civil strife, and this could have been a practical reason for its suppression. So Mary Douglas: it is possible, however, that these negative views of divination belong to the post-exilic period when reasons were being sought for Yahweh's permitting the Babylonian Captivity. In religious terms, regardless of the period in which we locate the prohibition, divination 'works', but it is false to Yahweh[64] – the same discomfiture as Christian authors felt in regard to pagan divination. Whatever the reason, the Hebrews followed a distinctively different path from their Near Eastern and Greek neighbours, however much Philo tried to assimilate Greek and Jewish practice in his Platonizing discussions of Hebrew prophecy.

Dreams may, however, have been responsible for the production of the long oracular pronouncements of the Hebrew prophets. In many cases their books are introduced with the information that they 'saw visions'.[65] The Book of Isaiah, a prophet active in the reign of Hezekiah (715–698 or 727–686 BC), is the longest and richest example of a collection of such 'oracles': though some of the oracles certainly belong to his lifetime, there is also later material from the reign of Josiah and even from the fourth century BC (Isaiah 24–7). How did the prophets see their visions? R.E. Clements (1996) has proposed that the prophets, too, saw dreams, though it is nowhere said that they practised incubation (indeed, where would they do it?), and we are perhaps to imagine dreams like those of Caedmon or (according to Synesius) Hesiod, where the vision simply comes to them. Joel 2:28 prophesies a day 'when I will pour out my spirit on all mankind; your sons and daughters shall prophesy, your old men shall dream dreams and your young men see visions; I will pour out my spirit in those days even upon slaves and slave-girls.' But they surely did not see Yahweh himself; they must have seen visions of events. A more practical use of the prophet's gifts is apparent in Isaiah 37, when King Hezekiah, anxious about the Assyrian invasion, sends Isaiah the following message. 'This is a day of trouble for us, a day of reproof and contempt. We are like a woman that has no strength to bear the child that is coming to the birth. It may be that the Lord your God heard the words of the chief officer whom his master the king of Assyria sent to taunt the living God, and will confute what he, the Lord your God, heard. Offer a prayer for those who still survive.' Isaiah's reply recounts 'the word of the Lord':[66] 'Do not be alarmed at what you heard when the lackeys of the king of Assyria blasphemed me. I will put a spirit in him, and he shall hear a rumour and withdraw to his own country; and there I will make him fall by the sword.' And so it turns out. Yahweh sends an angel to strike 185,000 Assyrians dead (Isaiah 37:36), and the result is Yahweh one, Ishtar nil – and Israel is saved.

Isaiah here made not so much a prophecy of the future as an assurance that Yahweh would do a certain thing, namely stop the Assyrians in their tracks, though he is not precise about the means to be used. God is not called in to give advice, but reassurance and revelation. The Prophets' Oracles of God (as Paul called them) became the model for a different kind of oracle with strong Jewish roots, the Sibylline prophecies (see chapter 12). Still, God continued to appear in Judaea in historical times: to Jaddus,[67] and even to Alexander the Great.[68] Jeremiah also made an appearance to Judas Maccabeus and gave him a sword.[69]

HEALING ORACLES[70]

The Greeks, as in so many matters, form a continuum with the practices of their Near Eastern neighbours from Mesopotamia and Asia Minor. But in their case the practice of incubation in the god's shrine is narrowed down to one very specific purpose: the seeking of a cure for illness. Disease is the most imponderable of irruptions into the course of life: not without reason does the Hippocratic tract *peri euschemosynes* ('on proper treatment') 5 say 'the philosophical doctor is equal to a god'.

If Greek epiphanic dreams were originally regarded as communications from the dead, it is only natural that it should be commonly heroes and not gods who appear at dream oracles[71] – though Apollo Ptöos himself appears in a dream to promise the gift of prophecy to a seer,[72] and Athena came to heal a sick person in Plutarch's *Pericles* 13.12–13. Tertullian, though he was chary of dreams as the work of demons, did admit that some dreams could be prophetic. He describes seven incubation shrines (*de Anima* 46.11–13) – Amphiaraus in Oropos, Amphilochus at Mallos, Sarpedon in the Troad, Trophonius in Boeotia, Mopsus in Cilicia, Hermione in Macedonia, Pasiphae in Laconia:

> the rest, with their origins, rites and traditions, and indeed the whole history of dreams, can be read in the substantial volumes of Hermippus of Berytus. It is a favourite doctrine of the Stoics that god, full of providence for human affairs, has endowed us with dreams; among the many other helps to the preservation of the techniques of divination, he especially intended dreams to be of particular assistance to natural foresight. This will be sufficient for those dreams which we must believe, even though we have a different interpretation of their nature. As for other oracles, where no dreams are involved, they must be the results of diabolical possession of the person in question, or else they try to fool us by using the tombs of the dead to perfect the deceit staged by their malignity, even counterfeiting some divine power in the form of a man. And through their deceitful endeavours they grant us the favours of cures, warnings and prophecies. Thus they hope to harm us when seeming to help us, and by their good deeds to distract us from the investigation of the true God by suggesting a false one to our minds. This vicious power is not restricted to the precincts of their shrines, but it roams all over with complete freedom. There is no doubt that the doors of our homes are open to such spirits and they impose on us in our bedrooms as well as in their own temples.[73]

Not all of Tertullian's list can be identified,[74] and it is far from complete. Another healing oracle is referred to by Strabo (14.1.44) at Acharaca near Nysa, where 'cures are prescribed by the gods. . . . Sometimes the sick give heed also to their own dreams, but still they use those other men, as priests, to initiate them into the mysteries and to counsel them. To all others the place is forbidden and deadly.' Another healing oracle at Tithorea also offered dream visions as cures.[75] Nor does Tertullian refer to the hundreds of healing shrines of Asclepius (below).

AMPHIARAUS

Among the earliest known, and one of the most important of the healing shrines Tertullian does mention, is that of Amphiaraus,[76] one of the legendary Seven against Thebes who descended into the earth in his chariot before the walls of Thebes and emerged at Knopia, not far to the south. His oracle was one of the seven tested by Croesus and, with Delphi, passed the test (Hdt. 1.46–50). But the site was subsequently moved to Oropos (Str. 9.2.10), which, though originally in Boeotian territory, came under Athenian control in 431 BC and remained so until the Boeotians reclaimed it in 412/11. The move to Oropos was the result of instruction by an oracle (presumably from Delphi), and one may imagine that the Athenians had something to do with the finding of the relevant oracle. Bringing one of the great anti-Theban heroes of the legendary past to Attic territory was a powerful move for Athens at a time when Thebes was a prominent enemy.

33 The Amphiareion, Oropos. The stoa for incubation.

As far as we know, Amphiaraus' function in Knopia had been purely oracular, but in Attica he quickly developed a role as a healing deity, and his oracular function in other spheres is little attested. In fact, we have only one case: that of Euxenippus[77] who was sent to sleep in the shrine in order to get advice about a territorial dispute between the sanctuary and two neighbouring tribes: the land was restored to Amphiaraus, but Euxenippus' opponent Polyeuctus claimed that the former had lied about his dream. The role of the oracle as legal arbitrator is rare though it was much commoner in Egypt (see p. 60, above). More typical is the dedication by the freed Jewish slave Moschus[78] in the mid-third century BC, who 'having seen a dream in which the god Amphiaraus and Health gave him instructions, according to the instructions of Amphiaraus and Health, made a dedication and inscribed it on a stele by the altar'. Curiously, the Church fathers seem to know Amphiaraus only as an oracular deity, not as a healer.[79] Also in the second century AD, Philostratus (*Imagines* I 27) describes an (imaginary?) painting of Amphiaraus beside the place where he used to meditate:

> a cleft holy and divine. Truth clad all in white is there and the gate of dreams – for those who consult the oracle must sleep – and the god of dreams himself is depicted in relaxed attitude, wearing a white garment over a black one, representing I think his nocturnal and diurnal work. And in his hands he carries a horn, showing that he brings up his dreams through the gate of truth.

Perhaps the god's healing role had faded away again by this date, when the cult of Asclepius had become widespread.

The reason Amphiaraus developed as a healing deity may be twofold. First, the method of consultation, by incubation, was one already familiar to Athenians (and others) as that used predominantly for healing. Secondly, he was brought in to Attica at almost exactly the same time as the healing god Asclepius, at the height of the plague in Athens; so his function as a frontier defender may have been intensified by his role as a protector from sickness. He also bore a strong iconographic resemblance to Asclepius, and his companions are the same; his biography exhibits several parallels, most notably his leaving his mortal life as the result of a thunderbolt from Zeus. Though Amphiaraus had not been a healer in life, he was a descendant of the seer-healer Melampus, and the gift may have run in the family. Both prophecy and healing are Apollonian functions, so the distinction is not that great.

Pausanias (1.34.1–2) describes how the consulter of Amphiaraus paid a fee,[80] underwent a period of fasting,[81] sacrificed a ram[82] to the hero and then slept on its fleece to await a vision of the hero. A thanks offering was also made, as Moschus' inscription shows; a cock is mentioned in Aristophanes' *Amphiaraus*.[83] The ram sacrifice is standard. Odysseus sacrificed one to call up the shades of the dead, and Strabo (6.3.9) tells us that those who wished to consult the shade of the prophet Calchas sacrificed a black ram first. The Sicilian historian Timaeus[84] reports that this rite was actually for Podalirius, and specifies: 'the Daunians are accustomed to sleep on fleeces at the grave of Podalirius and to receive oracles from him in their sleep. They are also accustomed to wash in the nearby river Althaenus, and to call on Podalirius, and to be healed, whence the river got its name, because it heals (*althainein*) wounds of those who wash in it.'[85] (One is reminded of the rather different prophetic function of the fleece in the story of Gideon, in Judges 6:36–40.)

Sleeping in the shrine on the fleece would produce a dream of the god. Whereas in the ancient Near East it had been the role of the priest to sleep in the shrine and to report to the consulter the vision he saw, in the case of the Greek god his appearance is direct and unmediated. The god appears and acts. As Synesius said, dreaming is a thoroughly democratic activity. Healing cults of this kind were an important aspect of the development of 'personal religion' in the Greek world.

ASCLEPIUS

This is even more notably the case with Asclepius, the most prominent healing god of antiquity. Asclepius was the son of Apollo by the nymph Coronis and was educated by the wise centaur Chiron, growing up to become a great physician (Homer, *Iliad* 4.405, 11.518). Pindar in his third *Pythian* describes how Asclepius got above himself and used his skill to raise a man from the dead. In anger at this defiance of fate, Zeus blasted both the healer and the victim with a thunderbolt. Although killed, Asclepius did not really die; he is usually termed a god rather than a hero despite his semi-mortal birth and sticky end. That end was only a beginning, for his cult, established first at Trikka in Thessaly (Str. 9.5.17), where no doubt his grave was shown, soon spread to Epidaurus, Cos and Messenia (Paus. 4.31.10).[86] His cult reached Epidaurus about 500 BC, and spread during the following century to Sicyon (Paus. 2.10.3) and Athens, where the god arrived in the form of a snake in a basket: at Athens the poet Sophocles had the job of tending the snake until the temple was ready.[87] When the god's cult reached Cos in the fifth century BC it was organized through a guild of 'descendants of Asclepius' (Asclepiadae) who maintained the great sanctuary there both then and after its rebuilding in the 360s BC. Both Cos and its mainland rival Cnidus became home to important medical schools, and the father of modern medicine, Hippocrates, was born and spent much of his career in Cos. In the fourth century BC Asclepius' cult moved also to Pergamon, which became another great healing shrine. In all these moves the god remained intact while multiplying, unlike a normal hero who was always confined to a single grave and cult site. Another sanctuary of high status was at Aegeae in Cilicia, listed in the *Miracles of St Thecla* along with Delphi, Dodona, Pergamum and Epidaurus.[88] By the Roman period there were over 900 Asclepieia – 171 in mainland Greece, 732 elsewhere.[89]

Asclepius' sons Machaon and Podalirius also acquired their own sites. As Aelius Aristides wrote, 'While Amphiaraus and Trophonius give oracles and are seen in Boeotia and Amphilochus in Aetolia, [Podalirius and Machaon] like stars dart everywhere over the earth.'[90] Machaon's was at Gerenia, his son Polemocrates' at Eua (Paus. 2.38.6), and Podalirius could be found at Smyrna in Asia Minor as well as in Daunia (above). Other gods also sometimes had healing functions, such as Dionysus at Amphicleia (Paus. 10.33.5), the hero Sarpedon (also called Apollo Sarpedonius) at Seleuceia,[91] and Heracles at Hyettos (Paus. 9.24.3); Asclepius shared the role with Pan at Troezen (Paus. 2.32.5). A few other healing sites were associated with different gods: Hemithea at Castabos, Pluto and Persephone at Acharaca, Apollo Myestes at Daldis.

The method of consultation of Asclepius and other healing deities was always by incubation: the patient slept in the temple of the god and awaited a vision that would lead to his cure. So the sanctuaries became something between a religious shrine and a sanatorium, while that at Aegeae became, in Philostratus' words,[92] 'a Lyceum and an Academy, since it rang entirely with philosophy'. Aristophanes provides a description of the procedures in his account of the visit of the blind god Wealth to a sanctuary of Asclepius to restore his sight: though the scene is fiction, and the mode burlesque, the details are presumably accurate. Beginning with a dip in the sea – 'just the thing for a frail old man', comments a bystander – the blind god is taken to the god's *temenos*. Sacrifices are made and his companions lay him down to sleep, and settle themselves close by; the attendant tells them to turn the lamps out and go to sleep. The narrator keeps an eye open and presently sees the priest going round examining the altars for leftover food items. After some scatological byplay,[93] the god appears and examines Wealth:

So then, alarmed, I muffled up my head
Whilst he went round, with calm and quiet tread,
To every patient, scanning each disease.
Then by his side a servant placed a stone
Pestle and mortar, and a medicine chest.

The god wipes Plutus' eyelids with a linen cloth, while his assistant Panacea (All-heal) covers his head with a purple cloth. The god clicks his tongue and two giant snakes slither out of the shrine, slip under the cloth and lick his eyes.[94] Then 'before you could drink ten pints of wine', Wealth sprang up, cured, and the god and the snakes disappeared into the temple. The rest of the night was given over to celebration.

34 Roman statue of the goddess Hygieia, first century AD. Note the snake, symbol of healing.

That this description is not just fiction is shown by the survival of some eighty accounts of cures effected in the temple of Asclepius at Epidaurus:[95] not one of the seven hundred inscriptions from Epidaurus mentions a doctor.[96] (No such formal records survive from the Asclepieion at Cos, and very few others.)[97] Several involve a cure from blindness (LiDonnici 1995, A18, A20, B2), in some cases involving the removal of a spear from the face (B12, B20). In another case a man with a growth on his neck is cured when a dog licks it as he sleeps (i.e. in a dream). So it need not be the god himself who appears to effect the cure; the same is the case in the Japanese cures discussed by Blacker[98] when leprosy or boils are cured by the dream of a boy licking the patient's body. The cures are often graphic: lice are swept away with a broom (B8); gout is cured when the sufferer's foot is bitten by a goose (B23). In a rather drastic example (B1) a mother dreams on behalf of her daughter who has dropsy: she sees the god hold her daughter upside down, cut off her head and drain the fluid out, then replace the head. The woman was evidently cured, as the existence of the grateful inscription shows.[99] A pregnancy that has lasted five years (A1) ends the moment the patient leaves the sanctuary, in the street. A urethral stone is cured by a simple wet dream (A14). A sore toe is healed by a snake (A17) and Melissa's tumour is cured by a viper (C2). A man with a sore in his belly was cut open by the god in the night: when he woke up, he was cured, but there was blood all over the abaton (B7). Examples could be multiplied. Many of the inscriptions refer to the fee paid, a tithe (C4) or a specific dedication (B13), and some to the failure of the cure when the fee was not forthcoming (B2: Hermon of Thasos was cured but didn't pay, so he went blind again).

An interesting example of a consultation about something other than healing is in no. 46 (Herzog, 1931):[100]

Callicrateia and the treasure. This lady, after her husband's death, being aware that he had concealed a treasure somewhere, but unable to find it by searching, came to the sanctuary about the treasure, slept and saw a vision. The god seemed to stand over her and said, 'The gold is in the head of the lion at midday in the month of Thargelion.' When day came, she departed for home and, on arrival, made a search in the head of the stone lion: this was an ancient tomb monument near her home with a lion's head on it. She found nothing. The prophet explained that the god did not mean the treasure was in the stone head, but in the shadow cast by the lion at midday in the month of Thargelion. Making a further search in the way decreed, she discovered the treasure and made the appropriate sacrifice to the god.

As Antonio Stramaglia (1992) has shown, this story belongs to a pattern found elsewhere in fictional texts from antiquity,[101] – and even in Plato (*Laws* 913d4–914a5), whose provisions often seem to have been inspired by the world of fiction. Does this mean that the record at Epidaurus is likewise fiction, a cautionary tale to remind readers that the god always earns his thanks offering? (The last line is surely part of the reason why it was inscribed.) If so, even Augustine fell for the story pattern.[102] He uses the story as part of his discussion of whether the souls of the dead can in fact appear in dreams, and suggests that they may just be images sent by angels; but the 'fact' of the dream that solved a financial problem remains. If the story of Callicrateia need not be fiction, is it then evidence for a miraculous intervention by the god? That question, of course, remains unanswerable.

In a papyrus of the second century BC (*POxy*. 1381), a narrator, perhaps of a longer fiction, describes his experience of healing by the Egyptian god Imouthes (Imhotep, the human physician become a god, and often identified with Asclepius):[103]

> It was night, when every living creature was asleep except those in pain, but divinity showed itself the more effectively; a violent fever burned me, and I was convulsed with loss of breath and coughing, owing to the pain proceeding from my side. Heavy in the head with my troubles I was lapsing half-conscious into sleep, and my mother, as a mother would for her child (and she is by nature affectionate), being extremely grieved at my agonies was sitting without enjoying even a short period of slumber, when suddenly she perceived – it was no dream or sleep, for her eyes were open immovably, though not seeing clearly, for a divine and terrifying vision came to her, easily preventing her from observing the god himself or his servants, whichever it was. In any case there was someone whose height was more than human, clothed in shining raiment and carrying in his left hand a book, who after merely regarding me two or three times from head to foot disappeared. When she had recovered herself, she tried, still trembling, to wake me, and finding that the fever had left me and that much sweat was pouring off me, did reverence to the manifestation of the god, and then wiped me and made me more collected. When I spoke with her, she wished to declare the virtue of the god, but I anticipating her told her all myself; for everything that she saw in the vision appeared to me in my dreams.[104]

This one may, like Callicrateia's, be just a story; but there were plenty of real healing 'miracles' recorded in inscriptions throughout Egypt.[105] Many of the cures from Epidaurus, too, are matter-of-fact in nature, and the record of the god's miracles reads not unlike parts of the Gospels. Such cures, like cures at Lourdes, defy explanation and are no doubt but a proportion of the outcomes for the many unhappy sufferers who appealed to the god. The Christian writer Origen, in the second century AD,[106] was the first of many Christian and rationalist critics to pronounce that such cures were probably faked, though he conceded that they might perhaps be the work of demons. This dilemma – fraudulence or evil spirits? – will bulk large in the writings of Christians on oracles in general (chapter 13), and in assessing their arguments it is important to remember that the evidence we have tells us about oracular healings that *worked*.

Though it may seem a misnomer to treat these encounters as oracles, since the god does not commonly speak, but simply acts, there are also cases when he does speak. A famous case is the Epidaurian inscription of M. Julius Apellas of 160 BC:[107] 'the god told me to use dill with olive oil for my headache'. The outstanding example is the experience of the rhetor Aelius Aristides in the second century AD who developed a personal relationship with Asclepius in his sanctuary at Pergamon.[108]

AELIUS ARISTIDES

Aristides was stricken by the first of a series of maladies when he was visiting Rome at the age of twenty-six. He became a chronic invalid for at least twelve years and, as Dodds says, his personality was transformed for life. 'Most if not all of his ailments were of the psychosomatic type: among the medley of symptoms which he reports we can recognise those of acute asthma and various forms of hypertension, producing violent nervous headaches, insomnia and severe gastric troubles.'[109] In his *Sacred Tales* Aristides provides a virtual spiritual autobiography describing his developing relationship with Asclepius. The reason that he was never cured is surely, as Dodds observes, that he needed the companionship of the god. Disease led him to his god, as Aristides gratefully says at IV.50. In the first of the *Sacred Tales* he describes a series of dreams and dream visions: while some of them depict bizarre events, such as his capture by Parthians who pour 'heartburn' down his throat, others are direct appearances of the god. 'The saviour indicated on the same night the same thing to me and to my foster father', telling the patient to apply a drug to a swelling; which was effective (1.66). In 2.7 'the Saviour began to make revelations'; he appears at one time in the form of a local notable called Sabrius (2.9), but later (18) 'He was at the same time Asclepius, and Apollo, both the Clarian and he who is called the Callixeinus in Pergamum. . . . Standing before my bed in this form, when he had extended his fingers and calculated the time, he said, "You have ten years from me and three from Sarapis",[110] and at the same time the three and the ten appeared by the position of the fingers as seventeen . . . and commanded that I go down to the river . . . and bathe'. After his dip in the icy water, Aristides felt a sense of contentment: 'Thus I was wholly with the god.' At another time (3.46) Sarapis and Asclepius both appear to Aristides together 'marvellous in their beauty and magnitude, and in some way like one another'.

As the recital continues, Asclepius informs his devotee that he is fated to die in two days unless he sacrifices some part of his body. A finger is agreed on, and then commuted for a ring. (2.26–7). Later, the god commands him to smear himself with mud and run three times round the temple (2.74–5); at another time he orders him to burn the tooth of a lion, grind it up, and use it as a dentifrice (3.36).[111] In AD 152 Aristides took a pilgrimage to the temple of Asclepius at Poemanenus in Mysia, where 'the god gave me oracles . . . and purged my upper intestinal tract' (4.5). In AD 165 Aristides walked from Myrina to the temple of Apollo at Gryneion, where he offered a sacrifice, and then on to Pergamon: it is worth noting that there is no mention of obtaining any oracles from the god at Gryneion, but then as an Apollonian oracle it would not have been specific to Aristides' needs (5.7–8). A year later, in December 166, he dreamed that he was studying Aristophanes' *Clouds*; when he woke up it was raining. Dodds (1965, 44) remarks that this is one of the few dreams that performs any predictive function, and not a very remarkable one at that, particularly in December. Aristides' communications with the god were not in general conducted to obtain a view of the future, but to nurse his hypochondria and to assure himself of the love and care of his chosen Saviour god.

EPIPHANIES

The experiences of Aristides in regard to Asclepius are in fact a sub-group of epiphanies.[112] Epiphanies, or appearances of the gods, had been recorded since early times, and two historians, Ister and Phylarchus, had written books about the epiphanies of Apollo and of Zeus respectively. If philosophers might be sceptical, 'those who do not absolve the gods from the care of humanity, but after going deeply into history conclude that they are favourable to the good and hostile to the wicked, will not suppose that even these manifestations are incredible'.[113] In general, one had to wait on the pleasure of the gods and reap the benefit,[114] or simply make a dedication.[115]

35 Pergamon, Asclepieion. The circular building, first century AD. This is perhaps where incubation took place.

A decree from Chersonese honours a man called Syriskos, the son of Herakleidas, 'because he recorded the epiphanies of the virgin (Athena) and described her philanthropic acts towards the kings and the cities'.[116] A number of individual epiphanies are recorded, among them the ones that concerned the enquirer of the oracle at Didyma (see chapter 4). A more extensive account is the official *Chronicle* from Lindos,[117] which describes a series of epiphanies of Athena to 'the rulers' over three centuries from the Persian War (490–79 BC) to the reign of Ptolemy I (323–283 BC). On one occasion the goddess appears to a retired priest on six successive nights to urge him to persuade the authorities to invite Ptolemy to give help against Demetrius (305–4 BC: ll.94–115).[118] Gods could be expected to appear in times of trouble, both public and private. In the third century BC, the goddess Artemis appeared to the Seleucid queen to demand that her statue, stolen by one of the Ptolemies, be taken home to Antioch.[119]

One such example is the story in Eunapius[120] of the sophist Aedesius (fourth century AD), who resorted 'with prayer' to a dream oracle, in which the god (not further identified) appeared to him and pronounced three hexameters which, on waking, Aedesius found had been written on his hand: 'On the warp of the two Fates' spinning lie the threads of thy life's web. If thy choice is the cities and towns of men, thy renown shall be deathless, shepherding the god-given impulse of youth. But if thou shalt be a shepherd of sheep and bulls, then hope that thou thyself shalt one day be the associate of the blessed immortals. Thus has thy woven thread ordained.' The portentous phraseology resembles that of other oracles from the third and fourth centuries AD (chapter 11) and is not typical of what we know of most dream oracles from the classical centuries.[121]

Another direct vision of Asclepius was experienced by a medical student named Thessalus who describes it in his *de virtutibus herbarum*.[122] He asked the god to comment on Nechepso's treatise on astrological medicine, which had failed to work for him: 'I was seated, and my body and soul were fainting at the incredible sight, for human speech could not convey the features of his countenance, nor the beauty of his adornment.'

As the Hellenistic age advanced, individuals tried deliberately to induce epiphanies and dreams to address their problems. These procedures are usually classified as magic rather than religion, perhaps because of the lack of an institutional setting. The Heliopolitan prophet Pachrates is said to have revealed a recipe for dream revelations to the emperor Hadrian.[123] The ingredients are worthy of the witches in *Macbeth*:

Take a field mouse and deify [i.e. kill] it in spring water. And take two moon beetles and deify them in river water, and take a river crab and fat of a dappled goat that is virgin and dung of a dog-faced baboon, 2 eggs of an ibis, 2 drams of storax, 2 drams of myrrh, 2 drams of crocus, 4 drams of Italian galingale, 4 drams of uncut frankincense, a single onion. Put all these things into a mortar with the mouse and the remaining items, and, after pounding thoroughly, place in a lead box and keep for use. And whenever you want to perform a rite, take a little, make a charcoal fire, go up on to a lofty roof, and make the offering as you say this [following] spell at moonrise, and at once she comes. . . . But pay attention to the one being attracted, so that you may open the door for her; otherwise the spell will fail.

Epiphanies did not have to come in dreams; but one god very commonly was summoned through dream visions, and that was Sarapis.[124]

SARAPIS

Sarapis appeared on the scene in the time of Alexander the Great and, like the older healing gods, presented himself to consultants through dream visions. Chronologically, the earliest recorded instance is the sleep of

Alexander himself in the 'temple of Sarapis' at Babylon during his last sickness.[125] This is a historical puzzle, since it is certain that the god Sarapis did not exist at this time: he was a deliberate creation of Ptolemy I designed to bolster Ptolemy's position as ruler of Egypt by creating a hybrid Greek-Egyptian god to appeal to the devotion of both groups of subjects. Ptolemy founded his cult following a dream.[126] The *Oracle of the Potter*[127] describes the god Sarapis as a 'private invention' of Ptolemy – and maybe it was the latter who inserted him into the story of Alexander's last hours. But according to the *Alexander Romance* (probably written in the Ptolemaic period: I.33), it was Alexander himself who discovered the new god when an eagle seized a sacrifice for an altar and deposited it on a different altar, thus revealed to be that of Sarapis. 'The god appeared to him in his sleep. . . . Then in his dream Alexander prayed to the god: "Tell me if the city of Alexandria that I have founded will remain, or if my name will be changed into that of another king." ' Sarapis foretells the future glory of Alexandria and concludes by revealing his identity through a riddle: 'put together two hundred and one, then a hundred and one again, then eighty and ten; then take the first letter and put it at the end, and thus you shall know who I am who have appeared to you'. By using the Greek letters that indicate the relevant numerals, Alexander (and the reader) may easily extract the name SARAPIS.[128]

Interestingly, a papyrus gives a record of another encounter between Alexander and the god,[129] which can be reconstructed as follows:

With . . . [e]yes [Ale]xander: [O great daem]on [become] visible [In a dream, en]ter into the [newly foun]ded city [and temple] for me, Sarapis. For [it is wor]thy of your service: [and ap]pear on the garme[nts wo]ven for you by the hands [of Oly]mpias, which [I lay on y]our knees. (The text becomes increasingly fragmentary from here.)

Not surprisingly, the substantial knowledge we have of practice as regards Sarapis' oracles is rather different from that in these stories. There is some slight evidence for a cult of Sarapis before Alexander, perhaps already at Memphis, where it had become Hellenized.[130] The earliest record of his invocation is the curse of Artemisia[131] (mid-fourth century BC): 'O master Oserapis and the gods who sit with Oserapis, I [pray] to you, I Artemisie, daughter of Amasis, against my daughter's father [who] robbed [her] of the funeral gifts and tomb. . . . As long as my cry is deposited here, he and what belongs to him should be utterly destroyed. . .'. The prayer reminds us how close together curse and oracle can lie: in both cases direct intervention by

the gods for a human purpose is invoked. A happier note is struck by
the repeated record[132] that the philosopher Demetrius of Phalerum, who
became adviser to Ptolemy II on the creation of the Museum at Alexandria,
was cured of blindness by a dream vision of Sarapis.

Dreams were key to the experience of Sarapis.[133] One Zoilus of Aspendos
describes in a letter of 257 BC to his friend Apollonius[134] how a dream
required Apollonius to found a new temple in the suburbs of Memphis:

> It happened that, when I was praying to the god Sarapis about your health
> and good relations with King Ptolemy, Sarapis pronounced oracles to me
> repeatedly in my sleep, telling me that I should sail across to you and
> display to you this oracle, to the effect that [you] should accomplish for
> him . . . an altar and sanctuary in the Greek quarter near the harbour and
> establish a priest and perform sacrifice on behalf of you (all). When I
> asked the god repeatedly that he should release me from this obligation,
> he threw me into great weakness so that I was actually in danger; then I
> prayed to him to cure me, promising that I would endure the burden and
> carry out the task he had enjoined on me. Quickly I recovered, and
> someone arrived from Cnidus who tried to build a Serapeum in this
> place, and gathered stones for the purpose; but later the god told him not
> to build it, and he went away. Then I went to Alexandria, hesitant to
> contact you about these matters, but about the business which we had
> agreed upon together, I delayed again for four months, because I was
> unable to come to you immediately. So it would be good, Apollonius, that
> you should go along with the decrees of the god, so that Sarapis will show
> himself merciful to you and make you in greater standing with the king,
> and more famous, after your health has been restored. Don't be alarmed.
> The expense on your part may be considerable, but it will release you
> from all your troubles. I undertake to act as your supervisor. Farewell.

Of course, we do not know the outcome, but the letter vividly documents
the immediate personal experience of this Greek businessman in Egypt:
this is not simply a cult imposed from the top down, but one that has a
life of its own in the hearts of its devotees, and indeed imposes arduous
demands on them.

At another time, another Apollonius founded another Sarapeum on
Delos, which was celebrated in a poem by Maiistas:[135] 'the god gave an
oracle to me (writes Apollonius) in my sleep that I should erect a Sarapeum
for him. The site was one which was advertised for sale: it was full of dung,
at the entrance to the agora; but because the god wished it the purchase was

completed, and the shrine was completely finished in six months.' Several
dedications at Delos to Sarapis were made by *oneirokritai*, indicating that
there must have been a professional staff of dream interpreters.[136]

A fragmentary papyrus[137] records how the god took mercy on a pauper
and cured him: 'the god appeared in the night beside him, and spoke:
"Thrason, you have in full the upshot of your Fate; not as Fate desired, but
against the will of Fate: for I change the Fates about . . . tomorrow, and after
the fourth hour souse and drink deep – having waited long without a taste
of anything – nothing but unmixed wine from a full-sized pitcher; and
after drinking . . . lie down and sleep. While you lie at rest, I will cure you." '
The sting in the tail is that the god transferred the malady to an unnamed
Libyan, who collapsed on the spot. We must perhaps deduce that the
Libyan had offended the god in some way, and that Sarapis showed both
his mercy and his anger in one neat operation.

Dreaming was perhaps a particularly common way of contacting the god
in Egypt. The *Instructions of Merikare* (2100 BC) state that dreams are sent by
gods to predict the future, and the pharaoh Tuthmosis even had a conversation with the sphinx in a dream.[138] In the Greek period Damascius[139] says
simply that 'dreams are oracles at Alexandria', and Dio Chrysostom (*Or.*
32.12) says that Sarapis appears almost daily at Alexandria. Strabo (17.1.17)
writes of the city of Canobus that 'it contains the temple of Sarapis, which is
honoured with great reverence and effects such cures that even the most
reputable men believe in it and sleep in it – themselves on their own behalf
or others for them. Some writers go on to record the cures, and others the
virtue of the oracles there.' The Greek author seems to evince a touch of scepticism about the superstitious behaviour of the Egyptians, 'even the great
ones'. However, Aelius Aristides in his *Hymn to Sarapis* was confident of
the god's powers: he protects health and property and gives 'every sort of
blessing, from the soul to material wealth'.

Perhaps only the great ones could afford to build temples on command,
or even afford the fees for incubation; but if you were an adept in magic, it
was open to anyone to obtain a vision of Sarapis (and, presumably, to ask
for his help):

On a jasperlike agate engrave Sarapis seated, facing forwards (?), holding
an Egyptian royal sceptre and on the sceptre an ibis, and on the back of
the stone / the [magical] name [of Sarapis?], and keep it shut up. When
need [arises] hold the ring in your left hand, and in your right a spray of
olive and laurel [twigs], waving them toward the lamp while saying the
spell seven times. And when you have put / [the ring] on the index finger

36 Elihu Vedder, *The Sphinx*. Like the Pharaoh Tuthmosis, the modern fellah listens for oracular words.

of your left hand with the stone inside, [keep it] thus and, going off [to bed] without speaking to anybody, go to sleep holding the stone to your left ear.[140]

All these varied procedures show how important it was to approach the god in the correct manner. Artemidorus makes it very clear that a dream of Sarapis will have the wrong effect if it does not take place in his temple. At 5.26 'someone dreamt that the name of Sarapis was engraved upon a bronze plate which was tied around his neck like an amulet. He caught quinsy and died within seven days. For Sarapis is considered to be a chthonic deity and has the same meaning as Pluto.' And at 5.94 'a man who was to receive an incision around his scrotum prayed to Sarapis for the success of the operation. He dreamt that the god said to him, "Undergo the operation with confidence. You will regain your health through surgery." The man died. For, as if he had been cured, he was destined to suffer no pain. It was quite natural that this should be the case, since the god is not an Olympian or celestial deity but rather a god of the Underworld.'[141] These might seem to be cases of the dream deceiving the dreamer, but it is surely rather a case of, first, not making the proper preparations and, secondly, not keeping your wits about you in the interpretation of an oracle that seems straightforward but in fact turns out to carry an unexpected meaning. The burden of interpretation lies with the dreamer. And as Sarapis says in an oracle collected at *AP* 14.70: 'Find not fault with the gods, but with the hour in which thy father sowed thee.'

CHAPTER 8

Dicing for Destiny

Someone said that Providence is the baptismal name of Chance; a believer will say that Chance is a nickname for Providence.

Duc de Chamfort, aphorism 62

Do-it-yourself Oracles

Humbler individuals could not perhaps afford to visit the great oracles, even the healing ones; yet anxieties about the future and what to do pressed on them as much as on the great. As Peter Green has eloquently put it, these were the 'dilemmas that faced a thinking man in a world where, no longer master of his fate, he had to content himself with being, in one way or another, captain of his soul'.[1] Green is speaking of the growing popularity of ethical handbooks, but the guidance that comes from the gods is not altogether dissimilar. So simpler methods of ascertaining the god's advice in crisis situations were developed, like the divination by *kledones*, utterances, which Pausanias describes as the form of consultation at the shrine of Hermes in the marketplace at Pherae. 'You come in the evening to consult the god, burn incense on the hearthstone, and fill up the lamps with oil; then you light them all and put a local coin on the altar to the right of the god; and then you whisper in the god's ear whatever your question is. Then you stop up your ears and go out of the market-place, and when you get out take your hands away from your ears and whatever phrase you hear next is the oracle.'[2] Just the same procedure is described by J.C. Lawson in rural Greece at the beginning of the twentieth century.[3]

Such a method is the acme of the aleatory approach, since there was absolutely no control over what you might hear. The god spoke through the random utterance. But more commonly some control was exercised, either by the use of the question requiring a yes-or-no answer, or by limiting the range of possible answers in some way. This was most commonly done by using *sortes*, or lots.

<h2 style="text-align:center">ORACLES BY LOTTERY</h2>

The use of lots is a basic and obviously aleatory way of determining a course of action. Most of our Greek evidence comes from the Roman period (first–second centuries AD), so it makes sense to consider briefly examples from an earlier stage of human history first.

One of the best-known and most complex forms of divination by lot is the Chinese *I Ching* (described in chapter 1).[4] This sophisticated divinatory system, which was old in the time of Confucius (sixth century BC), seems to have begun as a way of generating yes/no answers to questions. Each hexagram generated by the throws of the milfoil stalks was given a name and provided with an interpretation, so that a great many complex oracular utterances could be drawn from the throws. The complexity of the system enabled it to develop from a fortune-telling method to a book of wisdom, a development that we shall see also in the development of oracular texts in Greece in the late second and third centuries AD. But it should be noted that the *I Ching* is essentially a repository of wisdom drawn from human experience. It is not the voice of a god. The Greeks, on the other hand, seem always to have regarded the oracles acquired by lot as communications from a god.

Before turning to the Greek evidence we should consider another possible comparative example from a nearby culture that precedes our Greek evidence in date. The Hebrew Bible has several mysterious references to the oracular stones consulted by the High Priest, the Urim and Thummim (translated in the Septuagint as *deloi*, 'conspicuous [stones]').[5] This was a way of determining the will or advice of Yahweh from a consultation of the stones on the High Priest's breastplate. 'The lots may be cast into the lap, but the issue depends wholly on the Lord', says the Book of Proverbs (16:33). Descriptions of the operation are very obscure:

> Saul said to the Lord God of Israel, 'Why hast thou not answered thy servant today? If this guilt lie on me or my son Jonathan, O Lord God of Israel, let the lot be Urim; if it lie in thy people Israel, let it be Thummim.' Jonathan and Saul were taken, and the people were cleared. (I Samuel 14:41)

This seems to refer to a procedure like tossing a coin and calling 'heads' or 'tails'; but it seems that Urim could also be used alone: '[Saul] inquired of the Lord, but the Lord did not answer him, whether by dreams or by Urim or by prophets' (I Samuel 28:6). David consulted God using the ephod: 'When David learnt how Saul planned his undoing, he told Abiathar the priest to bring the ephod, and then he prayed, "O Lord God of Israel, I thy servant have heard news that Saul intends to come to Keilah and destroy the city because of me. Will the citizens of Keilah surrender me to him? Will Saul come as I have heard? O Lord God of Israel, I pray thee, tell thy servant." ' The Lord answered, 'He will come' (I Samuel 23:11–12).[6] But at II Samuel 5:23–4 the answer is not a simple yes-or-no response: 'David enquired of the Lord, who said, "Do not attack now but wheel round and take them in the rear opposite the aspens. As soon as you hear a rustling sound in the tree-tops, then act at once; for the Lord will have gone out before you to defeat the Philistine army.' This sounds more like the kind of advice that Ishtar gave to Esarhaddon in her dream appearances: but nothing is said in the biblical passage about David's method of consultation. The impression given is that it is unmediated, the direct result of prayer.

The problem is that by the time any of the books of the Hebrew Bible were written down, all forms of divination had been made illegal in Israel (it was the job of prophets now to ascertain the will of God), so it would not have been prudent or proper to describe the consultations in any detail. Descriptions we have of the operation of the Urim and Thummim come from a much later period.[7] The earliest description is in the *Letter of Aristeas*, a pseudonymous text, probably written in the second century BC in Alexandria, which gives an account of the commissioning of the Septuagint by Ptolemy II. Paragraph 99,[8] describing the High Priest's attire, reads:

> Upon his breast he wears what is called the oracle (*logion*), in which are set twelve stones of various species, soldered with gold, with the names of the heads of the tribes, according to their original constitution, each of them flashing forth indescribably with the natural colour of its own peculiar character.

Josephus in his *Antiquities of the Jews* (3.215–18) gives more detail, explaining that the twelve stones, stitched into what Josephus calls the *essen*, would foreshadow victory to those on the eve of battle.

> For so brilliant a light flashed out from them, ere the army was yet in motion, that it was evident to the whole host that God had come to their

aid. Hence it is that those Greeks who revere our practices, because they can in no way gainsay them, call the *essen logion* ('oracle'). Howbeit, *essen* and sardonyx alike ceased to shine two hundred years before I composed this work, because of God's displeasure at the transgression of the laws.

An even more elaborate description is given by the ninth-century AD Byzantine historian George the Monk (I.19):

When the High Priest wants to question God, he fixes on the ephod [a kind of scapulary] in the middle of his chest and places his hands underneath it, enfolding it in his palms as if in a box. Then Saul [who has not previously been mentioned in the passage!], wanting the priest quickly to prepare for war, instructs him 'Bring your hands together and raise up the ephod.' So then he looks at the ephod and asks God his question, directly and clearly to the diamond, which changes colour by divine power and by its changes indicates to the people what is to be. If it turns black it means death, if red, slaughter, if white the favour of God.

In addition there were letters of pure bronze,[9] one for each letter of the Hebrew alphabet, which the priest would bring before the Lord, placing them on his ephod and asking his question: immediately the letters would rise up through the power of God and make clear whether God was for or against. So, if the matter about which inquiry was made was according to God's will, only those rose up which indicated Yes, but if against his will, only those rose up which indicated No. Yes, and so it was with all other questions to the Lord, if they were in favour with him; but if he was angry at them, He would make no reply through these indicators nor through any other divine revelations and prophecies.

What all these passages have in common is a view of the High Priest's stones as essentially magical in their operation. God sends a miraculous sign according to certain prescribed schemata. The principle corresponds broadly to the attitude with which the spells in the magical papyri were performed; but it is not consonant with what we know of the operation of any other oracles contemporary with the age of Saul and David. Mesopotamia used lot oracles; the Hittite KIN oracle probably functioned by lot;[10] and Assyrian texts of the seventh century BC refer to 'incantation for oracular decisions with alabaster and haematite'.[11] So our best guess for ancient Israel may be that it worked by throwing stones with heads and tails to receive a yes or no answer. The throwing of two stones will give three possible answers – black + black, white + white, black + white – which would presumably indicate Yes, No, or 'inconclusive', so a series of, say, three throws would be necessary to give a Yes or No answer. Their use may have been developed into a more complex system, with a variety of coloured stones, that would produce a correspondingly more complex result (sufficient to warn the consultant to 'wait for the rustling in the tree-tops'): Mary Douglas compares the Yoruba form of divination with 'sixteen cowries'.[12] But if God was actually thought to speak through the operation of the Urim and Thummim, that may be a later construction put on the facts in the age when God communicated directly through prophets. It would, incidentally, also be the age in which Apollo was commonly said to be giving complex messages in verse to his consultants at Delphi.

In Assyria, 'Fates were determined by casting lots, but the deity determined how they would fall, and the results were written on the tablet of destinies.'[13] The lots lead the god to 'speak'. In the Book of Esther the lots are cast before Haman: 'It is Haman who decides the details for the king, as if he were the god giving the oracle deciding to exterminate the Jews.'[14]

GREEK LOT ORACLES

Fortified by these parallels, we may finally turn to Greek lot oracles. Pindar puts their use at the dawn of Greek time when he describes Mopsus taking the oracles on the Argo: 'At Jason's side/Mopsus the seer studied the will of heaven/by flight of birds and drawing of sacred lots,/and right gladly/ he gave the signal for the host to embark.'[15] No further description is provided, but one may imagine him using knuckle bones as Greeks did in historical times. In the *Iliad*, the lots for participation in the games 'leap out' of the vessel, which implies that each one is marked with an individual's name.[16]

Pausanias (7.25.6) describes the operation of a dice oracle, where the presiding god is Heracles, at Bura in Achaea:

> To consult the god you pray in front of the statue, and then take dice
> (Herakles has an enormous number of dice) and throw four on the table.
> For every throw of dice there is an interpretation written on the board.

For dice the Greeks used *astragaloi*, knuckle bones (which have four sides, called Chian [1], *hyption* or concave [3], *pranes* or convex [4] and *koon*, flattish [6]), and each throw had a specific name. Four *astragaloi* will give a possible thirty-five different throws, which according to a scholiast on Plato's *Lysis* (206e) could be for gods, heroes, kings, famous men and *hetairai*.[17] The method could be used as simple gaming, like poker dice, as well as in oracular consultation. Lucian (*Amores* 16) describes the unhappy lover casting dice to see whether his love for the marble Aphrodite of Cnidus will be requited:

> Charicles . . . would count out four knuckle bones of a Libyan gazelle and take a gamble on his expectations. If he made a successful throw and particularly if he was ever blessed with the throw named after the goddess herself, and no dice showed the same face, he would prostrate himself before the goddess, thinking he would gain his desire. But if, as usually happens, he made an indifferent throw on to his table, and the dice revealed an unpropitious result, he would curse all Cnidus and show utter dejection as if at an irremediable disaster; but a minute later he would snatch up the dice and try to cure by another throw his earlier lack of success.[18]

Similar procedures almost certainly took place at Ephesus and Claros, since coins of the former sometimes depict children dicing before the statue of Artemis,[19] while those of Claros' mother-city Colophon of the imperial period depict Apollo's *kithara* flanked by astragals.[20]

The most plentiful evidence for lot oracles in the Greek world comes from some two dozen sites in southern Asia Minor, concentrated in Lycia and Pisidia, and reaching as far north as Hierapolis and Laodicea in southern Phrygia.[21] There are three main types of oracle: (1) those consulted by five throws; (2) those consulted by seven throws; and (3) the simpler alphabetical oracles. The detailed labours of Johannes Nollé have made the study of these inscriptions much more straightforward. The first type, involving five throws, is known through eighteen examples.[22] In most cases the oracle consists of a pillar, some five feet high and two feet wide, set up in the agora, often with a statue of Hermes on top. In several cases a dedication by leading local citizens explains the inauguration of this public service. All can be dated to some time in the second century AD. The specimen at Kitanaura is a good example.[23] The inscription on the stone reads in part:

> According to the oracles of the god Hermes, Hermaios the son of Epi . . .
>   erected both the Hermes and the accompanying items at his own expense.
> A]AAAA E Zeus of Olympus
> Five Chians falling together speak as follows:

Zeus will give good counsel to your mind, stranger,
And will give success to your undertakings, in exchange for which
    you must
Pray to Aphrodite and to the son of Maia [sc. Hermes]
AA[A]AG Z Athena Areia
Four Chians falling together, and the fifth a three
Avoid enmity and evil when you come to the contest,
You will come and the grey-eyed goddess Athena will give you:
Your action will produce the desired result, if you strive at it.
AAAAD H The Fates
If you throw four Chians and the fifth is a four
Do not continue with what you are doing; it will not be to your advantage.
Your efforts will be difficult and hard to bring to fruition

A total of fifty-six possible throws was enumerated, each with its attendant three lines of hexameter advice. Presumably a table and a box of astragals were provided, as at Bura. An astragal has four faces, which were given the numerical values 1, 3, 4 and 6. The names of the throws are known from other forms of gaming: a Chian is a 1, for example, and a combination of five dice giving three 1s, a 6 and 4 (total 13) was known as Aphrodite.

A closely similar procedure is, or was, common in China.[24] Richard J. Smith describes what took place at the Huang Daxian temple in Kowloon. The worshipper shakes a bamboo container containing one hundred individually numbered bamboo sticks. When one falls out, he or she then 'casts a pair of crescent-shaped bamboo or wooden blocks called *jiao* to see if the stick selected was the "correct" one. These *jiao* are rounded on one side and flat on the other. If both blocks land flat side down on the ground, the answer is no; if one flat side is up and the other down, the answer is yes; if both flat sides land facing upwards, it means that the god is laughing – try again.' When the 'correct' stick is finally chosen, the number on the stick will be found to correspond to a printed message with the same number – a four-line poem accompanied by an explanation of its symbolism and meaning.

Such poems are also available in booklets and can be consulted for advice by whatever aleatory method the reader chooses (such as sticking a pin in a page dotted with numbers). Many are associated with particular gods or heroes, a favourite being Kuan Yin.[25] More enigmatic than the Greek verses, they stand in need of interpreters. Thus no. 56:[26]

The stream bubbles and sings over its bed of pebbles,
The wind is keen, the moon bright, the high ones are glad –

And after asking about the path of all your striving, see this:
The scent of the forest flowers comes from the right conditions.

is usually given an interpretation as follows:

Someone works very hard,
But nothing is achieved, even if he tries his hardest.
Therefore it is best to wait and see what happens.
In the end all will be well.

The Chinese consulter of such an oracle must come away with a similar degree of reassurance to the Greek one.

Why should such dicing seem to produce a destiny? The speaker in Cicero's *On Divination* 2.85 remarks, 'Pray what is the need, do you think, to talk about the casting of lots? It is much like playing at *morra*, dice, or knuckle bones, in which recklessness and luck prevail rather than reflection and judgment.'[27] Certainly reflection and judgement must be as little in evidence here as in playing roulette (though many would swear by their systems), but the point is that the oracular operation is put under the guidance of a god. The oracle, as Graf says, is not given by the god, but he or she guides the hand of the thrower. Albert Einstein famously said, 'God does not play dice' – but it may look as if he does, and the hero of Luke Rhinehart's novel *The Dice Man* eventually comes to believe that 'The Die is God' (189, cf. 107: 'with determination and dice, I am God'). Chance events, when looked at by the human eye, have a way of arranging themselves into a pattern.[28] A notable example of this is Darwinian Natural Selection, which has appeared to many to provide evidence for a Designer.[29] In fact, all that is required is infinite time. As Aristotle remarked (*de caelo* 292a28–34), 'to throw 1000 Chians with the dice would be impossible, but to throw one or two is comparatively easy'. If you wait long enough, the answer you need will probably turn up, but it is not like the infinite monkeys with typewriters who may eventually produce Shakespeare, because there is no testing, no natural selection.[30] This is not to say that chance, or randomization, can ever be a system. Chance has no memory. There can be no system for playing the roulette tables.[31] As Daniel Dennett has explained,[32] in any elimination contest there has to be a winner. So, although the chances of any particular person (or answer) winning a ten-round contest may be 1024 to one, when a particular answer emerges, you can say it was 1000-to-one against that happening, which 'must' show that more than chance is at play. Such self-deceiving logic is the stock-in-trade of those who think they have a 'system' for gambling. Consulting a series of oracles is a similar procedure.

The fact that Hermes is portrayed on the pillar does not mean that it is he who provides the answers, though some divinatory powers are attributed to him in the Homeric *Hymn to Hermes* (565ff.). Rather, Hermes is the messenger of the gods; he performs the function of the priest or prophet at a major shrine, and transmits the oracles of the god who is, as he usually is, Phoebus Apollo. As one of the oracles succinctly puts it: 'don't do it, but obey the oracle of Phoebus'.[33]

Though this group of oracles is a peculiarity of southern Asia Minor, the type is not unique. A similar method is involved in the Sanskrit *Pasaka-kevali*, or 'dice oracle', a poem of the seventh century AD or earlier.[34] Three throws of a four-sided die give sixty-four combinations, for each of which the poem offers an interpretation, first describing the throw and then telling the fortune.

The second type, with seven throws, has only three examples: Termessos (Pisidia), Selge and Perge. Though they could contain six hundred verses, only fragments have been recovered, but the essential structure is similar.

37 The oracle tomb at Olympos, second century AD. The inscribed verses are on the lower left block in the photograph.

The third type is simpler: there are twelve cases.[35] For example: A tomb at Olympos, overlooking the river valley from a hill crest, was provided by its thoughtful occupant with an inscribed series of twenty-four hexameter oracles, one for each letter of the alphabet. He thus ensured that his heirs and admirers would pay frequent visits to the tomb to pay him honours and make offerings. Bringing their own astragals with them, they could cast them into the little open chamber of the tomb and read off the appropriate answer (each Greek sentence begins with the appropriate letter of the alphabet):

A. You will carry off everything successfully: the god says so.

B. You will have the Pythian as your helper, with Fortune on your side.

Γ. The earth will return to you the fruits of your labours.

Δ. Violence is weak if it is not employed in accordance with the laws.

E. You will love to see the offspring of lawful marriage.

Z. Flee the great storm, lest you suffer harm.

H. The bright sun, who sees everything, sees you too.

Θ. You have the gods as your helpers on this path.

I. It will be a sweat; despite everything, you will survive.

K. It is hard to fight against waves; wait a while.

Λ. Reason, which dwells in everything, will demonstrate all clearly.

M. You must struggle; there will be change for the good.

N. The gift of victory crowns the oracle.

Ξ. You cannot harvest fruit from dry branches.

O. You cannot harvest where you have not sown.

Π. After completing many labours you will win the crown.

P. You will easily carry it off if you wait a while.

Σ. Phoebus says clearly, 'Wait, friend.'

T. You will get a release from your present problems.

Y. The enterprise has good promise.

Φ. If you work half-heartedly you will reproach the gods later.

X. You will turn the oracle to gold if you are successful, friend.

Ψ. You have obtained this just vote from the gods.

Ω. It is not beneficial to harvest raw fruit.

This is perhaps a case where the dead man was conceived as being a link to superior knowledge: it is not a god that speaks here, but wise great-grandfather, who now knows what is in the gods' minds. The similar inscription at Adada (Nollé 2007, 231–9) even begins with an invitation from the deceased's relics, somewhat ungrammatical but displaying its learning with a quotation from Homer:[36]

Lord Apollo and Hermes, lead us. Antiochos and Bianor: 'Sit down and enjoy the virtues of the oracles; for we have, from our ancestors, the "gift of prophecy that Phoebus Apollo bestowed".'

If none of the advice in the Olympos oracle and its congeners seems particularly profound or telling, that is perhaps the penalty of the rather rudimentary form of consultation. The more complex the method, the more detailed could be the answers given, and the greater the food for thought in interpretation.

In all these cases we are looking at a public monument, for everyday use; Robin Lane Fox goes so far as to compare the inscriptions to ATMs or cash-machines – you insert your number and obtain instantly what you need – and calls the provision of oracles in this region 'an industry'.[37] The oracles acquire authority from their being in verse, like the proverbs that many of them in fact replicate. ('Do not fight against the waves', Oenoanda 1, etc.; 'The winged crow is bested by the tortoise in running', Timbriada 6). Probably a similar method was used to obtain oracles from the 'flaming stone' that fell from heaven and came into the hands of one Eusebius:[38]

> The stone was a perfect sphere, whitish in colour and a span in diameter; its size was sometimes larger, sometimes smaller, and on occasions it acquired a purple hue. He pointed out to us letters inscribed on the stone and coloured with the so-called vermilion, through which it rendered oracles to the enquirer. And when he banged it against a wall . . . the stone gave out a soft whistling sound that Eusebius interpreted.

That types of oracle could overlap is shown by the interesting case of the inscription from Hierapolis,[39] where oracles could be obtained by choosing a letter from a pot and reading off the corresponding verse. This was found in the sanctuary of Apollo Careios (who is named in lines Σ and Ω), which stood directly over an underground chamber. According to Damascius in his *Philosophical History* (or *Life of Isidore*),[40] this chamber emitted deathly fumes. 'Even winged creatures could not pass over that pit without danger since everything which came within its ambit died. For the initiated however it was possible to descend to its lowest depths and stay there without suffering injury.' Damascius in fact did just that; also during his stay at Hierapolis he 'had a dream in which I was Attis and, at the instigation of the Mother of the Gods, I celebrated the feats of the so-called Hilaria, which signified my salvation from death'. Though no source states any connection between the poisonous fumes and the activity in Apollo's temple, the coincidence is curious, particularly as Damascius had under-gone an 'initiation' (as one might do at Claros) and had a dream vision during his stay. Dreams, vapours and an alphabet oracle: all are available here. The sanctuary became a place to inscribe important oracular texts. Besides the alphabet oracle, another block (later built into the cella of the temple itself) carried several further oracular texts, including a long response from Carian Apollo relating to the plague about which so many cities had consulted Claros:

> The sacred land (is angry) . . . whom my arrows killed.
>   Not you alone are being wasted by the raging sufferings of the deadly plague,
>   But many cities and peoples are groaning at the hateful treatment by the gods. To get rid of them, I order you to perform libations immediately and rich hecatombs. First, to Mother Earth, slaughter an ox from the herd in the four-square chamber with fragrant sacrifices, and when the fire engulfs it, drench the earth with honey-mixed libations.

And so on for Aither, Demeter and the heroes, 'and be mindful always of Carian Apollo: for you are of my race and that of the city-protector Mopsus'. Further, they must erect a statue of Apollo with his bow, and send choirs of boys and girls to Colophon to carry out further libations and hecatombs. The combination of these different texts builds up a rich picture of the sometimes feverish activity at this shrine of Apollo, in both sickness and health.

A mysterious bone plaque from Olbia, dating perhaps from the sixth century BC, may be another example of this kind of oracle. On the verso it bears the words 'To Apollo Didym[aios] the Milesian', and some other abbre-viated expressions. The reverse carries a text that may be translated as '7: the weak wolf. 70: the terrible lion. 700: the bowbearer . . . the healer. 7000: the wise dolphin. Peace to the city of Olbia. I bless. There I remember Leto.' There has been no consensus about the meaning of this object. The Russian excavator Rusayeva interpreted it as a document of the transition from a cult of Apollo the healer to one of Apollo Delphinios at Olbia. W. Burkert[41] proposed that the sevens represent periods of years, the whole being an account of a cycle of empires as in Daniel 7 and Vergil's *Aeneid* 1.261–82. Another possibility (I would like to suggest) is that the answers correspond to successive throws of a die, however these might be calculated. For each number thrown, you summon up Apollo in the guise indicated. All the epithets except the lion are well known as titles of Apollo. So if you throw a single seven, Apollo Lykeios can give you only feeble assistance. For 70, you get a powerful fighter, perhaps, and for 700, you get Apollo the healer with his bow that can send both disease and rescue. For 7000 you achieve the wisdom of Apollo Delphinios. Such a string of answers is anything but clear – it does not spell out the responses as the letter oracles do – and an added problem is that one can have no idea how the throws (if that is what they are) were arrived at. But the object does suggest that it was in some way used in obtaining the god's advice. One would love to know more.

THE ORACLES OF ASTRAMPSYCHUS

Sometimes the process of consulting an oracle could be further streamlined by predetermining the questions as well as the answers. This is what the fragmentary text on *POxy* 1477, from the late third century BC, is about. It is a list of predetermined numbered questions, which are as follows:

73. Shall I receive the gift?
74. Shall I be sold?
75. Shall I have help from my friend?
76. Will it be given to me to make a contract with the other party?
77. Shall I be reconciled with my son?
78. Shall I be granted furlough?
79. Shall I get the money?
80. Is the person abroad still alive?
81. Shall I profit from the business?
82. Will my possessions be sold by auction?
83. Shall I find a buyer?
84. Can I carry off what I intend?
85. Shall I become a beggar?
86. Shall I be forced into exile?
87. Shall I go on an embassy?
88. Shall I become a councillor?
89. Will my flight be halted?
90. Shall I be divorced from my wife?
91. Shall I be poisoned?
92. Shall I get what is my own?

Though the initial editor of the papyrus was puzzled by the modus operandi implied, G. Björck[42] suggested that it worked as follows. The consultation was in the hands of a priest or other master of the oracle

('Orakelmeister'), who alone could see the answers. The consultant must simply choose a numbered question from the list, which he had been given in advance; the fortune-teller would then work out the answer implied.

Clearly there are numerous possibilities for the fortune-teller to arrive at the answer. He (or she) might use a complex method of divination with sticks like the *I Ching*, or with arrows, like the Babylonians and the Arabs; it would even be possible to deal with questions like this by a method such as Tarot cards, though these were not used in antiquity, and with the latter it would be more normal for the consultant to conceal his question in his heart and interpret the fall of the cards. Since the questions only require a yes or no answer, a simple toss of a coin or an astragal would do the trick.

In fact, the papyrus has now been recognized as containing a fragment of an early version of the *Oracles of Astrampsychus*. Astrampsychus was a legendary Persian magician, somewhere in the long line of successors to Zoroaster enumerated by Xanthus of Lydia,[43] and was known as an author of love charms.[44] But in about the second century AD a Greek author compiled from earlier sources a complex fortune-telling book under his name. It was clearly popular since it survives in several versions, including some by Christian hands. In the preamble 'Astrampsychus' dedicates the book to King Ptolemy (unspecified) and describes it as a system of prognostication by numbers, invented by Pythagoras. There are ninety-two questions, each with ten possible answers. Several of the questions look familiar: 'Shall I be sold?', 'Shall I be a senator?', 'Shall I sell my cargo?', 'Shall I sail safely?', 'Is it time to consult the oracle?', 'Am I going to marry my girl-friend?', 'Will my wife stay with me?', 'Is the traveller alive?' The operation cannot be better described than by William Hansen:[45]

> Although it was possible to compose an oracle book of this sort in a straightforward manner, the designer chose not to do so, and on the contrary went to considerable pains to render the structure of his book as opaque as possible, doubtless in order to baffle the customer and increase the mystery attaching to the process. He staggered the ten answers to each question such that the first answer appeared as number 1 in its decade, the second answer appeared as number 2 in the following decade, and so on, until the ten answers to each question were distributed over ten different decades. But even that was not enough, for he then created eleven decades of dummy responses, increasing the number of decades thereby from 92 to 103. The extra 110 answers look as real as the others, but it is impossible for a questioner ever actually to reach them. Since he placed the mute decades at the beginning, he was obliged to number his 92 questions

12–103 (rather than 1–92) in order that no one might ever reach decades 1–11. Nor did even this satisfy him, for the author now shuffled all 103 decades, randomizing the sequence in which they appeared in the book. Finally, he added a table of correspondences, which while appearing mysterious was a key to the decades in their preshuffled state, although this fact was not apparent to the user. The overall result was a book that was easy to use but difficult to fathom, and this must have been his intent.

To use the book, the consultant would pick a question – e.g. 55, 'Shall I get the woman I desire?' – and then think of a number from 1 to 10. Let us pick 6. 55 + 6 = 61. In the table of correspondences, 61 leads you to decade 75. In decade 75, answer number 6 is 'You'll get the woman you desire to your ill.' If the god inspired you with a different number, say 7, 62 would lead you to decade 52, and the seventh answer in this decade is – just the same! Other possible answers are 'You'll get the woman you want' (49.1), 'You'll get the woman you desire and be rich' (42.9), and 'You won't get the woman you desire' (61.5).

Should one regard such *sortes* as oracles in the sense we have been exploring? The role of the god is very attenuated here, being reduced to the job of inspiring the consultant with the number to choose, from 1 to 10. Apollo could do better than that. And the answers would appear to be explicitly the composition of a human author: there is no suggestion that they are tailor-made for the occasion. (Of this alone it might be true to say, as Wood 2004, 17 says: 'the oracle knew the odds'; but how different from the procedures of the great Greek shrines!) Yet, though the answers – which probably cover most eventualities – are drawn from human experience, the process of randomization allows plenty of scope for the god's intervention. If a consultant could not see through the mathematics by which the book was constructed, the arrival at an appropriate answer every time could well seem magical or miraculous.[46] To that extent the procedure was more awesome than that of the yes/no lots of Dodona, or the one-to-one correspondences of the dice and letters in the public oracles of Asia Minor. Most importantly, the god guides you to a verbal answer. Which god would you choose to pray to for inspiration about the number? Surely you would pick Apollo. The god, though hidden or anonymous, is still speaking.

Oracles like Astrampsychus' became enormously popular. If you had a mind to, you could set yourself up as an oracle-priest with the slightest of preparations, as Apuleius describes.[47] The narrator, currently transformed into a donkey, finds himself in the possession of two priests, who 'devised a novel source of gain. They composed one oracular response to cover a number of situations, and in this way made fools of several people who consulted them on diverse matters. This was the response:

Why do the harnessed oxen cleave the field?
To make the seeds a luxuriant harvest yield.

The response could be applied to people contemplating marriage, or the purchase of a property, or going on a journey, or pursuing a band of robbers (the enemy would be 'harnessed' and profit would come from recovering their loot). For Apuleius this is mere fraud; yet it differs only in degree from the oracles of Astrampsychus, and perhaps in the degree of gullibility required of the consultants. Perhaps their real crime was that they had not worked hard enough (indeed, at all) to randomize the responses.

A different form of letter oracle was the device used by some friends of the imperial notary Theodorus at Antioch in AD 371/2:[48]

To find out who should be emperor after Valens, they set up a tripod which indicated the future to them. They claimed that the letters th, e, o and then d, appeared in the tripod, which virtually proved that Theodorus would come to power after Valens.

Naturally, Valens swiftly had the competitor eliminated, but to no avail since Theodosius soon succeeded him. The device seems to have been a combination of something like an Ouija board and a bar-football pendulum operating like a roulette wheel, coming to rest over letters around the circumference in turn.[49]

SORTES

If you could not devise sufficient answers yourself, another solution was to turn to a sacred book and seek the answers by choosing lines from it in a random manner. Homer's verses were being used as random oracles as early as the fifth century BC,[50] and the oracle of Zeus Belos at Apamea gave oracles in the form of Homeric verses.[51] As we have seen, the Asia Minor oracles sometime used Homeric verses. Pseudo-Plutarch[52] describes how Homer could be used as an oracle, while one of the magical papyri also describes a method for seeking oracles from the text of Homer by throwing dice.[53] Vergil could be used in the same way: the *Historia Augusta*[54] describes how wooden *sortes* inscribed with verses of Vergil were drawn at the Temple of Fortuna at Praeneste.

This method was even adopted by Christians[55] and can be found also in Jewish customs like that of drawing an oracle by asking a boy what line of the Talmud he had just learned (a mixture of book *sortes* and *kledon*).[56] Using the word of God in this way seems to have been acceptable to Christians who otherwise (like the Hebrews) spurned such aleatory methods of discovering what to do.[57] Augustine's teacher Vindicianus[58] insisted that in *sortes* and indeed astrology, it was no more than probability at work, when chance lots seemed to give the right answer. But God seemed to have sent Augustine a true word in his experience in the garden in Milan, where a chance utterance led to a random consultation of a book, which he describes in *Confessions* 8.12.29:

> Suddenly I heard a voice from the nearby house chanting as if it might be a boy or a girl (I do not know which) saying and repeating over and over again 'Pick up and read.' At once my countenance changed, and I began to think intently whether they might be some sort of children's game in which such a chant is used. But I could not remember having heard of one. I checked the flood of tears and stood up. I interpreted it solely as a divine command to me to open the book and read the first chapter. For I had heard how Antony has happened to be present at the gospel reading, and took it as an admonition addressed to himself when the words were read: 'Go, sell all you have, give to the poor and you shall have treasure in heaven; and come, follow me.'[59] By such an inspired utterance he was immediately 'converted to you.' So I hurried back to the place where Alypius was sitting. There I had put down the book of the apostle when I got up. I seized it, opened it and read in silence the first passage on which my eyes lit: 'Not in riots and drunken parties, not in eroticism and indecencies, not in strife and rivalry, but put on the Lord Jesus Christ and make no provision for the flesh in its lusts.'[60]

As usual, Augustine scorns the methods of the pagans, except when they can be recast as pieces of Christian theology.[61] This momentous conversion is a fitting culmination of the aleatory method of antiquity. Its legacy in the use of the Bible and *Saints' Lives* for the drawing of lots, the *Sortes Sangallenses* (three dice instead of five astragals) and *Sortes Sanctorum Apostolorum*[62] (a variant of those of Astrampsychus), the use of St John's Gospel, and even the use of *Sortes Vergilianae*, perhaps only shows how, while everything changes, everything remains the same. The Christian texts simply moved into the place previously occupied by classical authors, especially Homer, and God's word displaced those of the gods.

CHAPTER 9

Foreknowledge, Fate and Philosophy

It is impossible even for a god to escape from fore-ordained fate.

Herodotus 1.91, *Anthologia Palatina* 14.79

PHILOSOPHICAL QUESTIONS

As thinkers of the early centuries AD looked back on some eight hundred years of recorded oracular practice, both inscriptional and literary, they began to face the question of how and why oracles, apparently, worked, but also to ask themselves *if* they worked, or if there was some other explanation for their ability to foretell the future. Further questions arose, about the utility of such foreknowledge. A number of philosophers focused on the question of Fate, and their deliberations were strongly influenced by the need to fit a belief in the efficacy of oracles into any theory.[1] Stoics, indeed, constructed a theory of Fate precisely because they accepted oracles. Chrysippus made a collection of prophecies with a view to proving his doctrine of Fate. Posidonius wrote five volumes on prophecies.[2] But their 'hard determinism' raised hard problems that philosophers who disagreed with their position struggled to solve. Notably, many felt the need to allow for 'free will', and to deal with the corollary of absolute determinism, Cicero's 'idle argument', that choice and action are pointless. A belief in the stories of the oracles surely inhibited the development of disinterested argument about the question of fate, as much as a devout acceptance of Catholic theology impeded acceptance of Galileo Galilei's cosmology or a need to fit Genesis into the geological record impedes, even now, the disinterested discussion of the theory of evolution. Cicero, in a sceptical moment in *On Fate* (3.6) asked 'if there were no such word at all as fate, no such thing, no such force, and if either most or all things took place by mere casual accident, would the course of events be different form what it is now?' Chance may look like Fate, but to a religious mind Fate may also look like chance.[3] Epicurus and his followers rejected all form of talk about the gods, including prophecy and prayer; but Alexander of Aphrodisias[4] was the first writer to see that the myths about oracles had to be rejected in order to discuss fate rationally: 'Who when he heard these things [about Apollo's leading Laius to disaster] would not say that the absence of [divine] providence asserted by the followers of Epicurus was more pious than this sort of providential care?'

The problem of Fate could, and can, be resolved into a series of questions:

1. Is the future fixed?
2. If so, is it fixed by gods or by fate or Providence?
3. In either case, can gods know it?
4. If gods know it, can they change it?
5. Can they tell humans? (Can the examination of entrails, or study of the stars, as much as questioning the gods, tell of the future?)
6. Can humans take steps to avert the future that is foreknown and foretold. i.e., is there free will?
7. If not, is it in any way useful to know the future?
8. If it is possible to take such steps, can we in fact trust the gods' advice, or can prophecy fail?

This complex of questions was worried at by a variety of philosophers from Aristotle to Gregory of Nyssa,[5] and in those eight hundred years no consensus was arrived at. The oracles continued to do their work unimpeded.

Though the practice of oracles had not essentially changed since our earliest evidence in the sixth century BC, the philosophical tools for examining them had developed significantly. For Herodotus, oracles foretold what the gods were going to do, and as a result 'What was going to happen, happened.' He did not take the further step of seeing that this implied 'What happened was bound to happen' – though even Homer had realized that there was tension between the power of the gods and the decrees of Fate: his Zeus has to bow to *Ananke*, Necessity. Other historians, pragmatically, made little room for the gods in their discussion of human affairs. Thucydides had no time for oracles, and Polybius 36.17 remarked only that when men find an event difficult or impossible to explain, 'it is reasonable enough to escape from the dilemma by attributing them to the work of a god or chance'. Platonists in general followed a 'common-sense' view that events in the world may have many causes.[6] Plato seems at one time to distinguish three causes – Fate, Chance and free will[7] – though the later formulation by Plutarch probably owes something to Epicurean theory.[8] In fact, in the Hellenistic period, Chance came to take on some of the characteristics of a god, and for Aristotle Chance counted as one among many legitimate causes. Philosophers took an interest in Chance, and at least one, Demetrius of Phaleron, wrote a book on the subject. But other philosophers developed a more rigorous model in which the ruling divinity was not trifling in a random way, but operating purposively: the power at work was not Chance but Fate, which raised much more complex questions about future events and prediction.

Question 1. Is the future fixed? The first thinker to face up to the problems raised by statements about the future was Aristotle, and it would I think be generally admitted that he did not reach a satisfactory conclusion. Two passages, the second of them very famous, raise the issues.

First, 'That which was going to happen is not in every case what is now happening; nor is that which will in fact happen identical with that which is going to happen.'[9] This seems to be recognizing the observable fact that actions may go awry – 'the best-laid plans of mice and men gang aft agley' – whether by intention or involuntarily. Either accident or, if the action is voluntary, free will, must disprove the contention that the future is already fixed. Common sense, indeed, tells us that we can influence the flow of events, and Herodotus' theology was designed to show that we are not as clever as we think we are.

The second passage raises much knottier philosophical problems, because it is unclear exactly what philosophical problem Aristotle is posing. In *de Interpretatione* 9 he wrestles with the problem of 'the sea battle that will take place tomorrow'. His argument seems to be as follows:

There will either be or not be a sea battle tomorrow.
This entails:
'It is necessarily true that either there will be a sea battle tomorrow or there will not be'
('Necessarily true' means 'I know that x will be the case'.)
Does it therefore also entail:
'It is necessarily true that a sea battle will take place tomorrow' or 'It is necessarily true that a sea battle will not take place tomorrow'?

Clearly not, it would seem. The problem for Aristotle is that he has not disentangled the truth value of propositions. As Elizabeth Anscombe puts it,[10] it may be true that there will be rain tomorrow, but it is not necessarily true. To claim the latter would be a prophecy, and if it came to pass it would be a miracle. Aristotle thinks he is talking about knowledge and certainty, but in fact he is discussing necessity and its correlative, possibility. She quotes Ludwig Wittgenstein: 'the freedom of the will consists in the fact that future actions cannot be known. The connexion of knowledge and the known is that of logical necessity.'

Aristotle sees that assertions about the past and present are either true or false, and struggles to see how the same can hold of statements about the future. If, ten thousand years ago, X said that something would happen in January 2009, and Y said that it wouldn't, one of them was right: but did that make what he said 'necessarily true'? Aristotle saw that to conclude that it did was a false argument, but struggled to see why. The fact is that not everything that is, necessarily is. (Cicero's statement [*div.* 1.125] that nothing happens that was not going to happen is not a statement about necessity, but is merely trivial.)

But the question raised by Aristotle continued to run for some time. It should be clear that the issue of whether it is possible to make necessarily true statements about the future affects not only the reliability of oracles, but that of every other kind of omen and predictive method, including, for example, astrology. Alexander of Aphrodisias returned to the fray about the sea battle in *On Fate*, written *c.* AD 200, but by this time he had a different set of opponents to answer, namely the Stoics who held the determinist position, that everything that happens is fixed in advance and, furthermore, held that it is part of a divine plan. Stoics differed to some extent among themselves, but their position was to a considerable extent determined by their need to accept the validity of oracles as utterances of a provident God: they have thus to work out a doctrine of Fate that accommodates them.[11]

Question 2. Is the future fixed by gods or by fate or Providence? Most Stoics held a 'hard' determinist position.[12] Diogenes Laertius (7.149) attributes such a belief to the founder of Stoicism, Zeno, as well as Chrysippus, Athenodorus and Posidonius.[13] The whole universe is one endless chain of causation; everything is interlinked, so that one can read off, not only from prophecies, but from omens, from sacrificial livers, and from the positions of the stars, the way that fate is going to unfold. Furthermore, everything is to such an extent fixed that all events will, in time, recur in exactly the same conjunctions, an infinite number of times. 'When the same cause returns again, we shall, once more becoming the same persons, do the same things and in the same way, and so will all men besides.'[14] In such a universe, all that will occur in the future is fixed and a false statement about it is as impossible as an alternative outcome. God has already written the text of the play. As Plotinus (III.1.7) puts it, free will (τὸ ἐφ᾽ ἡμῖν) can thus not exist and our part will be like that of animals and babies, which go on blind impulse, and madmen.[15]

Fate, for the Stoics who take a simple view, is coterminous with Providence. 'Our school divides this whole question of the immortal gods into four parts, teaching first, that gods exist; second, their nature; third, that they order the universe; and finally, that they have the interests of the human race at heart.'[16] Marcus Aurelius (2.3) says 'The work of the gods is full of Providence: the work of Fortune is not divorced from Nature or the spinning and winding of the threads ordained by Providence.'[17] Seneca goes so far as to assert that Jupiter, Fate, Providence, Nature and the World are all names for the same entity.[18] All is for the best in the best of all possible worlds, and nothing can be otherwise. Marcus insists that the gods both care for us and communicate with us (2.11). They help men through dreams and prophecies,[19] not least healing oracles. Marcus counts among his own blessings from the gods 'that I was granted assistance in dreams . . . and the answer of the oracle at Caieta: "even as thou shalt employ thyself"' (1.17).[20]

The inevitable problem for those who believe in a benign Providence is, 'Why do the good suffer?' Seneca in *On Providence* offers what one might call 'hard providentialism', with the remarkable doctrines that 'No evil can befall the good man' (II.1); evil is illusory (III); the purpose of suffering is to give men exercise in goodness (IV.11): gods are like schoolmasters; and ultimately, the good man is superior to the god because he rises above suffering, while God is merely immune to it (VI.6).

In a rather different answer, Chrysippus' *On Providence* argues that evil is necessary in order for good to flourish and stand out.[21] Epictetus, too, explains away evil with the argument that it is all part of a larger plan if only we could see it.[22]

Philo's *On Providence*, written as an answer to a critic named Alexander who argued that the existence of evil proves that there is no Providence, brought forward three moral, but not very intellectually cogent answers: (1) sinners do meet their death and deserts eventually; (2) not everything is in the hands of God, and he is not responsible for the evil that occurs; (3) evil sometimes occurs in order to scour away other evil (e.g. an earthquake may kill good people as well as sinners – like God's destruction of Sodom and Gomorrah).

Pseudo-Plutarch's *On Fate*, probably written early in the second century AD, presents the common Middle Platonist idea that Fate and Providence are different things. Fate conforms to Providence, but not Providence to Fate (573B). Furthermore, there are three Providences, at different levels, 'to the end that god might not be chargeable for the future wickedness of which they would be severally guilty' (573F). As an Academic (a follower of Plato), this author rejects the premises that make things so difficult for the Stoics. Plotinus, a Neo-Platonist (*On Providence* I–II), holds to the Platonic idea that Providence rules the things above, Fate those below. The Aristotelian view is similar, that Providence is only concerned with higher-order movements in the universe. For Plotinus, the universe has existed for ever and is thus, with its faults, the best possible universe: 'Providence for the All is its being according to Intellect' (*On Providence* I.1). In the lower world, despite the rule of Fate, men have choices, and those who follow reason can approach the divine.

Question 3. Can the gods know the future? This is normally given an affirmative reply by Stoics and Platonists alike. Cicero (*On Fate* 14.32) puts the question very clearly: 'Carneades used to say that not even Apollo could tell any future events except those whose causes were so held together by nature that they must necessarily happen.' Or, as Alexander of Aphrodisias puts it, gods cannot make the diagonal of a square commensurate with its side, and neither can they foreknow the contingent. The Stoic answer was that all future events are determined; but, as Alexander of Aphrodisias notes,[23] 'those who make predictions along with advising someone to choose and do what he should, do not speak about the things they predict as things that will be of necessity'. Stoics even went so far as to suggest that the prophecy determines the future. This is not entailed, since the gods could, in principle, be ignorant of Fate. But of course if the gods and Fate are the same, then there is in effect no difference between predicting and causing future events. This is the position against which Alexander of Aphrodisias reacts so vigorously in *On Fate* XXXI: 'For prophecy is thought to be prophecy of the things that are going to happen, but they [i.e. the Stoics] make Apollo the author of the things he predicts[24]. . . . Yet according to what they say, at least, Apollo does not contribute to anything good for Laius, but strives and does all he can with a view to his house escaping nothing of all that is most holy and impious.' The Stoics cannot have it all ways, both believe in prophecies and believe in divine benign Providence. He concludes that the Stoics' assumptions should be done away with (p. 84.3)

Question 4. Can the gods change the future? This is much more problematic. Even Zeus in Homer had to bow to Necessity (p. 150). Nor can gods overrule the decisions of other gods (Artemis in *Hippolytus*).

Can omniscient God, who
Knows the future, find
The omnipotence to
Change his future mind?[25]

The Stoic answer is that he doesn't need to, the answer of their opponents has to be (if they believe in prophecy) that prophets can sometimes err: see question 8.

Question 5. Can the gods tell us? This must be given an affirmative answer by anyone who wishes to assert the value of prophecy, oracles and divination of all kinds. Examination of entrails presupposes that the gods' knowledge is revealed in their markings. Astrology is based on the assumption that our fates are written in the stars by the same hand that made the stars. And consultation of oracles is based on the assumption that the answers you get will come from the gods and indicate to you what to do. But therein lies the rub. The gods can only tell you what is going to happen if the future cannot be changed. Cicero expounds the problem very clearly in *On Fate* (28–9), in the course of his argument with the Stoic Chrysippus and his predecessors. Diodorus of Iasos, who was head of the Megarian school about 300 BC, and known as 'the dialectician', posed the problem acutely in his book *On Possibility*:

> If the connection of propositions, 'If anyone was born at the rising of the dog star, he will not die at sea' is true, the following connection is also true, 'If Fabius was born at the rising of the dog star, Fabius will not die at sea.' Consequently the propositions 'Fabius was born at the rising of the dog star' and 'Fabius will die at sea' are incompatible . . . a conjunction of incompatibilities which is propounded as an impossibility. Therefore the proposition 'Fabius will die at sea' belongs to the class of impossibilities. Therefore every false proposition about the future is an impossibility.[26]

Cicero sees that this argument is at odds with the idea of the Stoic thinker Chrysippus about prediction. Diodorus holds that whatever will happen must necessarily happen (13; the phrase echoes Herodotus), whereas Chrysippus wants to hold that things which will not be are also 'possible': 'that the reign of Cypselus at Corinth was not necessary although it had been announced by the oracle of Apollo a thousand years before. But if you are going to sanction divine prophecies of that sort, you will reckon false statements as to future events . . . as being in the class of things impossible.'

The question here is whether the gods could have foreknowledge of events that are contingent, not necessary.

Question 6. Can we take steps to avert what is predicted? Cicero calls the argument for total determinism the 'idle argument' – for if one yielded to it one would live a life of absolute inaction. If the future cannot be changed, there is no point in doing anything about it. If you are ill, there is no point in calling the doctor, for if you are fated to recover you will, and if you are not you won't. Chrysippus' reply (3) would be that whether you call the doctor or not is also fated: your mental movement that feels like a decision is actually determined by God.

Plenty of thinkers were ready to exploit this dangerous position. Diogenianus[27] pointed out that, if all is Fated, oracles are still useless because nothing can be changed.[28] Chrysippus' successor Carneades, who accepted the damaging nature of this argument,[29] took a less extreme view,[30] one that Cicero seems to have favoured, that Fate is identical with what is necessarily true, and this is all that the gods can know. His discussion is complex.[31] He distinguishes causal, logical and epistemic determinism: events have causes/it is true that they will occur/it is known that they will occur. But logical determinism does not entail either of the others. Only the event can make a proposition about the future true or false. But at the same time he insists that statements about future events must be immutably true or false. Yet stable truth value is the result of my action, not its cause.

If applied to the specific issue of oracles, this seems to suggest that if an oracle foretells a certain outcome, you are driven to take action that makes the oracle come true, or perhaps, you interpret your action as having made the oracle come true. In such a view, the inevitability of the fates of Oedipus and Croesus shows fate at work. But such a view is clearly not a common-sense one: it flies in the face of our sense that we do, in fact, make real decisions and that the choices we make in the garden of forking paths determine what happens next, even if we cannot foresee all the consequences. In a word, we think we have free will.[32]

To assert that we have free will is to deny the validity of prediction and prophecy, to deny in effect that the gods determine our fates. Epicurus was the first philosopher clearly to formulate a concept of free will.[33] Cicero said (*On Fate* 9.18) that he 'stood in terror of fate and sought protection against it from the atoms' by his doctrine of the 'uncaused swerve'. (The 'uncaused swerve' of one atom that, in Epicurus' cosmology started the formation of the universe out of the eternal rain of atoms would be, in modern geneticists' terminology, a mutation: the world began, not with a Big Bang but with a Little Ping.) He 'feared' (as Cicero puts it) that the Stoic arguments for divine control of the universe and predetermination of the future could only be annulled by the denial that things must have antecedent causes.[34] Epicurus was trying to 'save the phenomena', to accommodate the fact that we do, as a matter of fact, feel that we act voluntarily and that things don't always turn out the way we expect. A corollary of the Epicurean view is that prophecy must be false,[35] both on the grounds of the logic of this argument and, more broadly, because he denied that the gods took any active part in the world at all: everything is the result of the movements of atoms in the void. While not adhering to the atomist creed, Platonists insisted on the place of free will in human affairs,[36] and Cicero, as an eclectic thinker, also wanted to 'save' free will.[37]

While many, like Lucretius, may have felt that Epicurus' teaching freed them from the terror necessitated by knowing that one's doom is fixed, religious men of all persuasions were shocked by his atheism[38] (and his position was easy to caricature) and sought to save the phenomena of religion. Cicero lays out the position of Carneades (*de fato* 9.19):

It is not necessary for Epicurus to fear lest, when he admits that every proposition is either true or false, all events must necessarily be caused by fate; for the truth of a proposition of the form 'Carneades will go down to the Academy' is not due to an eternal stream of natural and necessary causation, and yet nevertheless it is not uncaused, but there is a difference between causes accidentally precedent and causes intrinsically containing a natural efficiency. Thus it is the case both that the statement 'Epicurus will die in the archonship of Pytharatus, at the age of seventy-two' was always true, and also that nevertheless there were no fore-ordained causes why it should so happen, but, because it did so fall out, it was certainly going to fall out as it actually did.

Question 7. If we cannot avert fate, is it nevertheless useful to know the future? Various answers can be given to this question.

(1) You can brace yourself for what is coming: Calasiris in Heliodorus 2.24 states 'My science had given me warning [of a change for the worse in his affairs] but not the ability to escape: for while it is possible to foresee the immutable dispositions of Fate, it is not permitted to evade them.' The holy man Apollonius of Tyana prophesied to the emperor Titus:[39] 'The gods had revealed to him that he must warn Titus to fear his worst enemies while his father lived, and after his death those closest to himself. "And how shall I die?" asked Titus. "The way they say Odysseus did," said Apollonius, "since

for him too, they say, death came from the sea." '[40] One remembers here also Tiberius' philosopher Thrasyllus, whose skill in prophecy the emperor tested by taking him for a walk along a cliff: 'I see,' said the prophet, 'that I am at this moment in great danger.' Impressed, the emperor allowed him to continue his walk.

Elsewhere Apollonius explains the principle, that the wise are able to perceive things that are about to happen.[41] Thus, in Christian texts, it is a mark of sainthood that one should foreknow the date of one's own death: the Far Eastern people, the Camarini, described in *Expositio totius mundi* 5,[42] are apprised of the day of their demise, as are the Blessed Ones of the *Life of Zosimus* (10–12).

(2) One can argue that the gods can also have foreknowledge of *contingent* events, i.e. events that may not after all occur. This is surely what would be needed for the power of oracles to be vindicated, for we see that the outcome foretold by the gods may come about in a roundabout way – by the false interpretation of a riddle, by the vain attempt to take a course of action that will defeat the oracle. (These are the 'myths of futile precautions' acutely discussed by Moreau 1990.) That is why there is so often an if-clause in oracles: the outcome is determined as soon as a cause occurs. That cause may be a simple efficient cause or it may, in terms of oracles, be an apparently unrelated event, an omen: a famous case is that 'When Birnam Wood shall come to Dunsinane' Macbeth will be defeated; or 'No man of woman born shall slay Macbeth' – but his slayer was Macduff who was 'from his mother's womb untimely ripp'd', i.e. not 'born' in the strict sense of the word. The cause or omen commonly seems to be an *adynaton*, something impossible, whose occurrence would be a miracle; but it turns out to occur nonetheless. The trees of Birnam Wood are cut down and carried as cover by the army.

In an example from Herodotus, the oracle told the Milesians and the Argives:

> *But when female conquers male and expels him,*
> *When glory in Argos redounds to her name,*
> *She will set Argive women a-plenty tearing their cheeks.*[43]

The Argives interpreted this as a prophecy of trickery by the Spartans, which caused them to take extra precautions. But it was only much later that Pausanias (2.20.8) connected this oracle with the story that the Argive woman Telesilla caused the Spartans to retreat from their attack – an interesting case, since he or his informants are reading into the oracle a meaning it did not have for Herodotus.[44]

This may, for the Stoics, resolve the problem of how prophecy can foretell the future even in a world that is not entirely ruled by Fate, but it still does not let the gods off the hook. If the gods know what is going to happen, do they also control it, or are they puppets in the hands of Fate? Alexander of Aphrodisias (*On Fate* XXX–XXXI) gave a more sophisticated answer, that God is not concerned with trivia but only with the big picture.[45] He differs from the Aristotelian view that divine Providence is concerned only with the heavenly bodies and not the sublunary region, and proposes that Providence is exercised by the Spheres rather than the Unmoved Mover: but it is nonetheless not concerned with details,[46] and therefore does not have total foreknowledge. He argues that divine foreknowledge cannot be used – as the Stoics wished[47] – to prove that Fate determines everything. 'Even gods cannot know what will come about if it is in its nature that it either may or may not come about.' The Stoics, assuming that the gods have foreknowledge and thus establishing that things come to be of necessity, in fact take away the power of the gods.[48] Any foreknowledge that is worth having must be of contingent events, of things that could equally well not come to pass. Thus Augustine[49] explicitly attributes foreknowledge to God but also free will to man. We, he says (meaning Platonists), do not deny the fact of prophecy, but neither do we take away its usefulness, since we allow that it is possible to take action in the light of prophecies. What use would advice be if everything was determined by Fate? If X would not have happened without the god's prophecy, then the outcome must be the god's doing.

The story of Laius and Oedipus, as so often, becomes the clinching case. Already in Sophocles, Oedipus felt himself in the grip of a machine: 'Zeus, what have you decided to do to me?' And the same sentiment closes the rationalist Voltaire's play *Oedipe*, when Jocasta says:

> *Priests, and you Thebans, who were once my subjects,*
> *Honour my ashes, and remember ever,*
> *That midst the horrors which oppressed me, still*
> *I could reproach the gods; for heaven alone*
> *Was guilty of the crime, and not Jocaste.* (See p. 7, above)

Alexander's conclusion, as we have seen (Question 3) is that the Stoics should reject their assumptions on account of the consequences rather than defend absurdities on account of the assumptions. But not everyone was swayed by his demolition. Later Neo-Platonists such as Proclus put forward the view (one could not call it an argument) that gods could foreknow even what is contingent.[50] They thus rejected the omnipotence of Fate: Porphyry[51] (F 339 = Eus., *PE* 6.4.2) calls magic 'a divine gift to undo the knots of Fate'.

(3) A third possible answer to Question 7 is to argue that there is moral benefit to be gained from knowing one's fate. Sedley (2007, 232) shows that for Stoics a knowledge of the future was regarded as helping you in your moral choices; it improved your attitude.[52] Eusebius (*PE* 6.11.19) put forward a similar argument: God foreknows what we are going to do, but we still have free will; but at 6.11.49 he explicitly states that we are deprived of foreknowledge (for Eusebius rejects oracles), in order that we shall struggle more forcefully against evil. Stoics thought we should struggle even though we couldn't change anything, because it would put us in tune with the universe.

(4) A fourth line of approach is possible. Does determinism take away *moral* responsibility?[53] From Homer to Calvin, actions have been subject to double determination. A god may be driving you, but still you can be blamed for your action. Alexander (*On Fate* 26) may be arguing with Chrysippus when he writes: 'If those things are attributable to us of which we can do the opposite, and if praise, blame, encouragement and discouragement, penalties and honours attach to such things, then to be wise and to possess virtues will not be attributable to those who possess them, because they are not capable of having the opposite vices. . . . But it is very odd to deny that our virtues and vices are attributable to us, and to say that we should not be praised or blamed for them.' Very odd, indeed.

Question 8. Can we trust the gods, or can prophecy fail? A hard-headed conclusion from the fact that prophecies are not always fulfilled, or divine knowledge fails (as in Apollo's failure to predict the destruction of his temple by lightning), must be that divine prophecy could, like human prophecy, sometimes fail: so Maximus of Tyre 13.2: 'Divine intellect does not hit its target every time, nor does human intellect always miss', and 13.8: 'These oracular utterances confuse my spirit, neither impelling me to outright contempt for prophecy, nor permitting me to put complete trust in human reasoning'. The same criticism is in Diogenes of Oenoanda:[54] 'Why is the coming to pass of certain predictions stronger proof that prophecy is real than the not coming to pass of others is proof that it is not?' But arguments like these were the thin end of the wedge: if divine prophecy might sometimes fail, why bother with it at all? Such was to be one of the main lines of the Christian attack on oracles developed by Eusebius in the fourth century, as we shall see.

Cicero's own discussion is the best place to conclude this consideration of philosophical aspects of prophecy. His complex argument leads to a firm statement about the place of oracles in Stoic thought (33–4):

Carneades held the view that . . . it was impossible for Apollo to foretell the fate of Oedipus when there were no causes fore-ordained in the nature of things making it necessary for him to murder his father, nor could he foretell anything of the sort. Hence if, while it is consistent for the Stoics, who say that all things happen by Fate, to accept oracles of this sort and all the other things connected with divination, yet the same position cannot be held by those who say that the things which are going to happen in the future have been true from all eternity, observe that their case is not the same as that of the Stoics; for their position is more limited and narrow, whereas the Stoic theory is untrammelled and free. Even if it be admitted that nothing can happen without an antecedent cause, what good would that be unless it be maintained that the cause in question is a link in an eternal chain of causation? But . . . 'cause' is not to be understood in such a way as to make what precedes a thing the cause of that thing, but what precedes it effectively.

The loss of large parts of Cicero's treatise prevents us from knowing for sure what his own preferred conclusion, as a Stoic sympathizer, would be. And perhaps, as he says in *On the Nature of the Gods* 1.10, one should not ask. But in another work, *On Divination*, he constructs a dialogue between a sceptic and a Stoic.[55] Taking himself the part of the sceptic, he speaks sometimes with an Epicurean voice and sometimes with an Academic/Socratic one. He clearly demonstrates (again) the weaknesses of the Stoic case, and Schofield concludes that the sceptical arguments put forward are *in fact* lethal to the acceptance of divination. But that is not to say that Cicero saw them as the last word. Even the famous anecdote in which he tells us that when two augurs met in the street (and he was himself an augur, responsible for divination from the flight of birds) they were unable to refrain from laughter, may be not so much a proof of scepticism about their profession as a comment on their unusual garb. Elsewhere Cicero professes himself favourable to the practice of divination;[56] but it is still possible that he had changed his mind by the time he wrote *On Fate*,[57] when Julius Caesar had got control of all the diviners. Or it may be that Cicero refused to take a position.[58] Or, more subtly, as Guillaumont concludes, he shared with Panaetius a belief in Providence while doubting divination: he would have expressed his position as favouring religion but rejecting superstition. Of course, one can draw the line between the two wherever one likes.[59]

If Cicero's actual position remains elusive, his marshalling of the arguments is powerful evidence of the discussions that took place in his day about divination and oracles. Religious behaviour that had been current for centuries was not going to be simply dismissed; rather, it had to be accommodated in a world view and intellectual climate that became ever more sophisticated. As we shall see, in the second and third centuries AD, oracles in fact experienced a revival of devotion that (one might think) made a mockery of rational thought.

CHAPTER 10

Sceptics, Frauds and Fakes

No man has ever seen or will see clearly, with knowledge, regarding the gods and all the other things I refer to. Even if he should come very close to the mark in what he says, still he does not know: *opinion is spread over everything.*

Xenophanes, fragment B34 DK

SCEPTICS

Despite this intense philosophical and scholarly activity applied to oracles, there were by the second century AD many who took an outright sceptical view of oracular activity. Indeed, if the stories of those who tried to bribe the Pythia, both from Sparta and as late as Heraclides Ponticus, are to be trusted, cynicism had set in much earlier. Scepticism could be consistent with belief in the gods: Xenophanes' scepticism (epigraph) in the sixth century BC implied that only the gods have perfect knowledge, while humans cannot know that they know anything.[1] We can only know what the gods tell us but we cannot be sure that we understand them, or even that we speak the same language.

But later, a more humanist view sidelines the gods. Intellectual distrust of the oracles is characteristic of several authors of the second century AD. Mostly the authors concerned are known to be Cynics, though some exhibit an Epicurean bent.

Dio Chrysostom's (AD 40–120) Discourse X, *On Servants*, is an account of a conversation of Diogenes the Cynic with an unnamed interlocutor who is on his way to Delphi to consult the oracle. Diogenes mocks him for 'making use' of the god as if he were a kind of slave, and brings forward the unusual argument that oracles cannot work because the languages of gods and men are mutually unintelligible. Even when men think they understand the god's command (this is a different argument, in keeping with the Cynic propensity to use *ad hominem* arguments indiscriminately), they can easily get them wrong, as Laius did when he failed to follow the god's initial advice not to produce a son. 'Afterwards both he and all his house were destroyed, all because he had undertaken to "make use of" Apollo when he lacked the ability' (25). Diogenes brings up another favourite argument, that about Croesus who misunderstood the god's advice that if he crossed the Halys river he would destroy a great empire. His third example is Orestes, who believed that Apollo had ordered him to slay his mother Clytemnestra. Diogenes concludes that it is of more importance for a man to know himself; 'afterwards, having found wisdom, you will then, if it be your pleasure, consult the oracle. For I am persuaded that you will have no need of consulting oracles if you have intelligence'(28). So Diogenes seems to share the view of Philostratus' Apollonius, that the wise man is himself able to make sound predictions. He also deliberately echoes both the Delphic maxim, 'Know thyself', and the wisdom of Socrates who knew already what the oracle told him.

A higher degree of scepticism is evident in two writers of committed Cynic persuasion. The first is Oenomaus of Gadara (fl. *c.* AD 120),[2] the only Cynic writer of the imperial period of whom substantial passages are preserved. This is because Eusebius in his *Praeparatio Evangelica* quoted long passages from his book, which may have been called either *Against the Oracles* or *Wizards Unmasked*. Oenomaus seems to have been moved to write his book by the experience of consulting the oracle at Claros himself on some commercial matter. Like Croesus, he set out to test the oracle, but in no spirit of piety. The response he received ran as follows:

> In the land of Trachis lies the fair garden of Herakles, containing all things in bloom for all to pick on every day, and yet they are not diminished, but with rain continually their weight is replenished.[3]

Understandably bemused by this response, his puzzlement turned to anger when he discovered that the same reply was seemingly being given to all consultants regardless of their enquiry. The oracle was, apparently, performing the same trick as the cheats in Apuleius. The second oracle he quotes, 'From a wildly whirling sling a man shoots stones and slays with his throws geese huge and fed on grass',[4] makes as little sense. To be sure such a divine pronouncement seems at once portentous and deranged: is it worth the trouble of trying to work out an interpretation? Many of the responses offered by the *I Ching* seem just as strange: what could one make of 'If the well is murky shoot the smelt; it is only (because of) the worn-out fish-trap',[5] unless there were a sage at hand to explain it? Obscurity may have kept the sanctuary staff in business.

Oenomaus does not absolutely discount the possibility that a god presides at Claros, or at Delphi; but he denies that anything useful is to be gained from consulting the author of pronouncements like these. The bulk of his argument (Eus. *PE* V.18–34) focuses on the deceits of the oracles who let down their supporters, like Croesus; on trivial or useless responses such as 'whichever you do, you'll regret it', banal medical advice; and how the oracles flatter tyrants, such as Phalaris. If even boxers can become heroes, then even a donkey could become immortal. The satirical and negative tone is thoroughly in keeping with what we know of Diogenes' practice and of what we saw in Dio's re-creation of the style.

The puzzle that Oenomaus' recorded responses leave us with is, How could the Clarian oracle have achieved the reputation it did in the imperial period (from Germanicus to Hadrian and beyond) if all it did was to issue stock responses that were at worst meaningless, at best chosen by some simple lottery from a set of stock answers? Parke's answer[6] is that the oracle was reformed by the time of Hadrian (r. AD 117–138), perhaps as a result of Oenomaus' attack; but this is hardly sufficient to explain why Romans were eagerly consulting it a century before. In any case the responses we know of from the first century AD (such as that to Germanicus), as well as the long inscribed oracles to other cities, seem to be reasonable, if orotund. We must perhaps conclude that there was a cut-price service for individual consulters, who would receive a standard but riddling reply which the staff would offer to interpret, while a full service was available for states who wished to consult the oracles on matters of great moment. Oenomaus picked his evidence to suit his argument.

FALSE ORACLES, FAILURES AND FAKES

If Oenomaus' attack coincides in time with Plutarch's period of 'decline', another piece of evidence for hostility to oracles comes from a fragmentary narrative preserved on a papyrus in Berlin.[7] The text is undated, but co-incidences of vocabulary suggest that it might belong to the same period as Oenomaus' tract. It describes an army's attack on Delphi under the command of one Daulis. Daulis addresses the *prophetes* in the following words: 'I am going to put an end to the deception of mortals by lying oracles. Who is this Apollo, what is this navel of the earth, wreathed in laurel, that they [utter?] things to terrify mankind? . . . The son of Leto rules in heaven, but we hold the earth, so the god should cease from proph-esying to men for gain, as if he were a starving magician: all these things are trickeries of yours, contrived for the purpose of fleecing clients.' These are strong words. The *prophetes'* dignified reply is fragmentary, but the tale probably ended with the ejection of the blasphemer and the re-establishment of Apollo's honour. However, the text shows that Oenomaus was not alone in his scepticism about oracles. The main charge is that oracles are mumbo-jumbo designed to relieve the gullible of their money. The accusation of greed against diviners goes all the way back to the fifth century BC, when Sophocles' characters show their unwisdom by laying into seers.[8]

The accusation of falsehood against the oracles is rather rare after Sophocles' Jocasta and Aeschylus' Thetis, though Porphyry found an oracle of Apollo in which the god himself asserts that he is telling falsehoods, and goes on to blame the conjunctions of the stars for his inability to prophesy.[9] The usual assumption, consistent with belief in the reality of the gods, is that failure of the oracle to be fulfilled is due to misunderstanding by the human recipients of the god's words. But Lucian in his *Dialogues of the Gods* (16) faces the issue of failure of the god to get it right, as well as his unscrupulousness. Hera is speaking to Leto:

> Apollo, who pretends to be so clever, with his bow and his lure and his medicine and his prophecies; those oracle-shops that he has opened at Delphi, and Claros, and Didyma, are a cheat; he takes good care to be on the safe side by giving ambiguous answers that no one can understand, and makes money out of it, for there are plenty of fools who like being imposed upon – but sensible people know well enough that most of it is clap-trap. The prophet did not know that he was to kill his favourite with a quoit; he never foresaw that Daphne would run away from him.[10]

The tirade modulates from the accusation of fraud to one of incompetence: Apollo does not even know what is going to happen to himself. The last accusation was taken up by Eusebius (*PE* 6.4.3), quoting Apollo's failure to foresee the destruction of his own temple by fire as evidence for the emptiness of oracles' claims.

ALEXANDER THE FALSE PROPHET

If Lucian could be so scathing about a god, it is little surprise that he should have no time for a mortal who set up in business as a prophet. One should beware of taking Lucian's as typical of any opinion among his contemporaries, but his blistering account of Alexander of Abonuteichos, the False Prophet, is a tour de force of invective which, apparently, contains a good deal of factual information.

Alexander was a native of Abonuteichos in Paphlagonia (later Ionopolis, now Inebolu), who claimed to have been a pupil of an associate of the sage Apollonius of Tyana. He decided to set up in business as a prophet, along with an associate, Cocconas. They buried in the temple of Apollo at Chalcedon some bronze tablets stating that a visit of the god Asclepius to Pontus was imminent, and then 'discovered' them and made them public.

If it would seem to defy belief that such a story could be taken seriously, one might read the account of the revelation of the Books of Mormon to Joseph Smith by the angel Moroni. They were found in a stone box near the village of Manchester, Ontario County, New York, under a stone on the west side of a hill:[11]

> Sept 1. 1823. He called me by name, and said unto me that he was a messenger from the presence of God to me, and that his name was Moroni. . . . He said there was a book deposited, written upon gold plates, giving an account of the former inhabitants of this continent, and the source from which they sprang. . . . Also, that there were two stones in silver bows – and these stones, fashioned to a breastplate, constituted what is called the Urim and Thummim[12] – deposited with the plates . . . and that God had prepared them for the purpose of translating the book.[13]

Alexander grew his hair and wore it in long curls, and entered the city affecting to be mad with divine inspiration. 'The two had long ago manufactured and fitted up a serpent's head of linen; they had given it a more or

38 The arms of Yale University, bearing the Hebrew words 'Urim wa Thummim'.

less human expression, and painted it very like the real article; by a contrivance of horsehair, the mouth could be opened and shut, and a forked black serpent tongue protruded, working on the same system.' A real serpent, from Pella, was also part of the equipment. Bishop Hippolytus (*Refutation of all heresies* 4. 28–42) has indignant fun with such tricks, even extending to the techniques used to induce a sheep to cut its own throat (30). Alexander's serpent puppet was employed to deliver oracles. Sometimes these were given in the form of rescripts attached to questions delivered and returned sealed, so that only the god's power could have divined the answer. Lucian describes how the wax seals were melted with a hot needle and resealed. Again, the technique is well-worn:[14] In *The Road to En-Dor* (1920), an account of the deliberate fraudulent conversion of an entire POW camp, and its Turkish guards, to spiritualism, E.H. Jones describes how the illusion could be maintained by receiving sealed questions which could be quietly steamed open before resealing with an answer attached. The spoken replies of Alexander's serpent were given through a speaking tube made from a crane's windpipe, a device also known from Egyptian and Phoenician oracles.[15]

Lucian describes the successful career of the prophet, who made up to 80,000 drachmas per year in fees. His activities extended even to blackmail and the establishment of a mystery cult. Many of his oracles seem to have concerned release from disease, either from plague (epidemic) in which case the god Glycon would send the victims to Claros, Didyma and Mallos, or individual sickness, as befitted a new Asclepius. Copies of his oracles were sent all over the empire.[16] Any suspicion that Lucian is making up his extraordinary tale is defused by the existence of coins depicting the god, and the discovery of statues of Glycon as far away as the west coast of the Black Sea and Antioch;[17] the latter was accompanied by a hexameter verse announcing that Apollo would keep the plague away. There was always room for a new healing god.

Lucian's pamphlet is addressed to an Epicurean called Celsus, at the latter's request. It is tempting to deduce that this Celsus is the same as the contemporary writer of 'Against the Christians' a tract preserved almost in its entirety by the Christian writer Origen (in *Against Celsus*), for the purposes of polemic. Celsus' attack on the Christians contains many points of resemblance to Lucian's attack on Alexander. Both cults employ trickery (Lucian 21; Celsus 73, 66–8), both appeal to fools (Lucian 15; Celsus 72–3), both call pagan cults to support their claims (Lucian 29: Claros, Didyma and Mallos; Celsus 110: Mopsus and Amphiaraus). It is interesting to speculate what the two texts would look like if the authorship were reversed,

39 Glycon, the snake-god of Alexander of Abonuteichos, second century AD.

and Celsus provided a philosophical demolition of Alexander while Lucian delivered a scurrilous attack on the self-proclaimed prophet Jesus. The latter, who shared his title Soter with the healing god Asclepius, benefited, however, from a better posthumous organization of his cult, even though he never made it onto coins of the Roman emperors.

It was perhaps not as difficult as one might imagine to set up a new cult at this time. If you did, oracles had to be part of the apparatus. Eusebius (*HE* 9.2–3) describes how the prefect of Antioch in the reign of Maximin (AD 270–313), Theotecnus, 'set up an image of Zeus the Friendly, with tricks and illusions; invented devilish rites, unholy initiations, and loathsome purifications; and even in the emperor's presence displayed his magic arts by spurious oracular utterances'. Speaking statues, attended by charlatan sorcerers, are again the subject of Lucian's *Assembly of the Gods* 12, and of his *Lover of Lies* in the story of Pellichus.[18] Oracles even come in as plot-drivers in ghost stories. Phlegon of Tralles, in his *Book of Marvels*, tells us of a hermaphrodite child born to the wife of the Aetolarch Polykritos, who had by then died.[19] The ghost of Polykritos appears and starts to devour the child, until only its head is left. The head promptly begins, like that of the murdered Orpheus, to utter an 'oracle': the author says that the utterance foretells the future, but in fact it offers practical advice, that the whole Locrian and Aetolian people should flee the land if they 'choose to escape a death in accordance with fate'. The story is perhaps to be situated in the third century BC, but its currency in Phlegon shows that it could appeal to an audience of the second century AD. The lesson we should perhaps take away from this assemblage of amazing tales is that belief (or credulity) continued strong in this period, and that no religious manifestation was complete without an oracle. Life without oracles was unimaginable. 'Faith – even a faith induced by fraud – is the most gloriously irrational and invincible phenomenon in all experience.'[20]

CHAPTER 11

New Questions for the Oracles: Platonism and Theology

Would that I had an oracle of Zeus or Apollo, that gives answers neither indirect nor ambivalent. I would not ask the god about Croesus' cauldron (that most witless of kings and most ill-fated of cooks!), nor about the measure of the sea or the number of the sands. . . . Let my answer be about Zeus, and let it come clearly from Apollo in Delphi, or from Zeus himself.

Maximus of Tyre, Oration 11.6

Plutarch and the History of Oracles

Late in the first century AD, Plutarch (c. AD 45–120) held office as a priest at Delphi. In several of his treatises he discussed the history and operations of the Delphic oracle and the sanctuary in general.[1] There was already a long-standing historical and antiquarian interest in oracles and divination. During the fifth century BC in Athens, oracle collections had begun to circulate widely.[2] Many were attached to the names of particular authors – the legendary Musaeus and Orpheus, as well as the real people Onomacritus and (perhaps) Bacis (though this may have been a generic name like Sibyl). Some of these were no doubt of hoary antiquity and could be brought out at any time of supposed crisis, like the Prophecies of Nostradamus today for moments of crisis like the millennium, or the atrocity of 9/11; others will have been collected by the poets mentioned by Plutarch, who hang around the Delphic oracle and transcribe its utterances. Herodotus (7.6) describes the career of Onomacritus, who had specialized in collecting the oracles of Musaeus, and had been expelled from Athens after Lasus of Hermione exposed him inserting some new lines into the text of Musaeus. Onomacritus then went off to Susa and plied the Persian king with oracles – but only ones that favoured the Persian cause.

There were many such men in classical Athens. They are a frequent butt of humour or invective in Aristophanes. When the Birds are founding their city of Cloud-Cuckoo-land, the first thing that happens is that an oracle-monger turns up and offers his services for the usual fee (*Birds* 958ff). Plutarch mentions (*Oracles of Delphi* 403E) the name of several historians who collected oracles, with Herodotus taking pride of place, followed by Philochorus (*c*.340–260 BC),[3] the author of a book *On Divination* among many other works, and Ister (*c*.250–200 BC),[4] author of books on the Epiphanies of Apollo and Heracles: perhaps it was in the former that he collected the oracles in both prose and verse that Plutarch mentions.

In the same mould was Apollonius Mokolles, the *archimystes* at Magnesia, who copied an old oracle about the Maenads.[5] It may have been a fake, but it seemed worth preserving. Most of the temples probably kept records of the oracles given in the past, and these were used by antiquarians.

In the fourth century BC Heraclides Ponticus, who had studied with both Speusippus and Aristotle, wrote a book *On Oracles*[6] which discussed dream oracles that came to Phalaris' mother and to Dionysius of Syracuse, as well as the interesting information that the Iamids at Olympia prophesied from the 'cracks in the skins of sacrificed animals, whether they were straight or not' (which reminds us of the Chinese divination from cracks in Oracle Bones). He also mentions the story of the priestess at Dodona who prophesied to the Thebans that they would win if they committed an act of impiety; whereupon they threw the priestess on to a bonfire.[7] He seems also to have discussed weather prognostication. We should very much like to know more about this obviously wide-ranging book. Diogenes Laertius (5.91) says that

> When their territory was visited by famine, the people of Heraclea besought the Pythian priestess for relief, but Heraclides bribed the sacred envoys as well as the aforesaid priestess to reply that they would be rid of the calamity if Heraclides, the son of Euthyphro, were crowned with a crown of gold in his lifetime and after his death received heroic honours. The pretended oracle was brought home, but its forgers got nothing by it. For directly Heraclides was crowned in the theatre he was seized with apoplexy, whereupon the envoys to the oracle were stoned to death. Moreover, at the very same time the Pythian priestess, after she had gone down to the shrine and taken her seat, was bitten by one of the snakes and died instantly.

This splendid cautionary tale may be quite untrue, fancifully derived from something in Heraclides' own writings, but it shows that the awe inspired by oracles remained as strong as ever.

In the third century BC Polemo (*c.*202–181),[8] a Stoic scholar with a particular interest in geography and antiquities, studied and copied inscriptions, dedications and paintings at major cult centres of the Greek world. F30 described the pillars and bronze cauldrons at Dodona: Stephanus describes him as one 'who understood Dodona well'. Polemo also told the story of Apollo Smintheus (F31) and his epiphany to a herdsman. His books included one of inscriptions, arranged by city (F79–80), one *On Wonders* (F84) and one *On the Fleece of Zeus* (F87–8: see Strabo 6.53 on the use of the fleece for purification in the rites of Amphiaraus). In the usual way of ancient scholars, he included somewhere a vigorous polemic against Ister.

Samos of Sicyon (or Athens) was an enthusiastic collector of inscriptions, known as 'the stonebreaker' (*stelokopas*).[9] Nicander of Colophon (fl. 130 BC), who at *Theriaca* 614 says that Apollo at Koropi endowed the tamarisk with prophetic powers, is said by the Suda to have written a book *About All the Oracles* and a *Prognostics in verse*, as well as a book on the poets of Colophon, which might have had something to say about the oracles of the Colophonian Apollo at Claros.

An extensive collection of anonymous oracles is in Book 14 of the *Palatine Anthology* (65–115, 148–150). Quite a few of these are Pythian oracles from Herodotus,[10] but others that seem to belong to early history are not in the relevant authors' works; many of them must be later compositions, like 67, which is a version of the oracle to Laius presupposed by the Oedipus dramas; 75, regarding the columns of the Temple of Zeus at Berytus; 148, addressed to Julian; and 115, addressed to Constantine. Number 72 is a curious oracle given to one Rufinus advising him to extract an oath from his own skipper, presumably that his ship is seaworthy: 'for such an oath not even do the gods, the splendid lords of heaven, dare to dishonour by their mouths'. Louis Robert argued that this Rufinus was the noted patron of the oracle at Didyma[11] and thus that this should be an oracle of Didyma.[12] It will have formed part of a collection which was used by Porphyry in his compilation, *Philosophy from Oracles* (see below). Whoever compiled *Palatine Anthology* Book 14[13] saw an affinity between oracles and riddles, for the preceding sixty-four epigrams are all riddles or similar brain-teasers, and several of the oracles are also riddles in form; 116–47 are also puzzles, mostly arithmetical. If the book did not take its present form before the Byzantine period, it, or its source, certainly drew on earlier collections, perhaps one of those mentioned above.

DECLINE OF THE ORACLES?

While these earlier writers showed a primarily antiquarian interest, Plutarch's tone in his treatises is nostalgic and melancholy. As is to be expected, Plutarch evinces a strong and simple trust in the operations of the oracle, which he finds not inconsistent with his position as a Platonist philosopher. For Plato, a God directs the things that happen in the world, and oracles are a part of that divine order. In *The E* (which refers to a large inscribed E that was prominent at the sanctuary), Plutarch calls Apollo 'a philosopher as well as a prophet', and suggests that his oracles take a riddling form because 'enquiry is the beginning of philosophy' (385C): the ambiguity of oracles promotes logical reasoning as men seek to understand them (386F). The E, which is identical in sound to the Greek word for 'if' (ei), is a reminder that 'if' is the philosophers' favourite word; and no doubt, though he does not say so, he thought of such oracles as 'if you cross the Halys, you will destroy a great empire'.

But things, for Plutarch, are not what they used to be.[14] For one thing, the Pythia no longer gives her oracles in verse: this (402B) militates against confidence in the oracle. His discussion of *Why the Pythia no longer gives oracles in verse* is structured as a dialogue, in which the various speakers give different opinions about the cause of the change, and even about the validity of oracles in general. The discussion wanders from point to point and is not easy to summarize, but the upshot is that a number of reasons are given why one should not be concerned about the change. The speakers agree that the style of the prophetesses of the past left something to be desired in comparison with the verses of Homer: Sarapion argues that one should not be looking for artistic skill in prophecies, while Theon suggests that the verse style should be laid at the door of the prophetess not the god. (Incidentally, it is taken as axiomatic that the verses are the utterance of the woman herself, not of a priest who tidies them up for public consumption.) Later, at 404D, he proposes that the god does not 'compose' but 'suggests' the oracles to the Pythia; and at 405E he points out that Love, too, may inspire poetry, but only in the poetically gifted. That bad verse should be replaced by commonplace prose is no cause for regret (397D). The speakers return to this topic later in the dialogue, with Sarapion arguing (402F) that scientific works are not less good because they are now written in prose, whereas in olden times verse was the norm. Theon, furthermore, points out that even in the past many important oracles were given in prose, for example the Spartan constitution (403E). This point is repeated at 405E, where Theon continues by affirming that prose oracles are easier to understand, whereas riddling language may breed suspicion of the oracle: ambiguity may in fact have been a ploy to protect the oracle and the ministers of the god from accusations of error, as well as from the displeasure of the great (407CD). The activities of the *chresmologoi* who hung around the shrine, he goes on, paved the way for wandering sooth-sayers and charlatans who made up oracles or 'took them by lot from certain treatises for the benefit of servants and womenfolk, who are most enticed by verse and a poetic vocabulary'. He might be referring to just the kind of oracles discussed in chapter 8, where itinerant prophets carry a board laid out like the inscribed verse oracles, or a book like that by Astrampsychus. If verse could lead you into falling for tricks like these, he seems to be saying, we are better off with prose that comes from the god himself.

The conclusion of the work, then, is that the present condition of the Delphic oracle is fine (408B). The world is at peace, political questions do not present themselves, but 'the interrogations are on slight and common-place matters, like the hypothetical questions in school: if one ought to marry, or to start on a voyage, or to make a loan; and the most important consultations on the part of states concern the yield from crops, the increase of herds, and public health', which it would be bombastic to clothe in verse. The priestess has a responsible attitude to her job, and we should be pleased at her simplicity, not cavil at her lack of grandeur.

Such is the main burden of Theon's argument, who perhaps represents Plutarch's own considered view. But the central portion of the dialogue (chapters 8–18, 398B–402E) gives the other speakers, Boethus the Epicurean, Diogenianus the Stoic and Sarapion the poet, an opportunity to discourse on other topics while the guides lead them from one sight to the next and offer their spiel. The antiquity of oracular practice, beginning with the arrival of the Sibyl at Delphi, is the subject of chapter 9. Boethus, of course, has the role of scoffing at all the stories of oracles and asserting that events are the result of pure chance. Diogenianus, on the other hand, gives a complex allegorical explanation of certain of the tales. Plutarch thus sets up a kind of exhibition of the varying approaches to oracles that had developed in the Hellenistic philosophical schools; the final statement of Boethus' scepticism (402C) is the occasion for the return of the dialogue to its main subject.

DAIMONES: THE PLATONIST EXPLANATION OF ORACLES

The reassuring conclusion of the dialogue, that one should be content with the present state of the oracle at Delphi, is further tested in the more far-reaching discussion in *The Obsolescence of Oracles*. Here, a meeting of several friends at Delphi becomes the occasion for a discussion of the reasons why so many of the ancient oracles of Greece are no longer functioning. Boeotia, for example, which was once home to very numerous oracles,[15] including the famous ones of Apollo at Ptoon and Amphiaraus at Cnopia, now has none surviving except that of Trophonius at Lebadeia. Again, the characters represent a range of philosophical attitudes, from the Cynic Didymus, who mocks and rails at oracles, to the traveller Cleombrotus, to Ammonius 'the philosopher', to the narrator Lamprias who may stand for Plutarch himself. The question that is posed, then, is how an oracle can 'die' unless the god who speaks in it loses his power. Does this imply that there are oracles which are not in fact divinely inspired?

The first answer which is reached is that the gods who speak in the oracles are not all gods, but *daimones* or demigods, and *daimones*, though long lived, can die. This is the occasion for Philip the historian to recount the famous story of the death of Pan. Epitherses, a teacher of grammar, once embarked on a voyage to Italy:

> It was already evening when, near the Echinades Islands, the wind dropped, and the ship drifted near Paxi. Almost everybody was awake, and a good many had not finished their after-dinner wine. Suddenly from the island of Paxi was heard the voice of someone loudly calling Thamus, so that all were amazed. Thamus was an Egyptian pilot, not known by name even to many on board. Twice he was called and made no reply, but the third time he answered; and the caller, raising his voice, said, 'When you come opposite to Palodes, announce that Great Pan is dead'. On hearing this, all, said Epitherses, were astounded and reasoned among themselves whether it were better to carry out the order or to refuse to meddle and let the matter go. Under the circumstances Thamus made up his mind that if there should be a breeze, he would sail past and keep quiet, but with no wind and a smooth sea about the place he would announce what he had heard. So, when he came opposite Palodes, and there was neither wind nor wave, Thamus from the stern, looking toward the land, said the words as he had heard them: 'Great Pan is dead'. Even before he had finished there was a great cry of lamentation, not of one person, but of many, mingled with exclamations of amazement.

The conclusion of the story situates the event in the reign of Tiberius (AD 14–37), which gave occasion for Christian commentators[16] to tie the moment to the destruction of the pagan gods by Christ's triumph in his crucifixion and resurrection. This of course was quite unknown to Plutarch, for whom the story is rather proof of the mortality even of the gods. Demetrius adds a footnote by remarking that many of the dead gods and heroes had taken up abode in or near the British Isles. After this Cleombrotus draws attention to the Stoic belief that all the gods will die except the one eternal and immortal God.

This injection of Stoic doctrine offers the opportunity to develop a Platonist treatment of the demigods or *daimones* who operate the oracles. The role of *daimones* in divination already had a long history: Plato (*Symposium* 202e–3a), described them as 'the envoys and interpreters that ply between heaven and earth, flying upward with our worship and our prayers, and descending with the heavenly answers and commandments . . . for the divine will not mingle directly with the human, and it is only through the mediation of the spirit world that man can have any intercourse, whether waking or sleeping, with the gods'.[17] Dwelling between the divine and human worlds, the demigods may choose to abandon their oracles, like instruments lying idle (431C).

Now Ammonius develops the view that the *daimones* are really disembodied souls. Lamprias, the narrator, asks why souls should need to be disembodied to perceive the future, and offers the answer that the body obscures the soul's vision (432C):

> Souls therefore, all possessed of this power, which is innate but dim and hardly manifest, nevertheless oftentimes disclose its flower and radiance in dreams, and some in the hour of death, when the body becomes cleansed of all impurities and attains a temperament adapted to this end, a temperament through which the reasoning and thinking faculty of the souls is relaxed and released from their present state as they range amid the irrational and imaginative realms of the future.

The best of seers, he says, is not the best guesser, as Euripides had stated,[18] but the most intelligent man.[19] He goes on to suggest that the prophetic skill is assisted by emanations from the earth (433C) which 'dispose souls to inspiration and impressions of the future'. Here he recounts the story of the original discovery of the oracle by a shepherd (see chapter 2) and argues that such exhalations may in time give out; thus the oracle of Tiresias at Orchomenos was brought to an end by a pestilence. The remainder of the dialogue, then, is devoted to discussion of the need for purity and preservation of the exhalations and the receptivity of the seer:

The power of the spirit does not affect all persons nor the same persons always in the same way, but it only supplies an enkindling and an inception, as has been said, for them that are in a proper state to be affected and to undergo the change. The power comes from the gods and demigods, but, for all that, it is not unfailing nor imperishable nor ageless, lasting into that infinite time by which all things between earth and moon become wearied out, according to our reasoning. And there are some who assert that the things above the moon, also, do not abide, but give out as they confront the everlasting and infinite, and undergo continual transmutations and rebirths (438CD).

With this melancholy conclusion Plutarch leaves the subject of the oracle in whose life he spent his service. But a ray of hope is provided by the story that Demetrius tells in chapter 45 about the shrine of Mopsus in Cilicia, which he had recently visited:

The ruler of Cilicia was himself still of two minds towards religious matters. . . . Since he kept about him certain Epicureans, who . . . have an arrogant contempt, as they themselves aver, for all such things as oracles, he sent in a freedman, like a spy into the enemy's territory, arranging that he should have a sealed tablet, on the inside of which was written the inquiry without anyone's knowing what it was. The man accordingly, as is the custom, passed the night in the sacred precinct and went to sleep, and in the morning reported a dream in this fashion: it seemed to him that a handsome man stood beside him who uttered just one word 'Black' and nothing more, and was gone immediately. The thing seemed passing strange to us, and raised much inquiry, but the ruler was astounded and fell down and worshipped; then opening the tablet he showed written there the question: 'Shall I sacrifice to you a white bull or a black?' The result was that the Epicureans were put to confusion, and the ruler himself not only duly performed the sacrifice, but ever after revered Mopsus (434DE).

The story recalls that of Croesus' testing the oracle (as well as the Athenian enquiry with the tin plates). The ruler is not identified but the presence of Epicureans ensures that it was thought of as having a more or less contemporary setting. This is proof that in many places the prophetic faculty remains alive and well.

Indeed, Plutarch had less cause for concern than he thought. Not only were the oracles of Cilicia flourishing, but the Greek world stood on the brink of a renaissance of oracular activity in Asia Minor. It was no doubt true that many of the older oracles had fallen into disuse, and Clement (*c.* AD 150–220), who was born a generation after Plutarch's death, also drew attention to the fact in *Protrepticus* 2.4:

> Do not therefore seek diligently after godless sanctuaries, nor after mouths of caverns full of jugglery, nor the Thesprotian cauldron, nor the Cirrhaean tripod, nor the Dodonian copper.[20] As for the old stump honoured by the desert sands, and the oracular shrine there gone to decay with the oak itself, abandon them both to the region of legends now grown old. The Castalian spring, at least, is all silent. So is the spring of Colophon; and the rest of the prophetic streams are likewise dead . . . Relate to me the utterly vain utterances of that other form of divination – I should rather say, hallucination – the oracles of Apollo, Clarian, Pythian and Didymaean, and those of Amphiaraus and Amphilochus; and if you will, devote to destruction along with them the soothsayers, augurs and interpreters of dreams. . . . Yes, and let the sanctuaries of Egypt and the Tuscan oracles of the dead be delivered over to darkness. . . . Partners in this business of trickery are goats, trained for divination; and ravens, taught by men to give oracular response to men.

In fact Clement protests rather too much. Some of what he says seems to be wish-fulfilment, though the trained goats are a nice detail.[21] In fact, as we know, in the second century AD many of the oracles underwent a revival, and Delphi shared in that success. Plutarch was incumbent at a bad moment, but no doubt what he wrote played its part in keeping the tradition alive.

THEOLOGICAL QUESTIONS

Concomitant with Plutarch's disillusionment at the triviality of the responses given by the Delphic oracle was a wider dissatisfaction with the kind of thing that oracles could be expected to do. The exposure of frauds like Alexander, curiously, did not diminish the oracles' status, for to expose a charlatan may not undermine the practice so much as reinforce it by emphasizing the need for experts.[22] Higher demands began to be placed on them, as by Maximus of Tyre (second century AD) when he looked for theological revelation from the oracle (epigraph). In another *Discourse* (41) he complains that Alexander in his interview with the god Ammon asked only where the Nile rises[23] (though as a matter of fact all the other sources make his questions considerably more interesting); he should have requested 'a single shared and public oracle to the whole human race'; and he goes on to suggest a suitable topic for such a response, namely the origin of evil.

Big questions like this were something new for oracles to answer, though there are forerunners visible in the Derveni Papyrus, according to which Orpheus 'says momentous things in riddles': theology requires interpretation.[24] In the late second and third centuries AD they began to be asked, especially at Didyma and Claros. An inscription from Didyma[25] seems to reflect an increase in religious experience in the second century AD: 'since from the time when Alexandra, priestess of Demeter Thesmophoros, assumed the office of priestess, never have the gods been so manifest through their appearances, partly through maidens and women, partly also through men and children, why is this, and is it auspicious?' The response is fragmentary – 'Immortals accompany mortal men . . . and make their will known and the honour which . . . .'[26]

According to the Christian writer Lactantius,[27] the oracle at Didyma had to field a number of questions about the immortality of the soul, the truth of the Jewish religion and 'Was Christ God or Man?' One of the most striking of Didyma's responses is that given to the emperor Diocletian when he was contemplating a persecution of the Christians: 'That the righteous on the earth are an impediment to the god's truth-speaking and on this account cause him to speak false responses from the tripods.'[28] (Fontenrose classes this as 'historical'.) Later the oracle found that its bread was buttered on the other side: when asked 'Was Christ god or man?' it replied 'He was mortal in flesh, wise in miraculous works, but convicted by Chaldaean judges he was nailed to stakes and reached a bitter end.'

Even if these three are Christian inventions, we can be sure that certain responses from the oracle at Claros reflect genuine theological enquiries. Cornelius Labeo, who wrote a book on *The Oracle of Apollo at Claros* in the third century AD (would that we still had it!),[29] recorded a response to someone who asked 'Which of the gods is to be regarded as the one called IAO [i.e. Yahweh]?' The oracle replied 'Men who have learned sacred mysteries should keep them hidden in secrecy. But if indeed you have small intelligence and a feeble brain, observe that Iao is the god above all gods. In winter he is Hades, at the beginning of spring Zeus, the Sun in summer and in autumn delicate Iao.'[30]

An even more remarkable response was given to an enquirer called Theophilus (Lover of God: the name raises suspicions), who asked whether Apollo or another god was God. Apollo tolerantly replied as follows:

There exists, far above the supra-celestial envelope, a limitless fire, always in movement, Eternity without limits: the blessed [sc. Gods] cannot know it, unless he the Sovereign father, after taking counsel in his own mind, decides to let them see him. There, neither does the *aither* bear stars with twinkling light, nor is the moon visible with her pale beams. No god meets him on his path, and even I myself do not encounter him as I whirl about shedding my rays in the *aither*. But there is a vast channel for the divine beacon that whirls around in a circle with a whistling sound. Even if one could touch that ethereal fire, one's heart could not divide it; for it is not to be divided: incessant in action, aeon is united with aeon by God himself. Self-born, self-taught, unmothered, unaffectable, unnameable by any word, dwelling in fire, that is God – and we his messengers are a tiny part of God.

This stirring pronouncement is known from the *Tübingen Theosophy* (see chapter 13).[31] The last three lines were quoted by Lactantius,[32] who noted that the whole response ran to twenty-one lines. The text was obviously somewhat fluid, and the same three epigrammatic lines make another appearance inscribed on the east face of the city wall in the remote Lycian city of Oenoanda.[33] Here they are followed by three further lines: 'Those who have learnt this about the nature of God, that he is the all-seeing *Aither*, should worship him at dawn, looking towards the rising sun.' The pronouncement made to Theophilus, which Lactantius knew as coming from Claros though the other sources do not locate the Apollo who speaks, became a kind of devotional tag which was adopted by the unknown worshipper at Oenoanda.[34]

'The parallel with the way in which Christianity laid down firm roots in the third and fourth centuries, by developing sophisticated and convincing philosophical explanations of its simple doctrines, is obvious, irresistible and entirely apt. The Oenoanda oracle is simply the tip of an iceberg of surviving literature which can be used to help illustrate this development. The oracular shrines of Claros and Didyma helped to disseminate this philosophical theology among the followers and sympathizers of the cult.'[35]

It would not be surprising if the god at Claros should give replies of this strongly monotheistic kind, for eight hundred years earlier the local poet Xenophanes had formed a not dissimilar view of the nature of God: 'One God, greatest among gods and men, in no way similar to mortals either in body or in thought. . . . Always he remains in the same place, moving not at all; nor is it fitting for him to go to different places at different times, but without toil he shakes all things by the thought of his mind.'[36]

Christian authors were fond of scouring the pagan poets for hints of monotheism, and John Malalas (III.13) cites a variant of the Clarian oracle

40 The oracle inscription at Oenoanda, third century AD.

as an answer to the Egyptian pharaoh when he enquired at 'the famous oracle in Memphis' [?] about the Jewish God: it runs (in prose) 'There will have descended from great heaven a celestial, everlasting and imperishable fire that surpasses flame, at which everything trembles – the sky, the earth, the sea and even the deep hell-dwelling demons shudder in fear. This is God, self-fathering, fatherless, a father son of himself thrice-blessed. We belong to a small part of the angels.' The terminology, including the reference to angels, suggests perhaps a Jewish origin for the Clarian tag as well.[37]

THE CHALDAEAN ORACLES

The use of oracles as a vehicle for theology is also apparent in the *Chaldaean Oracles*, which purport to be divine revelations in hexameter verses offering a complete cosmological and soteriological system, and moral and ritual instructions.[38]

> There is a certain Intelligence, which it is necessary for you to perceive with the flower of your mind. For if you incline your mind to it, perceiving it as you perceive something [else], you shall not perceive it. For it is the power of the strength that is visible everywhere, flashing with noetic divisions. And it is necessary not to perceive the Intelligence with vehemence, but with the outspread fire of an outspread mind . . .[39]

The *Chaldaean Oracles* came to have an enormous impact on the development of Neo-Platonic philosophy in the third and fourth centuries AD. E.R. Dodds[40] called them the 'last important sacred book of antiquity'. They continued to represent a pagan alternative to the Christian revelation right up to the time of Gemistus Plethon of Mistra (1355/80–1452), who believed them to be oracles of Zoroaster.[41] In fact the *Oracles* were composed in the late second century AD by a father and son, both called Julian, known as the Chaldaean and the Theurgist. They may well have been Babylonians, and their work certainly blended different eastern traditions in what Lewy called an 'Irano-Syro-Babylonian theocrasy'.[42] Athanassiadi (1999, 155) suggests that they put their work together in Apamea, a vigorous oracular centre at this time.[43]

Their title, *logia* rather than the traditional word *chresmoi*, implies revelation rather than response. In this they go one step further than the theological responses of Claros: the god offers theological wisdom, presumably as a consequence of invocation, though none of the fragments gives any hint of a dialogue form, a question by the worshipper to which the god responds. 'It is hard to be sure of the meaning of anything in the Oracles', wrote A.D. Nock.[44] The exiguous fragments that remain are concerned with the conjuring of the gods, a process called theurgy (god-working) to give revelations to the worshipper and to aid him in his quest to unite his soul with the divine. 'When you see the lunar daemon approaching, offer the stone called Mnizouris, while you pray.'[45] They are in effect Mysteries, giving men experience of the divine through the use of symbola.

The essentials of the doctrine are that the soul is divine and has free will; it can ascend and it will be reincarnated. The most extensive study, by Sarah Iles Johnston,[46] examines the beliefs and practices involved. Many of them are concerned with Hekate, goddess of the moon, conceived as a ladder between men and gods, a liminal point between the sensible and the intelligible worlds. From the moon[47] the *daimones* descend to earth to take charge of oracles, mysteries, salvation in war and so on: the *daimones*, that is, now do more or less what the classical gods did before, while the concept of 'god' has been pushed a level higher. The Platonist conception of the role of the *daimones* is foregrounded. The greater remoteness of 'god' necessitates the use of intermediaries and technical procedures. But alongside this technical aspect goes an increased spiritualization of worship, requiring purity of heart rather than merely ritual purity. (Two non-Chaldaean oracles in the *Palatine Anthology*, 14.71 and 74, require purity of heart when consulting the Pythia at Delphi.)

These texts and techniques were of particular interest to Neo-Platonic philosophers who sought to construct a pagan theology to equal the increasing sophistication of their Christian rivals. For example, the importance of Triads in the Chaldaean theology seemed to offer a counterweight to the Christian Trinity.[48] They seem to have become known to these thinkers after about AD 250. They strongly influenced Synesius and Iamblichus (AD 250–325), who settled in Apamea[49] where Numenius had created a Neo-Platonic ambience around the Oracle there; he wrote twenty-eight books on the Chaldaean theology, and thus turned them into a pagan 'canon'.[50] Though some of the oracles seem to be responses,[51] he oracles are much more like revelations in their content, setting the tone for a new 'image' for oracles.

Many later authors also studied the *Chaldaean Oracles*, including Arnobius (AD 253–327), Marius Victorinus (AD 280–363), Synesius (AD 370–413) and Proclus (AD 412–485). The latter regarded them as the most valuable product of pagan literature, and would have sacrificed everything else so long as he could save these and Plato's *Timaeus*.[52] Damascius made extensive use of them as an authority in *de principiis*, interpreting them as allegories, and quotes passages from them as New Testament authors quote scripture.[53] Even in the eleventh century, Michael Psellus (1018–1082) devoted several opuscula to the *Oracles*, which he may have known through Proclus, or through Procopius' refutation.

PORPHYRY, PHILOSOPHY FROM ORACLES

The most important from our point of view of the philosophers who made use of the *Chaldaean Oracles* was Porphyry. Porphyry (*c*. AD 232–303) was the last great pagan philosopher. Born in Syria (and named Malchus, of which Porphyry, 'kingly purple', is a translation), he wrote a large number of books, of which few survive in their entirety. His commentaries on Plato and Aristotle, his *Lives* of Pythagoras and of Plotinus, *On Abstinence*, and his edition of Plotinus' *Enneads* are preserved; but most of his metaphysical works are lost. His *Philosophy from Oracles* (again, the Greek word is *logia*, which is the word used in the Septuagint and by Paul [Romans 3.2] for the sayings of the prophets) represents a significant step in the re-categorization of oracles.

But when he wrote *Philosophy from Oracles* Porphyry may not have known of the *Oracles* or been convinced of their genuineness: his *Life of Plotinus* (16) refers to a large number of spurious or 'heretical' works that were circulating in Porphyry's youth. Hans Lewy (1978) argued that most of the *Philosophy from Oracles* is of 'Chaldaean' origin, and that understanding of the *Chaldaean Oracles* could be expanded by drawing into the discussion the oracles collected by Porphyry, as well as those in the *Tübingen Theosophy* (see chapter 13). Porphyry was certainly interested in oracles from an early age, since according to Eunapius (457) 'while he was still young he was granted an oracle different from the vulgar sort; and in the same book he wrote it down, and then went on to expound at considerable length how men ought to pay attention to these oracles'. Eunapius makes clear that *Philosophy from Oracles* was an early work. Porphyry also cited oracles in many of his other works, including *de abstinentia*, and notably in the life of Plotinus where he quotes a long oracle given to Amelius about the soul of Plotinus.

Lewy's view has not generally been accepted, though it is clear that *Philosophy from Oracles*, the *Tübingen Theosophy* and the *Chaldaean Oracles* are all offering material from a similar thought-world.[54] No extract from the *Chaldaean Oracles* is recognizable in the *Philosophy from Oracles*, though at F324 Porphyry does assert that 'only the Chaldaeans and the Jews' had found the way to god.

Later in life, after the death of Plotinus (AD 205–269/70), Porphyry did make use of the *Oracles*, mixing his own mysticism with their theurgic prescriptions, especially in his *de regressu animae* ('On the return of the Soul'). Augustine's extensive discussion of Porphyry's use of theurgy in *City of God* x, 9–29, shows how important they became for him.

Like Labeo in his collection of Clarian oracles, Porphyry in *Philosophy from Oracles* assembled authentic oracles inscribed on stone (many from Didyma) and from other sources, oracles that could be interpreted as providing a more sophisticated theology for pagan belief. Removed from their civic contexts, these utterances took on the character of sacred scripture.[55] The aim here was to beat the Christians on their own ground by philosophizing pagan religion. In fact, the existence of such collections actually led to the theologizing of oracles:[56] if you collect an oracle, it implies that it can be, and is going to be, reused with an application beyond its original occasion. Aaron Johnson (2010) interprets the *Philosophy from Oracles* as an educational compilation for Porphyry's students. Extensive passages of *Philosophy from Oracles* survive, many of them in the pages of Eusebius' *Praeparatio Evangelica,* where the author demolishes them as his most serious rival to the Christian revelation.

Oracles are given, Porphyry says in *Philosophy from Oracles,* as an aid to human blindness,[57] and in the preamble to the work[58] he insists:

> I swear by the gods that I have added nothing nor taken away anything from the responses as uttered, except to correct incorrect usage, or to clarify something, or to supplement metrical gaps, or to rephrase things that do not conduce to the main point; thus I have preserved the precise sense of the words, taking heed of the avenging justice that pursues impiety in such matters rather than that which pursues the transgressor on holy things. The present collection contains transcripts of many doctrines that are in accordance with philosophy, as the gods prophesied what was true; to some extent, too, we shall touch on oracular practice, which is beneficial both for contemplation (*theoria*) and for the purification (*katharsis*) of life. Such benefit as the collection offers, those will best know who, in their struggle to reach the truth, have prayed to receive a vision of the god and thus win respite from their uncertainty by receiving instruction from those who can be relied on in what they say.

The combination of the contemplative and the purificatory aspects of Neo-Platonic philosophical practice is made very clear.

In this early work Porphyry concentrates quite heavily on aids to ritual practice, whereas in later life he scorned theurgy in favour of a purely spiritual approach to divine enlightenment.[59] Though F305 refers to the riddling nature of oracles, Porphyry does not in general regard them as obscure, or as problems for solution. Following their instructions is seen as a straightforward matter.

The question arises whether Porphyry's collection is entirely genuine. Augustine (*CD* 19.23.2) contended that Porphyry had invented all of them. This is clearly untrue, though it is possible that some of them were fakes (not necessarily by Porphyry himself). His preface speaks for his honesty in diligently compiling a collection from various sources, and we may thus trust him for the genuineness of oracles that are not attested elsewhere.[60] F322 is a lament for the extinction of many of the old oracles of Greece, and in it the god avers that he speaks now only through Didyma, Delphi and Claros. From this one might deduce that these offered the main sources of Porphyry's collection. S. Levin (1989) believes that many of the oracles quoted are of Delphic origin, but other scholars are sceptical. Athanassiadi[61] suggests rather that most of them came from Didyma. Porphyry certainly cast his net widely, and continued to seek out oracles as his career progressed. The oracle he quotes on the soul of Plotinus (*Life of Plotinus* 22) poses an interesting question. Apollo said, in part,

> I am preparing to play a deathless hymn of song, weaving it about my gentle friend with the sweetest sounds beneath the golden plectrum of my well-tuned lyre. . . . Daemon, once a man, but now attaining the more divine lot of daemons, since you have loosed the bond of human necessity and in the vigour of your spirit have swum from the roaring billows of your bodily frame towards the shore of a peaceful headland . . .[62]

The response was given to one Amelius, and it may have been given at Apamea,[63] where we know that the oracle continued to function long after others had closed down. In form it is a hymn (cf. F325), and it may have been current as a text which could be reused, with insertion of the appropriate details, on the death of any great holy man.

The structure of *Philosophy from Oracles* is simple. As Gustav Wolff analyzed it, Book I is on the gods, II on the angels or *daimones*, III on the heroes and other 'terrestrial numina' (including Christ) that can interfere with divine activity. In some places (F344) it tends to henotheism, a position that Porphyry came to occupy with increasing firmness. In Book I, Apollo expounds the mysteries and outlines the rules for making effective sacrifices as well as for constructing images of the gods (especially of Pan and Hecate) for theurgic purposes. F309–13 and F328 offer self-descriptions by God along the lines of the Clarian oracles quoted above. F309 specifies the roles of the different gods (cf. *Tübingen Theosophy* 41). F314–17 are about ritual practice. F306 refers to constraining the gods, and in F342 the goddess Hekate refuses a response: this is one of the few passages[64] which suggests that actual oracular responses are involved, as distinct from revelations of the kind found in the *Chaldaean Oracles*. In F347 she is again reluctant to come when summoned.

A key doctrine is that although the gods are ruled by fate (338), magical actions such as binding of statues can override them (339): thus Hekate acquires a role analogous to that of Ishtar who can override the fate determined by the gods.[65] An important role of the gods is as astrologers: they determine the movements of the stars that in turn determine our lives

(331, 332, 333, 336): the gods are astrologers like men (335),[66] but they can get it wrong (340). The gods may lie (340, 341, 342), as a result of interference by the demons (F329).[67] This reminds us of the oracle to Diocletian (above, p. 180) that Apollo was being prevented by 'the righteous on earth' from speaking truly. This argument that hostile activity by other divine powers can interfere with the transmission,[68] as it were, is an interesting new contribution to the debate about false oracles that worried both Plutarch and the philosophers who discussed fate and free will.

Porphyry expects his readers to be surprised that the gods have something good to say of Christ:

> What I am going to say may certainly appear startling to some. I mean the fact that the gods have pronounced Christ to have been extremely devout, and have said that they mention him in terms of commendation; whereas the Christians, by their account, are polluted and contaminated and entangled in error.[69]

Augustine goes on directly to quote what Porphyry says of Hekate's opinion of Christ:

> that he was a devout man and that his soul, like the souls of the other devout men, was endowed after death with the immortality it deserved; and that Christians in their ignorance worship this soul.

The Jews, too, were let off lightly by both Porphyry and Apollo, as having, like the Chaldaeans and the Egyptians, some glimmering of divine truth:

> Steep and rough is the path to the blessed ones, and opening at first through brass-bound gates; but there are also paths not revealed by god, which those who drink the beautiful waters of the land of the Nile were the first of mortals to reveal by inexperienced practices. The Phoenicians, too, discovered ways to the blessed, as did the Assyrians, the Lydians and the race of Hebrew men.[70]

Apollo, however, was virulently anti-Christian. A man consulted the god to ask 'what god he should propitiate in order to recall his wife from Christianity'. Apollo's answer was:

> You might perhaps find it easier to write on water in printed characters, or fly like a bird through the air spreading light wings to the breeze, than

to recall to her senses an impious, polluted wife. Let her go as she pleases, persisting in her vain delusions, singing in lamentation for a god who died in delusions, who was condemned by right-thinking judges, and killed in hideous fashion by the worst of deaths.[71]

Although Porphyry's book was intended as an exegesis of existing oracles, Christians reacted to the book as an attack on Christianity itself. Augustine, after quoting Hecate's comment about Christ, goes on:

Is anyone so dense as to fail to realize that these oracles were either the inventions of a cunning man, a bitter enemy of the Christians, or the responses of demons devised with a like intent? For, surely, their purpose in praising Christ was to ensure that their vituperation of Christians would be accepted as truthful, so that, if possible, they might cut off the way of everlasting salvation, the way by which men and women become Christians.[72]

Because so many of the works of Porphyry are lost, questions have arisen as to whether the *Philosophy from Oracles* is identical with one or more other books known by different titles. J. O'Meara[73] argued that it was to be identified with *de regressu animae*, which seems to have a similar structure, but this has not been generally accepted.[74] More intriguing is the possibility that it is identical with the work *Against the Christians*.[75] Beatrice remarks that it does not look like a polemical work; but as we have seen, Augustine reacted to it as such. Porphyry was known as the most implacable enemy of the Christians of his generation. Active in the debate over toleration of the Christians, he may have taken part in the meeting called by Diocletian at Nicomedia which provided the emperor with the philosophical basis for the Persecution of 303–311.[76] It has generally been supposed that at this meeting he read from his book *Against the Christians*; but it may be that the *Philosophy from Oracles* would have served the purpose as well.[77] Whichever it was, the work of Porphyry brings the conflict of the old and new religions, and the debate over the validity of oracles, to a ferment which was only resolved with the abolition of pagan practice.

CHAPTER 12

'Ecstatic Predictions of Woe': The *Sibylline Oracles*

Self-begotten, undefiled, everlasting, eternal,
Master of heaven in might, measuring the fiery breath.
He holds the scepter of thunder with a rough firebrand,
And he soothes the peals of deep-sounding thunderbolts . . .
With your son, before all creation, you shared deliberations
With equal breasts, fashioner of men and creator of life.
Sibylline Oracle 8429–40, tr. J.J. Collins

If the oracles that Porphyry collected were outspokenly opposed to the new religion, the same cannot be said of the *Sibylline Oracles*, which were being composed in Greek at about the same time. These, despite their superficial similarities (in Greek, in hexameter verse), emerge from a quite different thought-world and social milieu from that of the Neo-Platonists. The Sibyl, though of Greek origin (chapter 6), took on a new life in the world of Rome as a purveyor of a theological interpretation of history. The best-known appearance of the Sibyl in literature is when she conducts Aeneas to the Underworld in Book VI of the *Aeneid*. Virgil's portrait of the Sibyl, however, is aberrant; he has clearly modelled her on the Pythia at Delphi in important ways: she is inspired by the *Delius vates*, namely, Apollo (6.10), and speaks in *horrendas ambages*, riddles that make you shiver (6.99). Another famous image of the Sibyl depicts her as immortal but impossibly aged, wizened and living in a bottle: when asked what she wanted, her only reply was 'I want to die'.[1] But to most Romans the Sibyl meant the *Sibylline Books*, the *Libri Sibyllini*, which were consulted in times of crisis or to explain worrying omens and prodigies. The story went that King Tarquin had been offered the chance to buy nine books of prophecies from the Sibyl, but balked at the price. In response, she destroyed three of the books but demanded the same price for the remainder. Tarquin found the price still too high (shouldn't it have come down now?), so she destroyed three more.

At last, sensing that he was missing the point, Tarquin agreed to buy the remaining three books for the price for which he might have had nine.[2] These books became a treasured possession of the Roman people and were regularly consulted, in the manner of the *Prophecies of Nostradamus*, when need arose. The practice is similar to that with the *chresmologoi* of classical Athens, except that in Rome it was institutionalized and lasted for centuries. Unfortunately, no author describes the procedure for consultation.

The *Sibylline Books* were consulted to elicit the meaning of omens, which are a much more common type of message from the gods than oracles in Roman history. Romans rarely consulted oracles, but sought meanings in strange events. Valerius Maximus starts his book of famous deeds with chapters on omens and prodigies: a Vestal Virgin carried water in a sieve without spilling any;[3] statues speak; a fire burns on Servius Tullius' head. Though Livy was sceptical, other authors (like Dionysius of Halicarnassus) revelled in such things, and Julius Obsequens even compiled a collection of prodigies from the references in Livy.[4] Often such prodigies are taken by the sources to describe them to be self-evident in their implications; but when they are not, it is often the *Sibylline Books* that are consulted.

A typical occasion for consultation was the birth of a hermaphrodite, as described by Phlegon of Tralles:[5] 'because of the event, the Senate decreed that the priests should read the *Sibylline Oracles*, and they made atonement and narrated the oracles'. A long passage of the books was found requiring sacrifices and propitiation of Demeter and Persephone. (The names are Greek because the books were in Greek hexameters.) In 228 BC a prophecy that Greeks and Gauls would come to occupy the city of Rome was nullified by burying alive a pair of Greeks and a pair of Gauls in the Forum. Such drastic reactions seem not to have recurred, but the books were regularly consulted in moments of crisis such as the death of Tiberius Gracchus (133 BC).[6]

In 83 BC the books were destroyed by fire, but a new collection was put together in 76 BC – from what sources is not stated, though the priests seem to have had difficulty. A long drawn-out episode in Dio[7] describes how the Temple of Jupiter on the Alban Mount was struck by lightning in 56 BC; consultation of the 'Sibylline verses' produced the following answer: 'If the king of Egypt come requesting any aid, refuse him not friendship, nor yet succour him with any great force; else you shall have both toils and dangers'. The response led to much debate, for it was well publicized by Cato and even translated into Latin to make it more accessible. It is not clear how the omen in question led the experts to just this pronouncement, but the way it becomes a subject of public debate much resembles the debate over the oracle of the 'wooden walls' in Athens in 479 BC (chapter 3).

It was probably at this time that an Etruscan prophetic book, the 'prophecy of Vegoia', was translated into Latin: it made use of a scheme of successive ages from cosmogony to apocalypse, not unlike the later *Sibylline Oracles*. The crisis-ridden atmosphere of the time made the Romans susceptible to this kind of writing,[8] and Etruscans had long been famous for their prophetic powers. Tarquin's semi-legendary queen Tanaquil, whose name is Etruscan, had the reputation of a prophetess and famously induced the appearance of a strange omen, an erect phallus in the ashes of the hearth.[9]

By the reign of Augustus many 'unauthorized' oracles were floating about (again, like the collections in classical Athens), and the emperor took steps to regulate their circulation. But they continued to pop up, and after the fire of Rome in the reign of the emperor Nero an oracle predicting the destruction of Rome in its 900th year gained wide currency.[10] T.P. Wiseman[11] makes an important point about this oracle:

> Why should the citizens have been afraid of the nine hundredth year of Rome? Surely they knew that AD 19 was *ab urbe condita* 771? All they had to do was go to Augustus' arch in the Forum and look at the list of consuls and triumphs; the AUC date was given for every triumph and for every tenth set of consuls. Why did the Roman people not believe so authoritative a source of information? I think the point is this, that all *human* knowledge is fallible. Only the gods know the truth, and only the *uates* – prophet or poet – is divinely inspired to reveal it.

So the Sibyl, or whoever the author of this particular oracle had been – and, on occasion, any poet – was the transmitter of divine knowledge, even if the words were not characterized as words of the god.

This entrenchment of the Sibyl in Roman culture was perhaps a surprising fate for a character who, as far as we can tell, had been an archaic Greek prophetess.[12] Romans had prophetesses (and prophets) of their own, from Tanaquil and Faunus to historical times.[13] Often, however, prophets in Rome were regarded as foreign types: Cicero refers to 'a Lydian diviner, one of Etruscan extraction'.[14] Sibyls had multiplied over the centuries, claiming origin from different parts of Asia Minor and often modelling themselves on the Pythia.[15] Several Sibyls were attached to

41 Domenico Beccafumi, *Tanaquil, c.*1519.

different places in Italy, including Cumae, Tivoli and finally the Lupercal in Rome.[16]

In short, no one knew who the Sibyl was, but her name came to be attached to books of oracles, of what Momigliano (1988) memorably characterized as 'ecstatic predictions of woe'. The Roman *Sibylline Books* were one thing; but from the Hellenistic age the name of the Sibyl came to be attached to a growing body of prophetic material in hexameter verse of Jewish origin, which was then reworked by Christians. In the end the thirteen books of the *Sibylline Oracles* amounted to a kind of history of the Roman empire and the coming of Christ, written in the future tense.[17] These 'oracles' are distinctively different from the other kinds of oracle we have been discussing, in that they are prophecies made by the Sibyl herself, not the words of a god mediated through her mouth.[18] In this they more closely resemble Old Testament prophecies like Jeremiah 46:1–51, 64.[19] Josephus quotes from *Sibylline* IV as 'an ancient prophet'.[20] Paul (Romans 3:2) called the Hebrew scriptures 'oracles of God', and this marks the shift of meaning of the word from 'response' to 'revelation' and even to 'prophecy'. Hebrew prophets are in the past, and this defining element is extended to the Greek Sibyl too. The Sibyl defends herself against the charge of madness like Cassandra's at *Sib*. 3. 817–18: 'when everything comes to pass, then you will remember me and no longer will anyone say that I am crazy, I who am a prophetess of the great God'. The *Sibylline Oracles* are not answers to questions put by enquirers. Lactantius makes this very clear:[21] Sibyls, like Old Testament prophets, are in the past, and their texts are for reading (and replicating).

Like the texts collected in the *Theosophy*, the *Sibylline Oracles* can be seen as prophecies by a pagan speaker of the Christian revelation. The Sibyl becomes a convenient mouthpiece for the new Christian view of the world that is superimposed on the Jewish one. In fact, Sibyl seems to stand for any 'prophetic female': Hermas (in the *Shepherd of Hermas*) thinks he sees her, until he realizes she is in fact the Church.[22] But their origin lies in Jewish apocalyptic literature. That in itself had not a few forebears in Hellenistic literature: the Egyptian demotic *Oracle of the Potter* and *Prophecy of the Lamb*, and the *Demotic Chronicle*,[23] predicting release of Egypt from the foreign oppressor; the Persian *Bahman Yasht*, which is likewise history in the future tense; and the poem *Alexandra* by Lycophron which is an account of Greek mythology couched in the form of a prophecy, and also in a highly allusive and obscure style designed to evoke the riddling quality that was supposed to characterize all the best oracles. In the *Sibylline Oracles* a collection of oracles merges with the reception of Jewish prophecy as a body of work of permanent import.[24] As such it became the model for many later books of prophecy, notably the sixteenth-century *Prophecies of Nostradamus*.

The *Sibylline Oracles* were aligned by Clement (*Stromateis* 6.v.42.3–43.2) with several other oracles: he refers to the Apostle Paul (in the pseudepigraphic *Preaching of Peter*), saying 'Take also the Hellenic books, read the Sibyl, how it is shown that God is one, and how the future is indicated. And taking Hystaspes, read, and you will find much more luminously and distinctly the Son of God described, and how many kings shall draw up their forces against Christ, hating him and those that bear his name, and his faithful ones, and his patience, and his coming.' The *Oracle of Hystaspes*, which foretold the downfall of Rome with the coming of Christianity, was attributed to the Persian king Hystaspes/Vištaspa, the name of both the father of Darius and the legendary protector of Zoroaster.[25] Few extracts survive, but its subjects included the fall of Rome and the end of the world with the appearance of the Son of God. Its themes are clear from the citations in Lactantius' *Divine Institutes*, for example 7.18.2: 'the pious and the faithful will separate themselves from the evil and will stretch out their hands with weeping and wailing, begging for Jupiter's promise: Jupiter will look upon the earth, hear the voices of men and destroy the impious'. It is possible that Hystaspes lies behind much of Lactantius' text, though this has been disputed.[26] Its origin may be in second-century Mesopotamia, and it may have been originally Persian or Jewish, but was plainly worked over to become a Christian text. It may be a misnomer to call it an oracle at all: Beatrice has argued that its title, *chreseis*, means 'extracts' not 'oracles' (which would be *chresmoi*). Be that as it may, its content was in line with that of other oracles of Christianity.

The *Oracle of Baalbek*[27] was also attributed to the Sibyl, in this case the Tiburtine Sibyl, 'seated on a rock on the Capitol, among the olive trees'. Consulted by the priests of the Hebrews about a vision they have seen of 'nine suns' shining on earth, she explains that the nine suns are nine 'generations', which run from the beginning of the world to the reign of Anastasius. Her prophecies foretell the birth of Jesus, the growth and persecution of the Church, and the calamities of the reigns of the emperors Theodosius, Valentinian and Leo. The end of time will come when Enoch and Elijah will make war on the 'ruler of perdition' and Christ will rule. A text like this goes beyond anything that we have met in our survey of oracles and aligns itself rather with apocalyptic literature like that of Pseudo-Methodius (sixth century AD). Such works are written by Christians to provide themselves with both comfort and hope as the expected coming of Christ receded ever into the future.[28]

There were plenty of oracles about the fate of Rome, current under the early empire, that could be adapted to Christian use.[29] Anything predicting the fall of Rome was grist to their mill, like the oracles quoted in Phlegon of Tralles' *Book of Marvels* 3.6–15, the first of them spoken by the Pythia, the rest by the general Publius in a state of ecstatic possession. The last is spoken by Publius' head after his body has been torn apart by a wolf:

> *To this land there will come a great and powerful Ares,*
> *Who will dispatch the armed folk to Hades in the darkness below and*
> *Shatter the stone towers and the long walls . . .*
> *These sure truths Phoibos Apollo has spoken to you,*
> *The Pythian, who sent his powerful servant and*
> *Led me to the abode of the blessed and Persephone.*

The corpus of *Sibylline Oracles* has a complex development and was put together over a period of at least seven hundred years.[30] *Sib.* 3 is the oldest – it even claims to incorporate a portion of an original prophecy by the Babylonian Sibyl (97–161) – and probably originates in Egyptian Jewish circles, foreseeing a Ptolemaic king as the Messiah. Momigliano compares it to the Book of Daniel for its periodization of history as well as to the Claros oracles in which Apollo makes pronouncements that seem to suggest the truth of monotheism. *Sib.* 11, which ends with Cleopatra, also belongs to the pre-Roman period. *Sib.* 4, from the first century BC seems to be an old political oracle like that of the Potter and the *Bahman Yasht*; it may have been the oracle that inspired Virgil in his fourth eclogue. Most of the rest focus on Roman history (*Sib.* 5 begins 'Come, hear my woeful history of the Latin race' and contains several oracles about Nero), and *Sib.* 13 is an important source for the history of the third century AD.[31] *Sib.* 14 is, according to one scholar who has studied it, 'the work of an ignoramus of insane zeal'.[32] Clement knew books 3–5, and Lactantius 3–8. The compilation was completed around AD 500 since the Prologue shows knowledge of the *Theosophy*.

The question of the *Sibylline Oracles'* generic affiliation has been clarified by Jane Lightfoot in her magisterial study of the subject (55ff): she aligns them with the genre of apocalyptic – itself a controversial term, defined by Hengel as a 'literature of revelation'. As John Barton argued, Second Temple Judaism saw a revival of the idea of prophecy, however the prophets were not now men who spoke to their contemporaries about the imminent effects of the wrath of Yahweh, but mystics who had a knowledge of the nature of the universe or, in Sibyl's case, of the future. Prophecy of future events was not a speciality of the Hebrew prophets, though Judith 9:5–6 makes clear that God had everything planned out: 'Thou hast done these things and those that went before and those that followed; thou hast designed the things that are now, and those that are to come. Yes, the things thou didst intend came to pass, and the things thou didst will presented themselves and said, "Lo, we are here".'[33] The Sibyl by virtue of her status as a prophetess has a mystical esoteric wisdom, comparable to that represented in the Wisdom of Solomon,[34] and running parallel to the knowledge of the other world purveyed in the Books of Enoch. Like the Jewish apocalypticists, she is both a teacher of ethics and a revealer of a new world order and God's plan for it, as well as of the nature of God.

The *Sibylline Oracles* tell history in the future tense and as an exemplar of a divine plan. They do not, however, set out to speak in riddles. (Puns are another matter: *Sib.* 3.363–5, 'Samos will become sand [*ammos*], Delos will become obscure [*adelos*], and Rome will become a single street [*rume*].') Allusiveness rules. They have nevertheless provided plenty of meat for historians to chew on. *Sib.* 13 is a good example,[35] for its narrative of events in the third century BC is reasonably straightforward but it omits names. Philip is 'a warrior who loves the purple' (21), the usurper Mareades, or Kyriades, is called 'a deceitful man, a foreign ally, a bandit from Syria' (89–90), and the rise of Palmyra is described in the words 'Then there will be a flight of Romans [from the Persians], but afterward the last priest of all will come, sent from the sun, appearing from Syria, and he will accomplish everything with deceit. Then there will be a city of the Sun' (150–4).

The *Sibylline Oracles* were unique in their wholesale adoption into Christian tradition. Clement may have regarded the Sibyl as a Jewish prophetess: 'I am not an oracle-monger of false Phoebus, whom vain men called a god, and falsely described as a seer, but of the great God, whom no hands of men fashioned in the likeness of speechless idols of polished stone';[36] but other Christian writers (and Clement elsewhere) concur in regarding her as a pagan.[37] Even as a pagan, Lactantius regarded her more highly than the flawed Hystaspes or the oracles of Claros.[38] Her great virtue, as the Byzantine preface to the collection makes clear,[39] is that she provides an encyclopaedic view of the history of the divine plan:

> I decided to set forth the oracles called Sibylline, which are found scattered and confusedly read and recognized, in one continuous and connected book, so that they might be easily reviewed by the readers and award their benefit to them. . . . For they expound very clearly about Father, Son, and

Holy Spirit [and the rest of the Christian revelation]. . . . In addition to
these things they clearly recount the things which are expounded in the
Mosaic writings and the books of the prophets. . . . In manifold ways they
tell of certain past history, and equally, foretell future events, and, to speak
simply, they can profit those who read them in no small way.

It is this absorption of the Sibyls into the Christian tradition that
earned them their place in the pictorial programme of Michelangelo's
Sistine Chapel and of the Cathedral of Siena. Given the Church's hostility
to all forms of pagan oracle, which we shall trace in our final chapter, this
was a remarkable apotheosis.

CHAPTER 13

Silencing the Oracles

Tell ye the king, the carven hall is fallen in decay;
Apollo hath no chapel left, no prophesying bay,
No talking spring. The stream is dry that had so much to say.
                                    The Delphic Oracle to Julian; tr. Sir William Marris

Lo, the gods that ruled by grace of sin and death!
They are conquered, they break, they are stricken,
Whose might made the whole world pale;
They are dust that shall rise not or quicken
Though the world for their death's sake wail.
                                    A.C. Swinburne, *The Last Oracle*

CHRISTIAN SUPPRESSION OF THE ORACLES

The Christian culture that succeeded pagan religion in the fourth century AD had a complex relationship with the classical past. The century between Constantine's acceptance of Christianity in 312 and Theodosius' abolition of pagan rites – including games and every form of worship – in 395 saw heated debate between the defenders of the old religion and the proponents of the new. The stakes were high. Pagan culture was all of a piece, and to demolish its religion was also to break up its societal bonds, its literary traditions and its whole shared frame of reference. T.S. Eliot once wrote: 'If Christianity goes, the whole of our culture goes. Then you must start painfully again, and you cannot put on a new culture ready made. You must wait for the grass to grow to feed to sheep to give wool out of which your new coat will be made. You must pass through many centuries of barbarism.'[1] Change 'Christianity' to 'paganism' in that first sentence, and it perfectly expresses the attitude of pagan intellectuals, from thinkers like Porphyry down to the merest teacher of elementary Latin or Greek. When

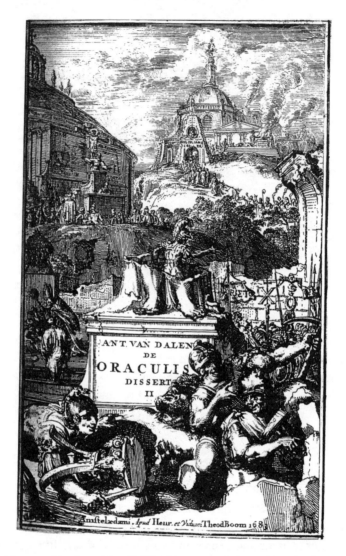

42 The title page of the first edition (1683) of Anton van Dale, *De Oraculis*, showing exultant soldiers destroying the pagan shrines.

Valentinian (AD 364–75) set out to make the Mysteries illegal, the proconsul of Greece 'said that this would make life unbearable for the Greeks' – upon which the emperor relented.[2] But it happened anyway in 395, and Eunapius[3] pointed out that it had been prophesied by the hierophant of Eleusis in Julian's reign. For every writer who exulted in the death of the oracles after more than a thousand years of operation,[4] there was another who hoped that they could somehow still be pressed into service.

Ideas about the gods had undergone enormous changes from the *polis* religion of the fifth century BC to the transcendental theology of the Neo-Platonists, but the gods still defined the way people thought and structured their lives. The conflict between abolitionists and re-users was a process that went on at least until the sixth century AD. The idea that paganism had 'lost faith in itself' by the middle of the fourth century[5] is not one that commands assent on further examination of the evidence.

The decline of the oracles, which Plutarch had prematurely lamented in the second century AD, became a plank of the Christians' arguments in the third and fourth. As early as the late second century, Clement in *Protrepticus* 2.4 had exulted (perhaps over hastily) in the inadequacy of the former religious centres (see p. 179). Tatian in a similar mode rages and sneers at the oracles, attacking even medicine because of its use of divination.[6] Origen (*c. Cels.* 7.3) speaks along the same lines, suggesting that the oracles are probably fraudulent but possibly the work of demons, in which case the Pythia who receives their inspiration through her vulva is certainly impure, and regards the healings carried out by 'sorcerers' as illusory.[7]

Such litanies of decline were to appear in other Christian authors in the next two centuries, notably Eusebius (AD 260–340) in his *Praeparatio Evangelica* (4.2.7–9; 5.1.2) and Theodoret of Cyrrhus (AD 393–460) in his *Cure of Greek Maladies* (10.46 and 105), which drew heavily on Eusebius. Gregory of Nazianzus (AD 330–391), a man steeped in Greek culture, described the flight of the old gods in his poem (II.7) intended to convert Nemesius, the governor of Cappadocia, to Christianity:

Let Phoebus announce the death of the gods that no longer exist. Self-fathered, unwed, motherless is he who destroyed my evil strength, in his final song. Castalia and Daphne, and the oracles of the oak – let them lie, never more to exercise their genius for witless men; also the Egyptian demon, Ammon the god whose words are empty; Branchidae too, and beetling Epidaurus. And the secret rites, as well as those open to visitors, the shame of former times in the nights of Eleusis, and the shrieking of Phrygian pipes that induces madness, the Corybants of Dicte, raving under arms, and the Bacchants who roam the mountains to honour the son of Semele. Also the evil apparitions of Hekate, and the evil deeds of the Mithras temple, as well as orgies no longer known to any; the howling of Cybele of the Galli who drink of the fruitful Nile in their androgynous shame, the tearful laments of Isis and Osiris; and Sarapis, a block of dry wood with his story of destruction.

The list goes on to include Apis, the rites of Artemis Orthia in Sparta, the Getic Zalmoxis and the Taurobolia. Bloody and gruesome as some of these rites are, it is impossible not to surmise that Gregory, as he piles up the Homeric epithets of these ancient practices, does not feel some regret for the colours of a world that is passing.

The famous 'last oracle' of Delphi given to the emperor Julian (epigraph) is usually regarded as a Christian forgery, but it has been suggested[8] that it may rather have been a genuine utterance of the Pythia in a plea for some attention to be given to the oracle and its buildings; this would not have fallen on deaf ears in Julian's case, since he conducted restoration work at many shrines, oracular and otherwise. The temple at Delphi does not seem to have suffered actual destruction until the fifth century AD.[9] In the interim, not one year is recorded without a prophet.[10] During the reign of Julian, the temple of Apollo at Daphne was burned down on 22 October 362, a disaster attributed by pagans to Christian arsonists and recorded by many authors both pagan and Christian.[11] But it was swiftly restored by the pagan emperor.

Some thinkers, both pagan and Christian, had an explanation for the growing inefficacy of the oracles. Christ was a powerful member of the tribe of demons that was interfering with the operation of the oracles. Christians deliberately set about disempowering the oracles by burying Christians close to them. When Julian in his short reign (r. AD 360–36) attempted to restore paganism, he removed a pile of stones which, it was said, the emperor Hadrian had piled across the Castalian spring in an attempt to prevent anyone else receiving prophecies that they might become emperor. The Caesar Gallus had also buried the bodies of Christian martyrs to prevent the oracle operating. 'And Julian, after invoking the god, decided that the bodies which had been buried around the spring, should be moved to another place.' After restoring the temple at Daphne, he took the precaution also of removing the bones of St Babylas from the shrine (Theodoret, *Cure of Pagan Maladies* X.48). Similarly, at Didyma, the growth of a Christian shanty town within the temple precinct was supposed to be the cause of its ceasing to operate.[12] Its failure to prophesy effectively inspired Diocletian's persecution of the Christians.[13]

Sometimes the oracles did speak, but in clear support of the new religion,[14] or at least to concede its power.[15] It is difficult to date many of these oracles, but it is possible that some belong to the third and fourth centuries AD, like the henotheistic oracles of Claros.[16] Some simply promote monotheism or other aspects of Christian doctrine, others are explicit about the impact of the new Christian revelation. Justin *(Apol.* I.18) lists a number of authorities, from Pythagoras to the Sibyl and the oracles of Amphiaraus and Dodona, who support the doctrine of resurrection. Lactantius (*div. inst.* 7.13.6) quotes Apollo announcing how God has arranged resurrection for the faithful, and at 1.7.2 and 4.13.2 he makes Hermes a prophet of the One God.[17]

The Pythia at Delphi, too, is alleged to have acknowledged Christ. When Augustus consulted her about who would be his successor, she at first remained silent. He sacrificed again and received the reply 'A Hebrew child ruling as god over the blessed ones bids me abandon this abode and return to Hades.' So Augustus returned to Rome and set up a new altar to 'the first-born God.'[18]

Many such oracles were collected in the fifth and sixth centuries AD which seemed to show the shrines yielding their power to Christ and acknowledging his supremacy. It is not impossible that some even did so; a thousand years later, in a similar situation, the adoption of Christianity in Iceland was enjoined by a prophecy given by the chief authority of the Norse religion, the Lawspeaker.[19] But most such oracles were plainly composed by Christians at a later date. Theodoret (10.43) insisted that the oracles had never predicted the new religion (which is presumably evidence that the numerous ones that do must have been composed later than Theodoret), but he is happy to assert that they flee precipitately from the new god:

> In fact, before the appearance of our Saviour, when darkness, so to speak, covered the earth, a kind of bandits and robbers, the evil geniuses of men, the maleficent demons, captured human nature by ambush with traps and snares and nets. But when the light of truth arose, they betook themselves to flight and abandoned their caves. That is why they cried out when she [truth] appeared: 'What have we to do with thee, Jesus, thou Son of God? Art thou come hither to torment us before the time? [Mattew 8:29], while others besought him not to send them into the abyss [Luke 8:31]. At Philippi, the spirit of Python cried out on the subject of the Apostles: 'These men are the servants of the most high god, which shew unto us the way of salvation' [Acts 16:17: the Bible text actually attributes the words to 'a damsel possessed with a spirit of divination', τινὰ ἔχουσαν πνεῦμα πυθῶνα.]

LEGAL MEASURES

But even gods who spoke in the form of Christ were not an acceptable option for most Christian writers of the third and fourth centuries AD. The threat of paganism was still too great, especially for those who remembered the persecutions of Diocletian or who experienced the reign of Julian. Human authorities had to help the new divine regime with its work of destruction. Laws had to be passed to deter pagan practice. Eusebius' *Praeparatio Evangelica* 4.135c describes with relish the 'cruel tortures before the Roman courts' that were applied in Constantine's reign to the priests of the oracles to force them to confess 'that it was all an artfully contrived imposture'. At 4.2.11 he mentions a prophet in Miletus who was sought out and killed. In the *Life of Constantine* (III.55) he describes the destruction of the oracular shrine of 'the hateful demon Aphrodite' at Aphaca in Lebanon: 'the devices of licentious error were at once destroyed, and a detachment of soldiers saw to the clearing of the site'. He also describes how at the shrine of Asclepius at Aegeae 'the vaunted wonder of the noble philosophers was razed to the ground, pulled down by a military force'.[20] The *Book of Miracles* of Sophronius (sixth century AD) describes how the cult of Isis had been maintained in secret in a private house in Alexandria for a hundred years after the abolition of paganism and the translation of the bones of two saints, Cyrus and John, to Memphis to replace her. Eventually the Patriarch, Peter Mongos (AD 482–90), had the house razed to the ground: two camel-loads of 'idols' were brought to the city and destroyed. A professor of medicine who openly mocked the saints suffered a back injury and went to incubate in the healing shrine of Menuthis. However, it was not Menuthis who appeared to him, but the two saints, who exultantly told him that his injury would only be cured if he went out in the streets wearing a donkey's saddle, bridle and bit, and shouting 'I am a fool and a sinner.'[21] Sophronius heartily approved this demonstration of the truth of the loving God of the Christians.

Divination was forbidden by law in AD 357 (*Cod. Iustin.* 9.18.5), a moment perhaps reflected in *Sib.* 7.55: 'Prophesy, Colophon, for a great fire is hanging over you.'[22] The Theodosian Code (9.16.9) provides that oracle priests can be tortured and 9.17–112 details various penalties for sorcerers and astrologers.[23] A high official named Fidustius who had used divination to reveal the name of the man who would succeed the emperor Valens was savagely tortured (AM 29.1.5ff.).[24] Ammianus describes in another place how people consulted the oracle of Besa in the Thebaid and were viciously punished 'exactly as if many men had importuned Claros, the oaks of Dodona, and the once famous oracles of Delphi with regard to the death of the emperor' (19.12.15).

EUSEBIUS

In addition, the oracles had to be comprehensively demolished on philosophical grounds, and that was what Eusebius (AD 264–339, bishop of Caesarea from 313) set out to do in his *Praeparatio Evangelica*. This enormous work, written between the years 311 and 320,[25] has been attacked by theologians as a hodgepodge of random arguments, and quite unoriginal;[26] in fact, it is a carefully structured work, and may be regarded as the intellectual underpinning of the Christian revolution.[27] Eusebius sets out to demolish the 'three forms of polytheistic error': he begins with mythology, continues with the philosophical-allegorical approach to classical religion, and in book IV begins on his third target, the religion of the polis. His discussion of oracular sites occupies books IV–VI; the remaining nine books treat the 'Hebrew descent' of Christianity (7–8), Greek borrowings from the Hebrews (9–14), and a discussion of Greek philosophical theology and its inadequacies (14–15). Eusebius' style is passionate and vehement but he argues his points against the authorities he dismisses, rather than just sneering as Tatian did. In constructing his arguments, Eusebius quotes verbatim very substantial amounts of earlier (pagan) writing on oracles, thus providing us with valuable material for the history of the subject.[28]

His method of argument is systematic:[29] he repeatedly demolishes (to his own satisfaction) a particular position about oracles, but then proceeds, 'If, however, we grant the premise, then . . .' and demolishes the next stage of the argument. His opening proposition is that the oracles are simply frauds, the work of charlatans who deliberately set out to deceive the people.[30] (Their motive is not specified, but presumably it would be power and advantage.) Pointing out that oracles often fail of fulfilment, he proposes that where they do succeed, it is simply the result of chance (IV.2, cf. IV.3.2). This view was in fact anticipated by Cicero and it is an easy conclusion to reach if one thinks of oracles as a kind of roulette wheel: there is a fifty-fifty chance of a simple statement proving true or false. Eusebius cites a number of authors who allegedly shared this view (IV.2.12), from Cynics and Epicureans to Aristotelians; he provides an extract from the Epicurean Diogenianus to support his view. It is piquant, incidentally, to see how the Christian author uses the arguments of the most notoriously 'atheistic' philosophical school of antiquity to strengthen his own. In this, as in so many other areas, we see how the arrival of Christianity represented a 'world turned upside down'.

The next stage of the argument is to hypothesize that oracles are not the result of fraud, in which case they could only work if the future is fated and can also be foreknown (IV.3.1). A further step in the argument is that, if everything is fated, there is little advantage in knowing the future since you cannot change it. Foreknowledge of evil increases suffering, while foreknowledge of good does not increase happiness because people hope for better things anyway (IV.3.7–9). If on the other hand one can guard against the future because it is foreknown, then fate cannot be immutable. In which case divination is useless. The argument is in fact compelling, and the example of Oedipus is brought in as so often: his parents tried to avert predestination by exposing the child, but they failed: the oracle came true anyway and so divination was useless to them (12–13).

> For example, Chrysippus himself says, à propos Oedipus and Alexander son of Priam, that their parents had employed every means possible to kill them in order to avoid the misfortune which had been predicted, but that they were unable to. He recognizes too that they themselves derived no advantage from the prediction of their misfortune, since fate determines everything. So all that goes, and it is already more than sufficient, to show not just the inconstancy but also the uselessness of *mantike*.

At this point, it may be noted, Eusebius has proved not that divination is false, but that it is useless, if Fate exists. He has not proved that Fate does not exist. He now goes on (IV.3.16) to consider the proposition that the oracles are true. Here he brings in extensive consideration of Porphyry's *Philosophy from Oracles*, which is used to show that oracles are part of the 'tyranny of demons' over mankind. The demons, '*daimones*', had been part of Greek supernatural apparatus since before Plato: the word itself implies only a demi-god, often a dead soul, but in Christian writers it comes to have its modern meaning of an evil spirit. This long discussion of Porphyry leads to the proposition (at the beginning of Book V) that the coming of Christ rendered the activity of the (evil) demons ineffective. He produces several arguments to show the mean nature of the demons: as Porphyry wrote (V.1.8): there is no help from the gods now that Jesus is worshipped. If the gods cared, why didn't they destroy the Christian religion? If the gods cared for mankind, why did they play so many evil tricks on them? This argument recurs at intervals throughout the book, from V.6 on Pan's random murders of humans to V.19, on Apollo's deception of his worshippers by ambiguous oracles that led them to disaster.

In putting together this part of his argument, Eusebius was able to summon Plutarch as a witness, with his melancholy and defeatist discussions of a religion that was, in fact, on the point of a tremendous flourishing. The demons can die: v.4.2, v.5.4, v.17. In fact they did die, in the reign of Hadrian (4.17.4, 5.1.7).[31] In v.10 Eusebius is able to use Porphyry's *Letter to Anebo* against its author: for at v.14 where Porphyry says that gods can make predictions come true because they know everybody's horoscopes, Eusebius is able to charge that this makes the gods no more than mere magicians.

At v.18 the argument gathers force and direction with the extensive citation of Oenomaus of Gadara's *Wizards Unmasked*. Oenomaus, who had begun from criticism of the absurd obscurity or triviality of certain oracles, is enlisted for an attack on the cruelty and wickedness of the gods: they cheat you with riddles, they demand human sacrifices, they flatter tyrants (35), and they give trivial or banal advice. The tone of the Cynic Oenomaus is close to that of Lucretius the Epicurean, *tantum religio potuit suadere malorum*, and indeed to that of a modern Lucretius such as Richard Dawkins; all the arguments that Eusebius here uses against pagan religion can equally be marshalled by a modern atheist against Christianity. But Eusebius, who thoroughly approved of the torture and execution of pagan priests by Constantine (though not with the same bloodthirsty fervour as exhibited by Lactantius in *De mortibus persecutorum*), did not take that further step.

At this point, Eusebius has shown to his satisfaction that oracles are fakes, but if they are true, they are the work of evil demons. He now returns to the question of Fate. Even the gods fear Destiny, he says (vi.2.2), and cannot help themselves. He cites from Porphyry[32] Apollo's oracle on the destruction of his own shrine. They can use Fate as an excuse for the failure of their own prophecies (vi.6.3). 'The demon, whose deceits lead people astray, protects himself by pretending to the foolish, such that if anything in the future should not fall out as predicted, he provides himself with a refuge for his unreliability in Fate (*heimarmene*). If Fate controls even the will, Eusebius concludes, there is an end of philosophy and religion (vi.6.5).[33] No praise or blame for good or bad is possible.

> If one must attribute to the stars or fate not only external events but even rational volitions, and if an inevitable Necessity compels human decisions, it is all up with philosophy, it is all up with religion (*eusebeia*): there will be no praise of virtue of good men, nor worthy recompense for ascetic effort, if Necessity and Fate have assumed total responsibility.[34]

Because this argument is to Eusebius (as it would be to us) morally objectionable, he concludes that humans must have, as they feel they have, free will (VI.6.21). Free will had been Epicurus' answer to the problem of change in a materialist universe: here again the Christian author uses an argument developed by an atheist. Perhaps aware that this doctrine leaves little room for divine purpose at all, Eusebius now brings in a new player, Providence:

> A sole all-powerful force, which circulates everywhere and which governs most often by divine reasons, unfathomable to us, which with a light hand directs the All and arranges most natural phenomena in accordance with circumstances, participates and aids in what depends on us and determines the necessary order for external events.

All events are caused by the Providence of God (V.6.45). To some readers, this new being might seem no different from Fate; but as above there is a moral judgement at play. Providence is the attribute of a good God, not the old gods who have been shown to be evil. It is also the attribute of a higher god than the demons who were subject to Fate in the old belief.

Most of the remainder of book VI is devoted to the refutation of belief in fate, making use of several philosophical authorities – not only Oenomaus, but Diogenianus' attack on Chrysippus, Alexander of Aphrodisias, and Origen's *Commentary on Genesis*. Eusebius even believes he has found an answer to the Oedipus conundrum (VI.7.24–7): Oenomaus cites Euripides for the idea that Oedipus' father Laius, having received the oracle that his son would kill him, was free not to engender a son. Further, Oedipus could have chosen not to be king. It is clear that Oenomaus' argument is only valid if free will is taken as a given; the point of such an oracle story is precisely that the oracle is fulfilled whatever action you take. The argument is a *petitio principii*, but Eusebius finds it serves his purpose. Astrology forms an important part of the case against Fate: at VI.11.3 he (Origen) considers whether the stars are signs of divine prescience, but points out that a prophecy is never the *cause* of the event.

Like Gregory of Nyssa, Eusebius rejects all pagan arguments for Fate; but he goes beyond Gregory in developing a positive Christian theory to replace it.[35] At VI.11.40 Eusebius finds himself arguing that free will exists even though God knows all our acts in advance. He knew that Judas was going to betray his son, and (40–2) he could judge that in any situation a certain result would or would not come about:

> If it is not possible that God should be deceived, it is possible that, in the case of events which might or might not take place, he should have

judged that they would or would not take place. More clearly, we may say as follows: if it is possible that Judas should be an apostle like Peter, it is possible that God should judge that he will remain an apostle like Peter; if it is possible that Judas will become a traitor, it is possible that god should judge that he will be a traitor. If Judas is going to be a traitor, God, by his foreknowledge of these two possibilities – given that only one of them can be realised – God will have known in advance, for he knows the truth in advance, that Judas will become a traitor. . . . God could say 'It is possible that he will do this, but also the opposite; given that the two are possible, I know that he will do this.'

If I understand this strange argument at all, it seems to say that God foreknows that Judas will betray his son. At this point one wonders how the God who sent his son to a painful death with foreknowledge differs from the Apollo who let down his servant Croesus, for example.

At VI.11.49 Eusebius argues that God has made men blind to the future because, if they knew what was going to happen, they would struggle less hard against evil. (The question why you should struggle against evil if your efforts are going to make no difference is not raised.) Having, by now, driven his argument into the ground but convinced himself that Christian religion is completely different from the religion it sets out to replace, Eusebius concludes his long discussion with a repetition of the conclusion that the oracles are frauds, and Christ has saved mankind from them (VI.11.82).

Reading Eusebius is an activity of a different kind from that of reading most of the Christian writers on pagan religion. Though I don't believe that his argument works in the end, he is formidably well read (to our great advantage!), argues intelligently and logically, and gives at least some opportunity to opponents to put their case. His conclusion is a clear one though, in view of the material I have assembled in this book, it must be wrong. Oracle priests were not crude frauds. But this is the only option open to Eusebius if he is to accept the existence of supernatural powers at all. He was intelligent enough to see this, where many other writers equivocated constantly between the two ideas, that oracles are frauds or that they are the work of evil demons. The dichotomy resembles that drawn by some modern anthropologists between religion and magic (see chapter 14); but Eusebius' simpler position is the same as that of Robert Burton in the *Anatomy of Melancholy*: 'Such fears have still tormented men in all ages, by reason of those lying oracles and juggling priests.'[36] He offers no alternative to oracles; they are simply fraudulent, obsolete and wrong.

CHARLATANS OR DEMONS?

Other writers did not solve the problem so categorically, and continued to equivocate between the view of oracles as simple frauds and the idea that they were the activity of dangerous and evil demons that required to be combated. Theodoret of Cyrrhus, for example, in his *Cure of Pagan Maladies*, written a century after Eusebius, made use of much of Eusebius' argumentation, but devotes most of his argument to the proposition that the oracles were the work of demons who had usurped the divine name (x.2).[37] He is able to use Plutarch as evidence for this (x.7). He cites many of the same examples as Eusebius to prove the malice of the demons.[38] Though at x.41 he quotes Oenomaus on the 'falsity' (ψεῦδος) of the oracles, he continues immediately with an account of the death of the oracle as the result of the coming of Christ. The removal of the body of St Babylas from the temple at Daphne is quoted (48) as an example of the power of Christian relics over the feeble, dying gods of old. He then proceeds to demonstrate the completely different quality of the prophecies of God himself, as found in Isaiah and the other prophets: they are not ambiguous, they are precise on events lying one thousand years in the future whereas Delphi and Dodona couldn't get it right three months ahead (x.60); and so on. The book then becomes a sermon on the prophets of the Old Testament.

Theodoret's purpose here is different from that of Eusebius. Where the latter was arguing for his own doctrine in a world that could, perhaps, still swing either way (as it swung back to paganism in the reign of Julian), Theodoret was writing in a world that was now legally Christian but where the ancient demons still seemed to pose a real threat.[39] Eusebius had set the death of the demons in the reign of Hadrian, but they were still causing trouble for Augustine a hundred years after Eusebius' death: this is the subject of *de divinatione daemonum*. For that matter, Michael Psellus in the eleventh century thought it worth devoting a treatise to the *Operation of Demons*, and in the seventeenth both Anton van Dale's *De Oraculis* (1675 and 1700) and Bernard de Fontenelle's *Histoire des Oracles* (1686)[40] continued to waver uncertainly between fraud and demons as an explanation for the success of the oracles. It was a pity for their case that even the oracles declaring the truth of Christianity had thus to be declared to be false.[41] The gods had not, after all, fled as precipitately as they were supposed to have, and pagan practices still continued in a nominally Christian world.

New Homes for the Oracles

People, it seems, were unable to manage without the kind of support and reassurance that oracles offered. It is a commonplace to compare the function of saints in Catholic countries with that of the gods of antiquity, and to contrast this with the Protestant interiorization of religion and rejection of 'magical' elements (though prayer as such usually seems to be excepted from the theologians' dismissal of attempts to work on the supernatural powers). In the fifth century AD one can watch the process of transfer taking place, as pagan shrines find themselves a new role under the tutelage of a Christian saint. One of the best-known examples is that of the shrine of St Thecla at Seleuceia on the Calycadnus.[42] In ancient times there was an oracle here of Apollo Sarpedonios. Only a few of its consultations are known – by Alexander Balas in the second century BC, by Queen Zenobia of Palmyra in the third century AD.[43] It seems that Apollo had replaced an earlier cult of Sarpedon, who is not otherwise associated in myth with Cilicia.[44] But later, Thecla, who had been a companion of St Paul on his journeys, settled in this place and worked many miracles of healing; when she died, her tomb became a place of pilgrimage and continued to provide healing (like that of the Neapolitan Doctor Giuseppe Moscati who died in 1927.)[45] If Sarpedon's dream oracle was, like so many dream oracles, a healing one (though the attested consultations have nothing to do with healing), then Thecla simply took over the modus operandi of a pre-existing cult. Or in other words, the use of the shrine was justified by the creation of a story about the healing powers of St Thecla. It is no surprise to find, in cases of sickness above all, that people continued to require the services of a supernatural healer – for human healers continued to be able to do very little. Theodoret (*Cure of Pagan Maladies* 8.69) may have supposed that martyrs were installed in shrines to drive out the old gods, but they seem to have picked up their predecessors' habits.

The process has been well documented for late Roman Egypt.[46] The same questions continue to be posed, by the same method of writing the enquiry on a ticket, but addressed now to 'the God of St Leontius', 'God and Christ', 'God Pantokrator'. The archive of the oracle shrine of St Colluthos of Antinoe contains seventy-one oracle tickets from the fifth century AD. As well as consultations at shrines, the use of oracle books was particularly prominent in late Roman Egypt; the *Book of Astrampsychos* may have begun its transformation into the *Sortes Sanctorum* in the hands of a Coptic monk.[47] Similarly, in the Byzantine East, a number of shrines of saints who heal by incubation are surely the successors of ancient healing shrines that were often unrecorded. In the seventh century AD an encomium was composed to St Therapon (i.e. healer, or nurse), at whose shrine, somewhere in Constantinople, the martyr would appear in dreams and heal the sleeper. Again in Constantinople, St Michael himself was known for having healed one Aquilinus of yellow fever by prescribing a medicine of honey, wine and pepper (Sozomen, *HE* 2.3). In the same century, Sophronius composed a praise of saints Cyrus and John, whose relics were kept near Canopus and who performed at least sixty-seven miracles of healing, 'without payment' (like Cosmas and Damian, the ἅγιοι ἀνάργυροι). Similarly, in the Latin West, the practice of incubation for healing dreams moved smoothly into the cult of saints Cosmas and Damian, and Gregory of Tours, who mentions them, tells also of other saints who performed the same function. In a cave on Monte Gargano an ancient oracle of Calchas had a church built over it in the sixth century AD: a sacred fountain continued to heal regardless of the presiding divinity (*Acta Sanct. Sept.* VII.xvii).[48] Even on Mt Athos it is said that a chapel of St Basil near the monastery of Iviron is built over an ancient oracle of Apollo, which had continued to operate until the Virgin Mary herself visited the place and put it out of action.[49]

CHRISTIAN ORACLES

Furthermore, the prestige of the old oracles remained so strong – as they functioned well into the fifth century AD – that they were repeatedly enlisted to bolster the Christian revelation. The finding of useful prophecies became not uncommon. Perhaps 'discovery' was the main source of many of these Christian oracles, just as it had been for the oracles that endowed Alexander of Abonuteichos with his mystical powers. In the first year of the reign of Anastasius (r. 491–518) a tablet was found after a great storm, washed out from the foundations of a temple at Delphi.[50] It contained words of 'the falsely named "god" Apollo' in response to a question about Christ:

> You should not ask me, for the last and final time, wretched servant of mine, what the glorious god and the spirit festooned all around, as it were with grapes, with monsters, light, rivers and Tartarus, air and fire, who drives me all unwilling from my home. . . . Woe, woe, Tripods, wail: Apollo has gone, gone, since a mortal, a man from heaven is compelling me [lines 9–24 omitted]. Christ is my god, who was stretched out on a tree, who died, entered the tomb, and rose from the tomb to the skies.

As early as Clement, Christ could be seen as a new kind of oracle. At *Protrepticus* 1.4P, after rejecting the prophecies of Orpheus and the like, he refers to Christ as 'my minstrel' who has 'come to bring an end to slavery to the demons'. A number of Christian authors wrote books collecting oracles that seemed to predict Christian doctrine, including Timotheos,[51] a shadowy figure who was the source of most of Malalas' oracles; Didymus the Blind, who used 'the non-Christian sages' as sources of several oracles quoted in his *On the Trinity* (ch. 27, Migne); and the lost *Chresmodiai Hellenikai* (below). As John Milton put it:

> *God hath now sent his living Oracle*
> *Into the world, to teach his final will,*
> *And sends his spirit of truth henceforth to dwell*
> *In pious hearts, an inward oracle*
> *To all truth requisite for men to know.*[52]

An intriguing story[53] tells how seven sages, including the wonder-worker Apollonius of Tyana, assembled in the house of an Athenian citizen.

> The conversation focussed on prediction of the incarnation of our Lord Jesus Christ. Their names are Apollonius, Solon, Thucydides, Plutarch, Aristotle and Chilon the philologist. The six philosophers said to Apollonius: 'Prophesy to us, o prophet of Phoebus: whose house will this be?' Apollonius replied: '. . . I announce to you the sole all-powerful God, one in three; whose imperishable Word will come to birth in a pure virgin. He will run through the world like a fire-bearing arrow, and will capture it and bring it as a gift to his father. And this will be the house of Mary, for such will be her name.'

One of the priests (where have they come from?) accuses Apollonius of lying, but he insists it is the truth. The other six philosophers then chip in with henotheistic pronouncements. Plutarch announces that God's Wisdom and Word encircle the world. Chilon says: 'This is he who is above the great heroes, an undying fire that excels the eternity of flame, at whom the heaven earth and sea tremble, and the depths of Tartarus, and the demons. He is self-fathered, unfathered, thrice-blessed.'

Another story in Malalas (IV.12), an obvious Christian invention this time, has the Argonauts consult Apollo somewhere near Cyzicus about founding a new shrine: the local Pythia responds: 'Do all that leads to virtue and honour. I proclaim only a triune, high-ruling God,[54] whose imperishable word will be conceived in an innocent girl. He, like a fiery arrow coursing through the midst of the whole world, will make it captive and bring it as a gift to his father. This will be her house and her name will be Mary.'

Apollonius appears again in a text purporting to describe a debate on religion at the Sassanid court.[55] It shows the oracles in dysfunctional mode, suffering heavily from 'interference' from the new god. A series of prophecies apparently relating to Alexander the Great is pushed into the service of the Christian message. The king summons a Greek and a Christian philosopher to explain the Greek prophecies of Christ. Aphroditianus begins by ordering his slave to read from the *Chresmodiai Hellenikai* the section called 'The Story of Cassander'.[56] This garbled account of Macedonian history leads to a consultation of the oracle at Delphi about how to handle the beautiful queen Doris. The Pythia, 'tasting the water of the spring', and ignoring the question completely, 'replied as follows: "Philip, son of Olympias, born at Pella, will travel across Asia and, encircling further regions with his mighty arm, will subdue it." They laughed at her and said, "Damn you, didn't we ask about a woman, not about a man from Macedonia?" ' They abandon Delphi and consult the 'priestess of Athens', Xanthippe. Complaining that they have come at an inauspicious time, she nevertheless prophesies: 'A certain young man, offspring of a mixed marriage, holding the unconquerable balance of god's unconquerable scales, will encircle the world like an egg, capturing everything with his spear.'[57] Abandoning this prophetess too in a rage, they decamp to the oracle of 'Great Phoebus Apollo' (location unspecified). A great voice is heard, saying, 'The tripod turns three times and the prophet speaks threefold as follows: the heaven-sent bringer of dawn dwells within matter, encased in chains of earth, fashioning a body for himself in the womb of a virgin. . . . He will tear down the lordship and every sacred shrine of yours, and will lead to the peak of blessed wisdom the honour of all fame [?].' Aphroditianus explains how the Macedonian, 'after attacking Persia at a bad time, returned at the right time, while Christ after being vanquished shamed those who plotted against him by overcoming them'.

In the tenth century the patriarch Photius (*Bibliotheca* 170) noted that he had read 'a substantial, indeed enormous, work in fifteen books and five volumes' by an author of the seventh century AD, which collected quotations and whole books by 'Greek, Persian, Thracian, Egyptian, Babylonian, Chaldaean and Roman authors' that were supposed to be in accordance with the Christian theological revelation. Such collections had been made from Clement's time onward. Prime among such works is one known as the *Tübingen Theosophy* which belongs to the early sixth century.[58]

The *Tübingen Theosophy*

P.F. Beatrice[59] notes that the author is well-read in Greek and Latin literature, and informed on magic and Zoroastrianism, but cites no Christian
authors apart from Cyril of Alexandria. He tentatively suggests as author
Severus of Antioch (*c.*465–538), who is known to have started life as a
pagan before being baptized in 488. The *Theosophy* is the most important
representative of the tradition of writing that attempts to save classical
literature by treating it in the same manner as the Old Testament, and
finding in it a foreshadowing of the Christian revelation.

The *Theosophy* does not survive in its entirety. The sole MS to survive
the Middle Ages belonged to Johannes Reuchlin (d. 1522), after whose
death it was taken to Strasburg, where it was destroyed in 1870 during the
Franco-Prussian War. But in 1580 Martin Crusius commissioned a copy,
which remained in Tübingen University Library; this copy was not
complete but provided only an epitome of the first part, as its author
explains:

> The author of the book entitled THEOSOPHIA states in his preamble
> that he first wrote seven books on True Belief (*orthe doxa*); then he wrote
> books 8–11 to show the prophecies of the Greek gods and the so-called
> theologies of the Greek and Egyptian sages, and in addition the verses
> of the Sibyls, chiming with the purport of holy writ and sometimes
> supporting the Cause of All, sometimes demonstrating the all-holy
> Trinity in one God.

It ends with a chronicle of world history from Adam to Emperor Zeno.

The book may thus have been designed as a refutation of Porphyry by
collecting oracles that trump the ones he had assembled. It includes quite
a number from his collection (27, 30, 41 cf. 309, 65, 85), as well as the
Clarian oracles (15–19, 21–4, 26, 33–9, 41–4, 52–4), including the longer
version of the one to Theophilus (13), some of the oracles of Hystaspes on
the fall of Rome, and quotations from Euripides (86), Menander (87–8),
Orpheus (55–6) and the Sibyls (80–1).[60] In *c.*7 the author of the *Theosophy*
writes (Erbse 1995, xxii): 'We must not reject the witness of the Greek sages
about God. Since it is not possible for God to appear and debate with men,
he stirs up the conceptions of good men to make them teachers of the
multitude. So, whoever discounts these witnesses, discounts also him who
inspired them.' Several of the oracles are utterances of Apollo expressing
his sense of new-found inadequacy: he laments his expulsion from shrines

(16–17), professes his ignorance of the creator (12), utters some 'negative theology' like that of the oracle from Oenoanda (21), as well as announcing to Byzas, the founder of Byzantium (19), and to other enquirers the theology of the Christian God (33–9). More explicit Christian theology is collected from oracles given in Coptos (46) and Elephantine (47), while one found in Cyzicus and in Athens in the time of Leo I repeats the prophecy of Christ from the Sassanid debate quoted above (53).

THE ORACLES OF LEO THE WISE

My final exhibit in this series of Greek oracles from more than a thousand years is a book of a kind that became common in the early Byzantine period: the *Oracles* of Leo the Wise. Many such oracle books were anonymous, as were the dream books that became equally prevalent,[61] and the name of Astrampsychos is a fiction; but the Byzantine emperor Leo VI (AD 886–912) became known as the author of an oracle book.[62] Leo himself did make use of diviners, and two actual predictions he made concerned the death of Constantine Ducas and that of his brother Alexander, but he was not a practising magician or sage. Perhaps the legend arose because his name was confused with that of Leo the Magician, a prominent intellectual and astrologer in the reign of the emperor Theophilus (*AP* 9.201). Leo can perhaps be seen as the successor to the Holy Man of late antiquity. The rise of the Holy Man is one of the most famous markers of the change of spiritual climate in late antiquity,[63] as the focus of reverence moved away from

43 A coin of Leo VI, The Wise, AD 886–912.

sacred places to sacred individuals. The Christian Holy Man was foreshad-
owed in the reign of Julian by pagan sages like Eustathius, whom the magi
regarded as a *goes*, a wizard or shaman, and who married Sosipatra who
turned out to be a prophetess. His eloquence and wisdom identified him
as a kind of oracle. The sophist Maximus (p. 427) 'spoke like an oracle'
and was able to interpret an oracle (Amm. Marc. 31.13.12–17, Penella 73).
Chrysanthius (Eunapius p. 433) gained a reputation as a wonder worker.[64]
So there was precedent both among pagans and among the Christian saints
for a wise man to exhibit privileged access to truth.

According to the chronicler Zonaras (Cedrenus II.274 app.), Leo turned
to oracles after his empress Theophano had failed to bear him a son. By
1200 he was well known as a prophet, many of his predictions being based

44 From a manuscript of *The Oracles of Leo the Wise*, 1577.

on those in the Book of Daniel. He became famed as a wonder-worker rather like Apollonius of Tyana, and his oracles were often copied. They take the form of a series of oracular poems, which are accompanied in many manuscripts by magnificent illustrations, among them five emperors, the wily dog-man and the flying serpent. They include both poems of ethical import and oracles of the fall of Constantinople and the end of time.

Wilfully obscure rather than riddling, they include utterances like the following:

10. Power.
Woe to you, city of seven hills, when the twentieth letter is admired on your walls. Then ruin and destruction of your rulers are near at hand, and of those who ruled unjustly. He has fingers like scythes, the scythe of desolation, and blasphemy against the highest.

13. Innocence
The dead man, unknown even by sight, is known to many even if none see him. As if rising from drunkenness, he will suddenly seize the sceptre of the kingdom. A fatal column seen in the sky, like an invisible herald, will cry three times: Depart in haste to the west of the seven-hilled city. You will find a man dwelling there who is my friend. Bring him to the royal palace – wise, calm, gentle, intelligent, skilled in knowing what is to come. Then, O city of seven hills, you will be powerful again.

Unmetrical, often ungrammatical, these oracles are pitiful descendants of the sayings of the Pythia sixteen hundred years before. They exceed by far the Sibyl's utterances in their metrical incompetence.[65] But nonetheless they are representatives of the same tradition.

In the *Oracles of Leo the Wise* we see many of the themes of this book reprised: the wise man who utters prophecies of doom or salvation recalls both the *chresmologoi* of classical Greece and the Sibyls of the Roman age, and their political content would not have come as a shock to Athenians and Spartans of the classical age. The use of his *Oracles* resembles that of the oracles of Astrampsychos and the *Sortes Sanctorum*; the content of the prophecies links the oracles of the Sibyl with the apocalypses of the early Byzantine age; the physical appearance of the illustrated manuscripts recalls that of Tarot cards; and the repeated consultation of the book in times of crisis parallels the employment of the later *Prophecies* of Nostradamus in the West. But for all that, Leo represents the Christianization of the form and a break with the pagan past: there is no consultation of his shrine nor any evocation of the dead or the demons. His prophecies are fixed, even though, like those of Nostradamus (and perhaps the pre-Christian Sibylline books), they can be endlessly reinterpreted. They were much employed during the period of the Ottoman threat; in 1535 his prophecies were applied to Charles v;[66] and in later centuries, Constantinople could be seen as a metaphor for the threat from Moscow. One of the first books printed in independent Greece was a book of oracles (1838).[67] The oracles of Leo are proof, if proof were needed, that the need to consult a spiritual authority for guidance in the affairs of life was not wiped out by the Christian revelation.

CHAPTER 14

Conclusion

It will never be that people do all these things out of pure stupidity.
Ludwig Wittgenstein, 'Remarks on Frazer's
The Golden Bough', ed. A.C. Miles and Rush Rhees,
The Human World 3 (May 1971, 28–41), cited in Tambiah 1990, 57

The Christian claim was that their religion was of a new kind, superior to and driving all value out of the religion of the pagan Greeks and Romans. During most of the time when modern scholars have studied the religion of the ancients, there has been an underlying assumption that this was indeed the case, that pagan religion was somehow a lower evolutionary form of religion, lacking in the personal and interior qualities of modern faiths such as Christianity and Islam, and perhaps even Judaism. Only in the last two generations (since the work of Dodds, for example) has there been a recognition of the richness of pagan religious experience. I single out the work of Robin Lane Fox as one of the best evocations of what it was like to take part in pagan religion in the early centuries AD.

Hand in hand with this assumption has gone the distinction contrived by the anthropologists between magic and religion. The distinction goes back to Malinowski, and has been followed by writers as diverse as Tylor, Tambiah and Keith Thomas.[1] Frazer saw an evolutionary progress in the successive emergence of magic, religion and science.[2] Keith Thomas implicitly sees English Protestantism as a casting off of the magical accoutrements of Catholicism. The hanging in chains of the Vicar of St Thomas' in Exeter in the Prayer Book rebellion, 'in his full Popish garb',[3] is an exorcism comparable to that of the oracles by the Christian martyrs.

The position might be compared with the outlawing of divination in the kingdom of Israel: as Tambiah (1990, 7) puts it, divination 'works', but is false to Yahweh. In the English case, the Protestant Church was hostile to soothsaying, sorcery and so on: regular annual excommunications were directed against wizards and witches.[4] Astrology was equally frowned on (Thomas 1971, 425 ff.). This hostility arose from a new concept of religion (Thomas 1971, 88) which emphasized it as an interior experience rather than a set of rituals: the change is comparable to that between the extensive rituals of pagan religion and the interiority enjoined by the Neo-Platonists and adopted by the Christians. It is a lower form of interaction with the gods which should be disallowed in order to forward the higher, purified, 'religious' (i.e. interior) kind of religion. It is magic and not religion, if one follows (as does Tambiah) a Malinowskian definition whereby religion is concerned with ultimate truths, whereas magic is the attempt to bend the powers to your will (magic objectively false, subjectively true). Though Porphyry moved away from theurgy towards a more spiritual interpretation of religion, and showed up some of the problems inherent in the idea of divination by the extremes of mere technical expertise involved in theurgy (or the magical papyri), no pagan would have rejected the tradition of a thousand and more years of oracles at work. For Keith Thomas, it was not religious opposition as such that led to the decline of magic, but the growth of a scientific spirit, with its implications of Whiggishness and Popperianism: magic, unlike science, never learnt from failure but simply explained it away.[5] Protestantism was the next step: it interiorized religion completely, rejected what did not 'work' and paved the way for atheism. The logical conclusion of this development of Protestant interiorization, this 'explicit individual questioning of authority' (Tambiah 1990, 12ff.) is not just scientific thought but atheism. Why not reject everything that cannot be experienced with the senses? Protestantism declared magic to be not just false but inefficacious, in an echo of Eusebius' critique of the oracles.

As we have seen, a considerable body of theory grew up about the apparent failure of oracles to work, either through a failure of human understanding or because of interference by hostile demons. The same principles were applied in astrology too (cf. Tambiah 1990, 30); failure was usually explained by inaccuracy in the premises. Ancient and early Christian thinkers never developed a way of testing procedures comparable to the scientific method of falsification. It is true that reason sometimes wipes out superstition: Tambiah (1990, 132–3) cites the case where the development of a smallpox vaccine led to the demise of the smallpox goddess in Sri Lanka. But this is not what Eusebius and his co-religionists were doing.

But perhaps the dichotomies are too harsh? Even Malinowski had recognized that magic and religion arise from the same source: 'Both magic and religion arise and function in situations of emotional stress: crises of life, lacunae in important pursuits, death and initiation into tribal mysteries, unhappy love and unsatisfied hate.'[6] Just so in the introduction I drew attention to such 'crises of life' as the occasions for the consultation of oracles. In despair one seeks help and reassurance that cannot be found from within. The oracles may 'work' because they fulfil a social/psychological function, even if they don't come true. Wittgenstein subtly commented (Tambiah 1990, 61): 'That which is characteristic of ritual action is surely not a view, or opinion, whether it is now correct or false, although an opinion – a belief – itself can be ritualistic, can belong to the rite.' The distinction called 'magic and religion' might better be termed 'ritual and interiorization'. And the material collected in this book has surely shown that the rituals of oracle consultation are anything but incompatible with an interior conception of the gods. States that consulted Delphi or Claros were not performing magic spells, and the many personal enquiries show how close to the heart were the concerns people brought to the gods. Not just the theurgy of Porphyry, or the questions asked about theology in the third century AD, but the debates of the fifth century BC, the appeals to the Egyptian gods in the Hellenistic period or the treks to dice oracles of the second century AD, all spring from the same inner motivation: to understand the nature of the crisis and thus to find a way out. The Christians did not succeed in wiping out the oracles, because they represented an answer to a need. Their new religion was not of a different kind, or if it was it failed to be strong enough to change human nature. Malinowski's final sentence in his seminal essay is 'I think we must see in [magic] the embodiment of the sublime folly of hope, which has yet been the best school of man's character' (90).

This failure of Eusebius to drive his point home draws attention to the most profound point about oracles, namely that they do work. The blame falls on the questioner if they don't – for getting the question wrong, or for misunderstanding the answer, or taking the wrong action, or (like Oedipus) for thinking it was possible to evade it. You reject the god's advice, whatever it may be, at your peril.

Failure never disproves the system. You may doubt the message, but never the god.[7] Sometimes this may be no more than a studied vagueness in the conditions, such as Liebeschuetz detects in the rules of Roman divination: 'a very effective inbuilt mechanism to shield it both from rational criticism and from refutation by events'.[8] But 'in a culture in which the possibility of divination is taken for granted apocalyptic reversals may make no obvious dent on belief in divinities'.[9] If the message you extracted from whatever method you chose – poisoning chickens, throwing dice, examining entrails, jumbling milfoil stalks, consulting an ecstatic – turned out wrong, that was because you did not try hard enough to understand it. Rationalizing explanations such as bribery and bias (or fraud) 'are unsatisfactory because they underestimate the true believer's power to forgive and forget, to explain away particular failures and even misdeeds'.[10] But even if God speaks through random events, that does not mean chance, or randomization, can ever be a system. Chance has no memory.[11] There can be no system for playing the roulette tables, or the oracles.[12] Cicero already knew it was true that the oracles, however dressed up in theological garb, were no more than a form of roulette. That is not necessarily a reason not to run your life by them.[13]

But, quite apart from Christian observance, many people still bring their questions to oracles of all kinds: the fortune-teller, the astrologer, the spiritualist medium, even the doctor.[14] John Milton[15] was over-optimistic in his belief that the birth of Christ had put an end to all such mummery:

> *The Oracles are dumm,*
> *No voice or hideous humm*
> > *Runs through the arched roof in words deceiving.*
> *Apollo from his shrine*
> *Can no more divine*
> > *With hollow shriek the steep of Delphos leaving.*
> *No nightly trance, or breathed spell,*
> *Inspires the pale-ey'd Priest from the prophetic cell.*

The human mind does not change so much, and the questions people pose are no different from the one that Alexander asked Sarapis, 'Lord, when am I going to die?'; or Thulis asked Sarapis, only to be murdered the moment he left the shrine; or Oedipus asked the Pythia, or the city of Troketta asked Claros, 'How can we be freed from this torment?'; or the people of Lycia asked the dice oracles, 'Will my harvest be successful?'

In his poem 'The Oracles' A.E. Housman, like Milton, asserted that the ancient oracles were all silent; but he concluded:

> *I took my question to the shrine that has not ceased from speaking*
> *The heart within, that tells the truth, and tells it twice as plain*
> *And from the cave of oracles I heard the priestess shrieking*
> *That she and I would surely die and never live again.*

The response was the same as that given to Alexander; the moral Housman draws is the fortitude of the Spartan warriors at Thermopylae – simple endurance of the destiny that men must bear and none can escape. For Housman, no gods help. The voices of the bicameral mind are silenced. We are on our own. Is it better that way?

Notes

INTRODUCTION

1. Harrison 2000, 147: If oracles were the exclusive business of professionals, getting answers would be too easy. Bribery was a common accusation: Flower 2008, 204.
2. Clement, *Stromateis* I.134.4 gives a list of early Greek prophets that includes Asclepius, Tiresias, Onomacritus, Mopsus and Aristander. In 135 he moves on to Hebrew prophets. Whether Mohammed was a *kahin* or some new kind of prophet was a matter of controversy: Fahd 1997, 240. Even a king could sometimes give oracles: Plutarch tells us that Demetrius Poliorcetes was seen as so godlike that his pronouncements were received as oracles: Plut., *Demetr.* 13; cf. Athen 6.63, 253DF = Duris of Samos *FGrH* 76F13.
3. The word 'divination' demands comment. The English word is from the Old French *devin*, i.e. a divine, a theologian but also a soothsayer, which in turn is from the Latin use of *divinus* (normally as an adjective, but also as a noun), which can define a person as inspired by a god, able to foretell the future: Cic., *de prov cons 38, sapientes ac divini fuistis*; Cic., *de fato15, Chaldaeos ceterosque divinos*. Divination in common usage, and in this book, refers to techniques of ascertaining the will of the gods and, sometimes, predicting the future.
4. E.g. J.G. Frazer cited on p. 70.
5. As Sax Rohmer seems to in his *The Romance of Sorcery*.
6. Fontenelle 1971, 55.
7. Wood 2003, 155.
8. Wood 2003, 250: 'The gods appear whenever we think we know more than a human creature ordinarily could, and they disappear again when we turn to ask them what to do.'
9. Boyer 2001, 343, 371ff. (citing Mithen).

CHAPTER 1 WHY DID THE GREEKS CONSULT ORACLES?

1. Historical examples where plague led to the consultation of oracles: the Peloponnesian War (Thuc. 2.54); plague in Asia Minor in the second century AD, at Pergamon, Troketta and elsewhere (Claros oracle, Oesterheld (=Merkelbach and Stauber) 2, 8, 9, 11, etc.; the oracle at Didyma was founded following the assistance of the inspired shepherd-boy Branchus in a plague, Callimachus fr. 194.28 and fr. 229. King Alyattes was cured of disease after he rebuilt the temple of Athena which had burnt down: Hdt. 1.19–22. In Hdt. 9.93.4 Apollonius consults the oracle regarding the cause of barrenness. A questioner at Dodona (Eidinow 64 = *SEG* 19 [1963], 149 no. 427) asked whether a storm had been caused by pollution.
2. Compare the Hittite king Mursilis' prayer – 'for what sin is this plague sent upon us?' – cited in Dodds 1951, 69: see McQueen 1986, 116. On sickness as punishment see Parker 1983, 235–6. At Plutarch *Greek Questions* 293ef, the oracle advises consultants to bury a girl whom Apollo has caused to hang herself. Cf. Epimenides DL 1.110f, Plut., *Sol.* 12.1–4.

3. The content of the oracle is first spelt out in the Argument to Euripides' *Phoenissae*, and represents the form of the tale that became canonical after Sophocles: 'Laios, son of Labdakos, you ask the blessing of children's birth./You will have a son of your own, but this will be your fate:/To die at the hands of your son. For so decreed/Zeus son of Cronos, acceding to the loathsome curse of Pelops/Whose own son you carried off. He asked all this would befall you' (tr. E. Craik). It is a moot question whether the curse of Pelops is expected to be in the minds of the audience of *Oedipus the King*. Cf. Aesch. *Septem* 800–2. Comparable motifs are widespread in folktale: see J.G. Frazer's appendix 9 to the Loeb edition of Apollodorus, 370–6; Propp 1975; Wood 2003, 77ff.

4. Mastronarde (ed.), *Phoenissae* 1994, 19.

5. Compare Adam's anguished question to God in John Milton's *Paradise Lost* 10.741ff.: 'Did I request thee, maker, from my clay/To mould me man, did I solicit thee/From darkness to promote me, or here place/In this delicious garden? . . . inexplicable/Thy justice seems.'

6. Sloterdijk 1985, 15.

7. Goldhill 2009.

8. Oppenheim 1964, 211–12, cf. 224.

9. Aeschylus, *fab. incert.* Fr 350 Radt., from Pl. *Rep.* 383a7, cf. Eus. *PE* 13.3.35. The lines form the epigraph to C.P. Cavafy's poem 'Perfidy'. Athenagoras *pro Christianis* 21.104 p. 252c refers also to Apollo's killing of Hyacinthus. At Aeschylus, *Cho* 1030–2 Orestes trusts in Apollo's promise; but the audience is not to know that he is right to do so, and is likely to think he is deceiving himself, until the denouement of the next play, *Eumenides*. See Flower 2008, 132–7, on scepticism about seers.

10. *De brevitate vitae* 1.3: 'life is long if you know how to use it'.

11. Teles, *Reliquiae*. ed. O. Hense, p. 43.

12. Also in other literatures: e.g. Vafthrudnir's sayings 52 (p. 48), Gripir's Prophecy 24–5, 51–2 (pp. 146–9) in Larrington 1996.

13. Stoneman 1992, 102.

14. Hypereides, *Euxenippus* 19; Carney 2006, 96.

15. *SIG* 252 N.5–8.

16. The exception to this generalization is an oracle recorded in the Greek Anthology, said to have been given to Olympias when she enquired how her son was going to conquer the Persian empire (AP 14.114). It alludes to his early death and burial in Alexandria, in obscure language; and its origins are equally obscure:

    The Persians have killed my worshipper with a violent hand, and native dust covers his corpse; but if anyone swiftly shows his white bones to Phaethon [the sun], he will shake the great empire from within. He lies within Asia, on a small island, next to the laurel and the streams of the old man of Pelius; make inquiry of Phoceus, the diviner man who will show you the way, who dwells by the sands of the Aparnis.

17. One wayward account (Maximus of Tyre 41.1) says that he asked where the source of the Nile was to be found. Perhaps he was thinking of the story of Zoser consulting Imhotep about the source of the Nile: he was favoured with a vision of Khnum: Nock 1934, 370.

18. Diod. Sic. ii.14.3–4.

19. Appian, *Syr.* 56.

20. Appian, *Syr.* 63. For the type of unexpected outcome cf. Shakespeare *2 Henry IV*, iv, 5, 235–40, where the oracle that the king is to die in Jerusalem is indeed fulfilled – but not in *that* Jerusalem.

21. Str. 6.1.5; cf. Livy 8.24.1; Justin 12.2.3 and 14.

22. A similar story is told of the Seleucid pretender Alexander Balas, who was warned by Apollo Sarpedonius to beware of the place that bore the two-formed one. The birth of a hermaphrodite at Abae seals his doom. The story is an interesting combination of omen and oracle.

23. Propp 1968, and cf. Propp 1975.

24. See Winkler 1982; Said 1997.
25. *Agamemnon, Ion, Phoenissae* are all built around Fate. The Theban legend is particularly full of prophecies from Stesichorus (Lille Papyrus 76 abc) onwards: P. Parsons, *ZPE* 1977, 7–36; tr. in West 1993, 92–4.
26. Zonaras 7.11, cf. DH 4.69.3, Livy 1.56.20, Wiseman 2008, 297 (cf. 307).
27. Oppenheim 1964, 224; Lloyd 2002, 24ff.
28. Mastronarde (ed.) 1994, 19. For Cocteau, the gods had simply 'set a trap' for Oedipus: Wood 2003, 74.
29. Goldhill 2009.
30. The form is the same as the oracle to Telesicles (Fontenrose 1978, Q56) that the first of his sons to meet him will be a poet. See p. 15 below.
31. *Collected Tales* III.238.
32. Boyer 2001, 347; cf. Harrison 2000, 243–5, Parker 1985/2000, 81.
33. Boyer 2001, 92.
34. Blacker in Loewe and Blacker 1981.
35. Flower 2008; see also Shapiro 1990; Dillery 2005.
36. Bottéro 1974.
37. *Epinomis* 984d–6a, cf. *Symposium* 203.
38. Leick 2001, 235ff.
39. Livy 1.39.1–2, Cic. *div.* I.121.
40. Paus. 9.11.5.
41. Clay 2004, 99.
42. Ogden 2001. Lists are given at Deuteronomy 18:10–11, Aeschylus, *Prometheus Bound* 482 ff. and AR I.4.3. Van Lieshout 1980, 215, counts ten such lists in Greek literature.
43. See chapter 7, section: 'Epiphanies'.
44. Cf. Parker 2005, 119.
45. At Astypalaia the priest of Atargatis was designated by lot: IG XII.3.178, and examples could no doubt be multiplied. Parker 1996, 125–6; Connelly 2007, 48–50. At Plato, *Laws* 856 a question of inheritance is to be decided by choosing ten names by lot, reporting them to Delphi, and allowing the god to make the final choice. Cf. Jaynes 1977, 240, 305.
46. Demetrius of Phaleron fr. 81 Wehrli, cited in Polybius 29.21, Cic. *de fato* 3.6.
47. A possibility intriguingly explored in Guillermo Martinez, *The Book of Murder* (2008). See also Eus. *PE* 4.2.2.
48. Bottéro 1974; the idea was taken up by the Stoics.
49. Keightley 1985.
50. A more complex method using 49 yarrow stalks is perhaps the standard procedure: see Wilhelm 1951, appendix 721–3; also Shaughnessy 1996.
51. Needham 1954, vol. 2. 336, 337; 304–45 are a discussion of the *I Ching*, 346–95, of other forms of divination, and scepticism.
52. Vernant 1974, 23.
53. Bottéro 1974, 152.
54. Bottéro 1974, 116–25.
55. Tacitus also describes, rather obscurely, a method of choosing best of three among bark strips inscribed with runes (cf. *Edda* 12) and of divination from the neighing of horses; Herodotus 4.67.1–2 describes how the Scythians use bundles of twigs, but the procedure is not clear; perhaps it is similar to the *I Ching*. The Persians did the same according to Deinon, *FGrH* 690F3. The very similar technique used by the pre-Islamic Arabs, employing arrows without points (*istiqšam*) is condemned by the Qur'an (5.90): 'O you who believe, intoxicants and games of chance and (sacrificing to) stones set up and (dividing by) arrows are only an uncleanness, the devil's work; so shun it that you may succeed:' Fahd 1966, 177–83.
56. Hdt. 4.94.3.
57. Huson 2004, 253, specifically counsels against approaching the Tarot with questions requiring a yes/no answer.
58. Bottéro 1974, 127; at 152 he suggests that divination in fact succeeds 'prophetism', and that its propensity for classification (as, I might add, in China), makes it a forerunner

of a scientific method. But divination is not scientific because it is not falsifiable; rather, it takes every step to avoid falsifiability.

59. Graf 2009 explores Apollo's oracular and other functions, which include music, archery, plague and rape – a combination that needs some intuition.

60. Isaiah answered a question for Hezekiah, and Ishtar answers the enquiries of Esarhaddon, but the model is much less common outside Greece.

61. Jaynes 1977; see also Dawkins 2006, 392-3.

62. He uses a rather restrictive definition of consciousness as meaning essentially conceptualization.

63. See Mithen's diagram on 163; and for the elaboration of the metaphor, 245.

64. Du Bois 2009, 6. Dodds' idea of a shaman is rather different (1951.24): it encompasses, first and foremost, intellectuals like Pythagoras and Empedocles. The latter proclaims oracles at B112.9-10 DK, cf. OF Test 87.9; Philochorus in Clem., *Strom.* 1.121.134.4.

65. Black Elk/Neidhart 2000, 157.

66. Athanassiadi 1999, 151 (footnotes omitted).

67. Du Bois 2009.

68. Evans-Pritchard 1976, 126.

69. Sarapis makes the point to Alexander at *AR* I.34.

70. Cited in Smith 1991, 259; cf. 14, 173.

71. Oppenheim 1964, 211-12.

72. Dalley 2007, 196.

73. Huson 2004, 248-9. Compare the paradox of time travel: if you can go back in time, you may create a parallel universe, e.g., by murdering your parents before your birth.

74. Xen. *Mem.* 1.4.14ff.

Chapter 2 Possession or Policy: The Case of Delphi

1. Ecstatic, automatic speech is a repeated feature of shamanistic trances: Eliade 1964; see also Bottéro 1974, *c.*90, 92 on the Babylonian case, where the *muahhu* or *apilu* speaks in the first person, as god.

2. Van Dale 1683 counted 261; a modern estimate (Hajjar 1990, 2236ff.) suggests 'several hundred' in Greece alone. Curnow 2004 managed to identify 124 in Greece, 62 in Turkey, some of them quite suspect.

3. Bottéro 1974, 91-2; Smith 1991, 222-30.

4. Maurizio 1995, 83.

5. This is probably not correct: vase-paintings occasionally depict the questioner face to face with the Pythia, and stories like that of Alexander's brutal manhandling of the Pythia imply that the questioner came directly before the prophetess.

6. Calasso 1993, 150.

7. *Homily on Ist Epistle to the Corinthians* 29.12.1: see Johnston 2008, 40. See also Gregory of Nyssa, *contra Fatum* 173b, Origen, *contra Celsum* 7.6: 'Apollo's sole source of delight was in the private parts of women.'

8. Dittenberger *Sylloge*² 790; the subject of a brilliant evocation by Louis Robert 1948a.

9. Parker 2005, 157: our information is everywhere scant on what actually took place at religious festivals.

10. On sitting down, compare the testimony of Emily Ounsted, p. 36 below.

11. Parke and Wormell 1956, 20.

12. As recounted in the *Homeric Hymn* to Apollo, Euripides' *Iphigeneia in Tauris* 1244-82, and the Delphic Paean (*Coll. Alex.* 141); see Sourvinou-Inwood 1987, and p. 34-5 below.

13. Du Bois 2009, 170.

14. *National Geographic News*, 14 August 2001. See further Johnston 2009, 47-50; Graf 2009, 64-71 and 183.

15. Whittaker 1965, 30 cites an anthropologist, M.J. Field, as saying 'I have never seen fumes inhaled to induce dissociation'; and cf. n. 37 where he (not surprisingly) expresses scepticism about Robert Graves' claim that magic mushrooms were used at Delphi.

16. Dodds 1951, 73.
17. Lloyd-Jones 1965, 67.
18. Lucian, Pausanias. Iamblichus seems to favour the view that the trance is self-induced by extreme piety, but speaks in metaphors of 'clouds of divine fire', and likewise at Claros and Didyma: *de Myst.* III.11.
19. Also Graf 2008, 70 (cautiously).
20. Cf. Maurizio 1995, 86.
21. Gurney in Loewe and Blacker 1981.
22. Sourvinou-Inwood 1987.
23. Dodds 1951, 64–71.
24. *Meno* 99c.
25. At *Timaeus* 71bd he even seems to approve of hepatoscopy; God wrote the messages on the livers.
26. *Anatomy of Melancholy* I.1.1.4.
27. Du Bois 2009, 124.
28. Du Bois 2009, 224.
29. D'Este 2008. See also the epigraph to this chapter. Cf. Du Bois 2008, 88: 'a seemingly passive opening of the self to another's communicative agenda'. The importance of such revelations is underlined by the tongue-in-cheek title of the 'Free Guide to Holistic Glastonbury': *The Oracle.*
30. Maurizio 1995, 81 provides a Chinese parallel example.
31. Calasso 1993, 144. Bowden 2005, 28 n. 15 gives the choices: venal (Daux)/political (Forrest)/medizing (Parke and Wormell).
32. E.g. Parke and Wormell 1956, 33.
33. Heraclides in *DL* 5.91; Hdt. 6.66; Thuc. 5.16.2.
34. Plut. *Alex.* 14.6, Diod. Sic. 17.93.4.
35. Fontenrose 1978, H 20.
36. Fahd 1997.
37. Fontenrose 1988, 46.
38. Also Strabo 9.3.4.
39. Golding 1995, 92 and 102.
40. Nilsson 1951.
41. Connelly 2007, 219.
42. Like the Sibyl's: Lightfoot 2007, 165. Fontenrose 1988, 102, remarks that inscribed Delphic verses are generally poor: the later ones are uniformly bad while the early ones are competent (194ff.).

CHAPTER 3 THE RIDDLES OF THE PYTHIA

1. Manetti 1993, 19. Heliodorus' novel is similarly punctuated and directed by oracles, dreams and prophecies.
2. Eus., *PE* 5.20.8, from Oenomaus: the god deliberately deceived Croesus, despite his piety. Cf. Strabo 6.1.5 and Parke and Wormell 1956, II no. 595, on Alexander the Molossian (variously ascribed to Delphi or Dodona).
3. Kapuscinski 2007.
4. God is not Fate: Mikalson 2003, 148–9.
5. Mikalson 2003, 152 n. 56.
6. Herodotus 7.57 makes clear one's duty to understand the oracle.
7. Thomas Browne, 'Of the answers of the Oracle of Apollo at Delphos to Croesus King of Lydia', *Miscellanies* XI (III.36). Other misunderstandings of the oracle: Herodotus 3.64 (the wrong Ecbatana). Hdt. 9.33 (Tisamenus and the 'five contests'), Diod. Sic. 16.91–2 and 20–9 (you will eat and sleep in the besieged city[but as a prisoner]). Manetti 1993, 25 offers a thought-provoking typology of misunderstandings.
8. Shaughnessy 1996, 8–9.
9. Eus., *PE* 5.19.4, from Oenomaus.

10. Like Euripides in his characterization of Artemis, who abandons her devotee Hippolytus to his fate.

11. Cf. Vernant (ed) 1974, 23; Maurizio 1995, 82; Manetti 1993, 19.

12. Betegh 2004, 365.

13. The contest of Calchas and Mopsus is also relevant here: see chapter 6. So too, perhaps, is Heraclitus' aphorism that 'men die because they cannot join the end to the beginning'.

14. *Homo Ludens* (1949). In *The Poetic Edda* (Larrington 1996, 244), Odin puts riddles to the prophetess in a contest of wits: he knows the answers but is displaying his superior power.

15. But Bremmer 1993 argues that the skin was not Epimenides' own, but a leather scroll.

16. Struck 2005.

17. Cf. Alcibiades II.147b, poets hide meaning in riddles.

18. Oppenheim 1956, 227.

19. Arnott 1989, 155. The same story is told in slightly different language by Chime Radha Rinpoche in Loewe and Blacker 1981.

20. A similar case in I Samuel 6, where the Philistine diviners test whether it is the God of Israel who has destroyed Ashdod and sent on them a plague ('and they had emerods in their secret parts' – NEB: 'tumours'). They send the Ark of the Covenant, which they have looted from the Israelites, filled with treasure on a cart drawn by two cows. 'And see, if it goeth up by the way of his own coast to Beth-shemesh, then he hath done this great evil: but if not, then we shall know that it is not his hand that smote us; it was a chance that happened to us.' (I Sam. 6:9).

21. Livy 1.36.2–6, cf. Cic. *div.* 1.17.32.

22. Val. Max. I.8 ext. 8; alluded to by Cic. *de Fato* 5–7 = Posidonius F 104 Kidd; cf. Strabo 14.1.39.

23. Diod. Sic. 22.9.5, where the maidens are taken to be Athena and Artemis; Cic. *div.* 1.37.81, Val. Max. I.1 ext. 9. PW 325, Fontenrose 1978, Q 231.

24. Paus. 10.10.6, PW 525, Fontenrose 1978, Q 36.

25. Plato, *Apol.* 21b–d.

26. Political questions were also taken to Didyma, Hdt. 5.11.12, al, but less commonly.

27. Livy 1.56.4–7: the king sent envoys to seek an explanation for a prodigy that had occurred. Cf. Graf 2009, 89.

28. Kirchberg 1965.

29. 1.165–7, 1.174, 2.158.5, 5.89, 6.135, 6.139.40, 7.169, 7.178–9, 8.36, 9.93–4.

30. 2.147, 3.57–8, 4.179, 5.1, 6.19, 6.77, 8.20, 8.77.

31. 2.139, 3.16.6, 4.163, 5.92, 6.98, 7.220, 9.33.

32. 4.161, 6.52. The laws of Sparta were the result of divine decree in the distant past: Q 8–10, Herodotus 1.67. Lycurgus, the lawgiver of Sparta, was appointed to his role by the Delphic oracle, which also decreed what lands it would be proper for Sparta to possess in the Peloponnese. In particular they would be rulers of Tegea, but only if they bring back the bones of Orestes from their burial place in Tegea to Sparta itself (Hdt. 1.67, Q90, cf. Q91 and H7). See Parker 1985/2000, 90f.

33. 5.42.5. Colonization oracles are fairly widely attested elsewhere. Few cities, in fact, in the ancient world could be established without the guidance of the gods. Numerous inscriptions refer to colonizing missions supported by the oracle, and even Fontenrose, whose scepticism about the historicity of most Delphic responses is very high, allows a fair number of colonizing responses into his category of 'Historical Responses': H6 (Spartans in Trachinia), H14 (Parians to Pharos in the Adriatic), H56 (an inscription with a query from the Parians leading to the foundation of Pharos – accepted by Parker 1985/2000, 85–7). See Parke and Wormell 1956, 49–81.

34. 2.174; cf. 6.66, 8.114.

35. Morgan 1990; Bowden 2005, 3; cf. Betegh 2004, 89–90: professionals can turn to the oracle to discover whether a particular action is sanctioned.

36. Parke and Wormell 1956, 162; Forrest 1982.

37. E.g. Synesius, *On Dreams* 3.3, Maximus of Tyre, *Oration* 13.1.

38. This famous oracle has been much discussed. Evans 1982 and 1988 considers that this was a real, historical consultation in 481 or 480 BC: a prose oracle was rendered which referred to the wooden wall, and this was later reworked as a myth. Alternative views are that it is an ex post facto fabrication from Delphi (Bowden), or a piece of 'semi-oral tradition'. Note that the oracles cannot be detached from the narrative.
39. Parker 1985. Cf. Kirchberg 1965, 116–20: the obscurity of oracles lays a compulsion on people to work out their meaning.
40. Betegh 2004, 365, citing Manetti 1993, suggests that the debate moves the question away from the religious sphere; for Bowden (2005, 133) it *enforces* religion.
41. Nicely analyzed by Kirchberg 1965, 116–20.
42. The magi are religious professionals and go by the book, concentrating on omens, predictive dreams (Hdt. 1.107, 119, 128, 7.19) and on technical divination (X, *Cyr.* 8.311, E, *Or.* 1495). Their kind of mageia is teachable: Pl., *Alcib.* I. 122a. D.L. 1.7 says they could make the gods appear to them. See also Hdt. 1.132, 140, 7.43, 113, 9; and 1.140 on their role at funerals. Pl. *Rep.* 364b5, *Lys.* 909ab. For Hippocrates, *On the Sacred Disease* 2 and Heraclitus fr. B14 DK the word Magi is equivalent to charlatans. Some interesting data on later Persian divination – by sneezes, random utterances, playing cards, chickpeas and the severed heads of goats – are collected by Mahmoud Omidsalar in *Encyclopaedia Iranica* s.v; also at www.iranian.com/Sep96/Iranica/IranicaDivine/IranicaDivine.html. Khosrow II Parviz divined his own death and the demise of the Sasanian Dynasty from the accidental fall of a quince from the top of his throne.
43. Lloyd 2002, 41, suggests that it was easier for professional oracle interpreters to look like charlatans in Greece than in China because there was no bureaucratic structure in which they could function: they had to be freelances or, in the dubious phrase, 'independent scholars'. Diviners, on the other hand, had a settled social role.
44. See e.g. Connelly 2007, 254.
45. Connelly 2007, 53–4; Henrichs 1978.
46. *IG* 12.3.248; Fontenrose H54, *SIG* 977, 29032; Lupu 2005, 36–8.
47. Bowden 2005, 137.
48. Parker 1985/2000, 101–5.

CHAPTER 4 FROM EGYPT TO DODONA

1. Cf. Soph. *Tr.* 1166–7.
2. The Sun and Moon trees are already in Ctesias (fifth century: F45, 17 and 57), but there is no hint that they give oracles. An oath is sworn by a holy tree in Livy 3.25.6. On the motif see Stith Thomson, *Motif-Index* (Thomson 1955–8) 1311.4, 1311.4.2.
3. Parke 1967a, 23–6.
4. Suda agrees.
5. LXX: 'when you hear the voice of lamentation of the enclosure of the grove'.
6. Moses of Choren, the fifth-century AD Armenian historian (I.20), mentions oracles given by the rustling of a tree at Altintepe.
7. Fontenrose 1988, 78–9. But there is never any mention of a role for water in the prophetic process, as there is at the other major oracles, even though Zeus' title here is Naios, 'of the spring'.
8. Birds are commonly observed as part of the divinatory process, and in Rome the officials called *augurs* did nothing else. For a list of bird omens with interpretation see *Sylloge*[3] 1167. Alexander's talking crow is celebrated in Posidippus epig. 35, which is the last of a series of epigrams (21–35) about bird omens.
9. Parke 1967a, 75–6.
10. Černy 1962; Schenke 1963; Lajtar 2006; Frankfurter 1998, 145ff.; Kakosy in *LdÄ*.
11. Curnow 2004 lists the following: Abydos (Sarapis, incubation and Bes); Bacchias (Sobek: papyri survive); Buto (Leto/Wadjet: Hdt. 2.83); Canopus (Pluto/Sarapis, and lot oracles); Elephantine (Khnum: papyri survive); Heracleopolis Magna (Harsaphes/Heracles); Karanis (Soknopiaos); Kellis (Seth); Koptos (Min); Memphis (Apis: children give the

oracles); Ombos (Horus – healing and incubation); Oxyrhynchus (Taweret: movement of statue, and incubation; cf. Parsons 2007 175ff., 189ff., 208); Philae (Isis); Pselchis (Thoth); Siwa (Ammon – movement of statue); Soknopaiou Nesos (papyri survive); Talmis (Mandulis – incubation: see Nock 1934); Tebtunis (Sobek: papyri from fourth century BC, showing alternative answers); Tentyra (Hathor – healing); Theadelphia (Sobek – movement of statue); Thebes (Amun) and Deir al-Medina (Amenhotep I: see text).

12. Maybe the sky-god Gad, since, unusually, this Apollo's image has a beard: Lightfoot 2003, 463–4.
13. The whole story is unlikely to be Lucian's invention, since Macrobius describes a very similar operation at Heliopolis: Sat. 1.23.13–16, where Jupiter is carried on a *ferculum* (carrying-frame).
14. Other juridical consultations of Egyptian oracles: Hdt. 2.174, cf. 6.66, 8.114.
15. Schenke 1963, with examples from 1300 and 1200 BC.
16. See p. 53.
17. More examples are collected by Parsons 2007, 175; cf. 189ff., 208, on Astrampsychos and dice oracles; Schenke 1963, 75.
18. Most of them are now conveniently accessible, with translations, in Eidinow 2007.
19. Parke 1967a, 36–8.
20. Eidinow 2007, 64; Parke 1967a, 261–2 no. 7 (= SEG 19 [1963], 147 no. 427).
21. 'There is an object that represents one of the highest peaks of civilization, with respect to which all others we are familiar with are but waterd down derivatives: the bronze caldron. In the China of the Shang Dynasty it became the cult object around which people's lives revolved. . . . In Doric Greece, the cauldron was made in just the one dominant form: the tripod.' Calasso 1993, 150–1, a suggestive passage.
22. *Protr.* 2.11.1.
23. *PE* 2.3.1, cf. Theodoret, *Cure of Greek Maladies* 10.3.5; Johnston 2008, 66–7.
24. Cic. *div.* 1.34.76; cf. 2.32.69, where the speaker derides such portents.
25. Gurney 1952, 133 is a Hittite example: a dog upset the sacrificial bread.
26. Parke and Wormell 1956, I.242.
27. It is also in Heracleides Ponticus, fr. 135 Wehrli.
28. Hyperides, *For Euxenippos*, 25.
29. Parke 1967a, 125. A word of caution on Strabo's testimony: Strabo also found Onchestos deserted, whereas Pausanias, two hundred years later, found it flourishing (9.26.3).

CHAPTER 5 THE GODS, THE HEROES AND THE DEAD

1. Bonnechère 1990.
2. Curnow 2004. In very many cases he quotes no sources for his listings. I have been unable to verify the cases of Argos, Lousoi (Paus. 8.18.7 makes no mention of oracles), Lykaion (Paus. 8.38.5 makes no mention of oracles), Gortys, Eutresis, Thermos (Odysseus) and Ichnae. At the sanctuary of Earth at Aigeira the priestess was selected for virginity by a test of drinking bull's blood (Paus. 7.25.8); though lamb's blood was used to obtain oracular inspiration at Larisa (Paus. 2.24.1), there is no mention of oracles here.
3. Paus. 10.35.2: 'there used to be an oracle'.
4. Paus. 9.2.1.
5. See p. 46.
6. Paus. 9.23.3: the oracle was revived under Cassander but died out around AD 50; Levi 1971 ad loc.
7. Plut., *de Defectu oraculorum* 412b.
8. On its later history see pp. 116–18.
9. Paus. 9.11.5. 'You made your offerings, left the shrine with your hands over your ears, and the first words you heard on coming out and removing your hands were your oracle.'

10. Paus. 7.21.5.
11. Paus. 7.22.2.
12. Hdt. 7.111.
13. Paus. 1.40.5.
14. Strabo 7 fr. 1a – later moved to Dodona.
15. Paus. 2.32.5.
16. Paus. 8.37.11: 'the god used to give oracles'.
17. Bouché-Leclercq 1879–82, 1,150.
18. Omitted by Curnow. See above, pp. 28–30.
19. There was another on Mt Cithaeron; Paus. 9.3.5.
20. Dio. 41.45, Larson 2001 ch. 4.5.3. She points out that the oracle-monger Bacis is sometimes presented as a 'nympholept': Ar. *Pax* 1070, Theop. 115F77, Fontenrose 1978, 145–65.
21. See the comprehensive treatment by Ogden 2001, and also Bremmer 2002, ch. 6.
22. Collected especially in *PGM* IV.
23. *TAM* V.2.384, no. 1055; Nollé 2007, 247; Robert 1937, 131ff.
24. Cumont 1913, no. 136; Robert 1937, 132–3.
25. Ogden 2001.
26. I Samuel 28:7; see Isidore, *Etymologiae*, 8.9.11, 8.19.13.
27. Cited from Bialik and Ravnitzky 1992; 515.94.
28. J.W. Waterhouse's painting, *Consulting the Oracle*, is an imaginative depiction of such a scene.
29. Ogden 2001, 208–16. There are four 'dead-head' spells in *PDM* LXI 79–94 and *PGM* IV 1928–2005, 2125–39, 2140–4: see Johnston 2008, 171, 174.
30. Tr. Bürgel 510–4.
31. Betegh 2004, 76, cf. 79 on magi.
32. Ogden 2001, 231–50 is a full discussion of this interesting topic.
33. Phlegon, *Book of Marvels* 2: see the translation by W. Hansen, Exeter 1996, 28–32.
34. See above, pp. 19–20.
35. Plutarch, *Consolation to Apollonia* 14, also Cic., *TD* 1.115; Ogden 2001, 74. See further ch. 7.
36. Pl., *Phaedo* 66e.
37. Levi 1971 ad loc.
38. The reference is to Hippol., *Refut. omn. haeres.* 4.28–42, esp. 36, on how an accomplice may create an apparition. Frazer's words represent well the rationalist view that it is one of the purposes of this book to combat. Other examples: Rufinus, *Ecclesiastical History* II.23 on the magnetic statue of Sarapis at Alexandria; Fontenelle 1971, 171–2.
39. Paus. 2.35.4–10; Ogden 2001, 25.
40. Paus. 3.25.8; Plut., *de sera numinis vindicta* 360E.
41. *SHA* Hadrian 14.7 – if one is to believe this author.
42. Lightfoot 2007, 211.
43. Qu. Sm. 6.469–91; Ogden 2001, 29–42.
44. Guthrie 1952, 35ff.
45. The oracle of the dead at Koroneia, listed by Curnow 2004, seems to be a chimera.
46. Paus. 1.17.4–5; Clement, *Protr.* 10P, cf. Eus. *PE* 2.3.1.
47. Ogden 2001, 43–60 is a comprehensive account.
48. Dakaris 1993, 22.
49. But compare the rites for Amphiaraus, pp. 116–18 beow.
50. Bonnechère 2003 is a comprehensive treatment.
51. We might have learnt more of the shrine's procedures from the comedy *Trophonius* by Cratinus. However, the fragments that survive are nothing but strange words quoted by lexicographers, and a reference to abstinence from fish (F 236 KA).
52. Springs are significant at Delphi (Castalia) and at Dodona, where the title of Zeus, Naios, refers to flowing water. According to Ephorus (*FGrH* 70F20 = Macrob. *Sat.* V.18.6–8), every response from Dodona enjoined the consultant to sacrifice to the river Achelous. There is no other evidence for this custom.

53. 1.37.4; Habicht 1985, 156ff.
54. Paus. 4.32.5–6 mentions that a few survive. See those collected in Levin 1989, including *IG* VII 4136 (second century BC) and *SIG*³ 635B. Bonnechère 2003, 364–7 gives a list of the recorded consultants: thirty-five in all.
55. Amyntas IV.
56. *IG* VII 3055 = *LSCG* no. 74 = F. Salviat and C. Vatin, *Inscriptions de Grèce centrale* (Paris 1971, 89 l.4). The inscription also mentions visitors from Locris (four), Tenos (two) and Chalcidice.
57. Luc. *Dial mort* 3 (255 Rabe).
58. Plut. *Obsolescence of Oracles* 434c.
59. When Plutarch, later, suggested that the oracles were operated by the *daimones*, these dead souls are very different from the heroes of the classical period: Platonism has made its mark, and Plutarch is not speaking of the heroes.

CHAPTER 6 THE ORACLE COAST: SIBYLS AND PROPHETS OF ASIA MINOR

1. Merkelbach and Stauber 1998, I 03/07/06.
2. Heraclitus frag. B92DK = Plut. *The Oracles at Delphi* 397b.
3. Parke 1988, 54ff discusses Burkert's suggestion. See also Oppenheim 1956, 237.
4. Bottéro 1974, 88–95, who also suggests that such women were ancestors of the Chaldaean Sibyl.
5. See below pp. 79–80 on Mopsus.
6. McQueen 1986, 112, cf. 116.
7. Cic. *div.* 1.41.91. But it is not certain whether there was an oracle at Termessus. Photius 204 mentions one at the similarly named Termissus (in Caria); but cf. Frei 1990, 6.8.1.
8. Nice 2005. Posidippus epig. 34 celebrates another seer from Termissus, Damon, skilled in the observation of birds. According to Posidippus epig. 35, Alexander achieved his three victories over the Persians after seeking a response from a talking crow that gave responses of the hero Strymon of Thrace.
9. Parke 1985a, 55.
10. Nicolaus of Damascus *FGrH* 90 F 68.8.
11. Parke 1988, 60–3.
12. Strabo 14.1.27.
13. In Hesiod's version, F278 MW.
14. The story pattern, in which a defeated seer forfeits his life, is repeated. See Lycophron 424–30, Apollodorus 6.2–4.
15. From Pherecydes, *FGrH* 5 F 142.
16. Strabo 14.5.16; Apollodorus epit. 6.19 with Frazer's note.
17. For what follows, Metzler 1990. See also Bremmer 2008. It has been argued by Barnett 1953 that Mopsus was a real person who lived *c.*1220–1170 BC.
18. Paus. 10.32.4 with Peter Levi's note.
19. Levi 1971 mentions some interesting parallels.
20. Robert 1937, 74–89.
21. Strabo 13.3.5.
22. *Sacred History* 5.7–8. Cf. pp. 123–4.
23. Bean 1954, 85–6.
24. Buresch 1889, 71ff.
25. Athen 4.149d.
26. Philostr. *Heroikos* 15.2–3; 15.5–7 for the oracle to the athlete, which takes a riddling form; 16 (healing); 23ff (his tale of Troy).
27. Str. 12.8.17 and 13.4.14; Dio. Cassius 68.27.3. Damascius ap Phot. *Bibl.* 344. b. 35 describes the 'way down under the temple of Apollo'. See Parke 1988, 180–4, who also mentions a fume-filled cave at Nyssa (Str. 14.1.43) which, remarkably, had healing properties.
28. The Italian excavators argued for a Hellenistic date, but opinion now favours the high Roman empire: see Lloyd-Jones and West 1966; West 1967; Guarducci 1978.

29. Aelian HA 12.30.
30. Two final scraps. At Hieracome, the oracle issued pronouncements in verses which Livy (38.13.1) called *haud incondita*, not unskillful: see Robert 1948. Strabo 13.1.3 mentions one at Zeleia, defunct in his day.
31. The main treatments are Parke 1986, Fontenrose 1988, Günther 1971 (archaeology), Busine 2005, McCabe and Plunkett 1985 (the responses).
32. Callim. Fr. 194.28.
33. Hdt. 1.92.
34. See Fontenrose 1988, 37–9.
35. Parke 1986, 42; Fontenrose 1988, 55.
36. Fontenrose 1988 no. 25, second century AD, the longest from Didyma.
37. Connelly 2007, 40–1; on the case of Satorneila, 44.
38. Busine 2005, cat. 5 and p. 179.
39. The novelists Heliodorus 10.7 and Achilles Tatius 2.28 describe such tests carried out in shrines.
40. Lucian's assertion that she 'chewed bay leaves' (*bis acc.* 1) can probably be discounted.
41. Busine 2002.
42. Iambl. *Myst.* III.11.124.
43. Cf. Paus. 7.21.3 on Cyaneae; at Antioch, Nonnos, scholion in Greg. Naz., *or.* 39 no. 14; see Burkert 1994 n. 39, who compares the effect to that of a crystal ball.
44. Du Bois 2009, 59ff., 113–14.
45. Fontenrose 1988, 84.
46. For the doxography see Fontenrose 1988, 79–80.
47. Günther 1971, 119–22.
48. They are collected in Fontenrose 1988, 177–244. See also McCabe and Plunkett 1985 (569–81 for the verse oracles).
49. Also F 27 and F 29, F 30, F 31, F 32 on the location of an altar.
50. Dio. Chr. 40.13–15; 45.3–4. See Jones 1975 who argues for Didyma as the origin of the prediction. This is rejected by Fontenrose 1988, 243.
51. Heraclides Ponticus fr. 50.
52. Hdt. 1.158.1.
53. The novelists frequently use oracles as plot-movers. Another example is Heliodorus' *Ethiopica*, which uses both the oracles and the token motif from Euripides' *Ion* as plot devices. See Said 1997.
54. There was a sympolity of the two cities in the late fourth and third centuries BC: Robert 1936, 165ff.
55. Merkelbauch and Stauber 1996 collect the known responses. See also the catalogues of Busine 2005 and Oesterheld 2008.
56. Merkelbach and Stauber 1996, 2, 20.
57. Possibly for Sardis: Merkelbach and Stauber 1996, 11 = 1998, 03/02/01. See Graf 1992.
58. Merkelbach and Stauber 1996, 13 = 1998, 09/06/01.
59. Merkelbach and Stauber 1996, 15–16.
60. Also Anacreontea 12.5 on the water.
61. Iambl. *Myst.* 3.11.
62. Plut. *Apopth. Lac. Lysander* 10, *Mor* 229D. The same anecdote, but with no mention of an oracle, at *Antalcidas* 68 (217CD) and *Adoxoi* 236D; cf. *FGrH* 546 F 1b.
63. *IGRRP* 4 nos 1586, 1587; *OGIS* 530.
64. See Parke 1988, 221; Oesterheld 2008, 120 n. 223.
65. Lane Fox 1986, 175.
66. Chandler 1971, 135.
67. Lane Fox 1986, 173.
68. H. Jones in the *Road to En-Dor* (1920) describes how he acquired necessary background information for the responses from his fake oracle by asking leading questions and reading other peoples' letters.

69. Ferrary 2005: there are twenty-four from Crete, especially from Hierapytna, and several from Laodicea on the Lycos, Chios, Phocaea, Heracleia, Tabae, Iconium and Aphrodisias, from AD 130–186.

70. E.g. Of the Laodiceans: 'in the proconsulship of Lamias Aelianus, when Aelias Gallios was prytany, when Artemidorus was priest, Pythion the son of Artemisios was prophet, and Asclepides the son of Demophilos was thespiode; secretaries Krito and Alexander son of Krito; paidonomos Latranios son of Berylos; attendants Diagenes Menagoras son of Seleukos; leader of the hymn Permissos son of Nothippos . . .'.

71. Stark 1955, 108–9. I have not been able to trace the original of her 'waspish answer to a deputation from the rival oracle in Ephesus, refusing to help those "who are not in the habit of coming to ask here" '. Busine 2002, 14 (= Merkelbach and Stauber 1996, 11) and 51 are the only ones referring to Ephesus.

72. Cf. Busine 2002, 175: oracles that were given for one city might be set up elsewhere too; one given to Ephesus regarding its cult of Artemis was subsequently set up also at Rome.

73. Tac., *Annals* 2.54. Above, p. 94.

74. Ael. Arist. 15, p. 312.5 (AD 147).

75. 'Heis eti chronos' (one more 'time', i.e. year) or 'eiseti chronos' (a long time still).

76. Buresch 1889, no. 24; Busine 2002, cat. 93.

77. Paus. 8.29.3–4. Jones 2000.

78. See Amm. Marc. 23.6.24. Coins of Lucius Verus depict an image of Apollo Pythoktonos, slayer of the Python (of plague?): BMC Lydia 351.

79. Buresch 1889, 10ff., *IGRRP* 4, no. 1498 = Merkelbach and Stauber 1996, 8. Translation in Parke 1985a, 150–1.

80. Parke 1985a, 144.

81. Merkelbach and Stauber 1996, 9.

82. Merkelbach and Stauber 1996, 2.

83. Merkelbach and Stauber 1996, 4–7; West 1967 and further bibliography in Parke 1985a., 249 n. 14.

84. A. Souter, *Cl Rev.* 11 (1897), 31; Parke 1985a, 162. A similar response found at Nicomedia probably also came from Claros: Merkelbach and Stauber 1996, 13; see Merkelbach 1975, 100.

85. *IGRRP* 1, no. 767.

86. Parke 1985a, 159.

87. Merkelbach and Stauber 1996, 15.

88. Robert 1966, 91ff.

89. Merkelbach and Stauber 1996, 16; see Robert 1960, 546 n. 1.

90. But Gonzales 2005 disputes the attribution to Claros.

91. Parke 1985a, 160ff., Busine 2005, 184ff.; Merkelbach-Stauber 1996, 24.

92. *Chiron* 4 (1974), 511–13.

93. *ZPE* 161 (2007), 113–19.

94. Graf 1992.

95. Gonzales 2005.

96. Gonzales 2005: Side, Iconium, Syedra, Bubon, Kyaneiai, Oenoanda, Myangla, Xanthus, Sidyma and twenty others; coins of Cyaneae, Podalia and Arycanda depict an armoured warrior.

97. Nollé, 2001, no. 378.

98. Alexander Polyhistor *FGrH* 273 F131; Hecat *FGrH*1 F 256 = Strabo 14.3.6.

99. Servius Auctus in V. *Aen.* 3.332.

100. *TAM* II.420.

101. The insistence on the virginity of the priestess is marked in an inscription of the late second century AD (*TAM* II.174), which records an oracle on the matter delivered 129 years earlier. Discussion: Parke 1985a, 190–2.

102. Servius in V. *Aen.* 4.143.

103. *TAM* II.905, XVII E.10ff.

104. 7.21.3; Parke 1985a, 193–4.
105. *FGrH*770F5 = *TAM* ii.174.
106. Bean 1978, 130–3.
107. *FGrH*770 F 2; Aelian, *NA* 12.1, cf. 8.5 Plut. *de Sollertia animalium* 23, p. 976 c, Plin. *NH* 32.17. Athen 8.333–4.
108. Aelian, *NA* 12.1, Parke 1985a, 197. Something similar also occurred at Limyra, if this is not simply a confusion of names in Pliny (Bean 1978, 143), and at Labraunda. Another zoological oracle is referred to by Aelian (*NA* 11.2) in Epirus, where snakes give 'oracles of prosperity' by accepting food offered to them.
109. Those from the temple are described by Bean 1962, 6–8.
110. *IGRR* iii.711–14.
111. Plut. *de def orac.* 434d.
112. Cf. Luc. *Assembly of gods* 12: 'That is how Apollo here has fallen into disrepute; it needs but a quack (and quacks are plentiful),a sprinkling of oil, and a garland or two, and an oracle may be had in these days wherever there is an altar or a stone pillar.' Clement, *Stromata* 1.134.4 lists this oracle with several others in the vicinity.
113. *Philopseudes* 38.
114. Plut. *de sera numinis vindicta* 563d.
115. Dio. 72.7.2. See Mackay 1990, 2110ff., xiii.
116. Str. 14.25.9; Mackay 1990, 2110ff., xii; Nissen 2001.
117. Diod. Sic. 32.10.2f; Zosimus 1.57.24.
118. See p. 201.
119. Eusebius, *Life of Constantine* 3.55.
120. Balty 1981; possibly the oracles were lines from Homer. The oracle remained important in the third century AD.
121. Lucian, *On the Syrian Goddess*; see ch. 3.

CHAPTER 7 DREAMS AND HEALING

1. The idea of the wandering dream-soul is found in China (Laufer 1931) as well as in Greece, where Democritus proposed that the soul in sleep has special modes of cognition (van der Eijk 2005, 172)
2. Xenophanes (B34) rejected all forms of divination on the grounds that only the gods have certain knowledge: Cic. *div* 1.3.5, cf. S., *OT* 499–512; Harris 2009, 226–7. See Lesher 1978.
3. *Philosophical History* 9c Athanassiadi.
4. Cf. *Epinomis* 985c for a similar point.
5. Harris 2009, 213, citing Bartsch 1989, 85–94; Said in Heintz 1997.
6. Harris 2009, 138.
7. Lamoreaux 2002, 84.
8. Lucr. 5.1161–82 and 4.757–962; Harris 2009, 242.
9. *De anima* 47, Harris 2009, 215ff.
10. Mikalson 1983, 39–40, Harris 2009, 173 and 175. Dream oracles are regularly tested in Mesopotamia: see below, p. 111.
11. Genesis 37.5–11, 40.1–41.14, Qur'an 12.36–42.
12. Aesch. *PV* 484 ff.; Walde 2001, 13–15.
13. Theorists such as Aelius Aristides and Artemidorus distinguish meaningful (prophetic or diagnostic) dreams from non-significant ones that simply recycle the residue of the day's experiences: Aristides calls such dreams *parerga*. Walde 2001, 76.
14. Harris 2009, 101–6.
15. Aristander, Alexander's seer, wrote a book about Alexander's dreams: Hughes 1984; Nice 2005, 94.
16. *De sera numinis vindicta*, 566 BC.
17. Robert 1937, 131ff; Nollé 2007, 247. Another example: Paus. 4.16.7–8. Dr Giuseppe Moscati's tomb in Naples became a place of pilgrimage for those seeking healing: Walde 2001, 49.

18. Sophronius, *Narratio miraculorum SS Cyri et Johannis*.
19. Augustine, *On the care for the dead*, 13.
20. Harris 2009, 146.
21. Eur. *Hec.* 70–97.
22. Cf. *PGM* iv.210.
23. *Alexander Romance* i, 8.
24. Dodds 1965, 39 is dubious; Harris 2009 more positive.
25. Achilles Tatius 1.3 explains that foreknowledge acquired through dreams allows us to prepare ourselves for what is going to happen. A similar justification for oracles: Ch. 9, pp. 157–60.
26. The fragments are collected by Del Corno 1969; see Walde 2001, 122ff.; Harris 2009, chs. 3–4 (123–278).
27. Lloyd 1978, 252–9. Galen, too, used dreams to diagnose ailments. Even for the Babylonian interpreters, dreaming of stars could have a diagnostic function: Oppenheim 1956, 205.
28. *Aristides* 27 = Demetrius of Phalerum, fr. 96: dream-interpreters sit about at Athens with their tablets, waiting for custom.
29. And in *On Dreams*. Van der Eijk 2005, 179–86.
30. Aristotle's theory was adopted by Arab writers on dreams, notably Ibn Sina, in classifying dreams as 'remnants of the day', wish-fulfilment and imbalance of humours. Of prophetic dreams there is also a threefold classification into enigmatic or coded, visionary or literal, oracular (where the god appears). Lamoreaux 2002; Fahd 1966/1987, 247ff. There were numerous Arabic dream books, from the translation of Artemidorus made by Hunain ibn Ishaq to the original work of Pseudo-Achmet, written AD 813–1000. Herophilus (*c*.3 BC) had a fourfold classification: god-given, clairvoyant, random, wish-fulfilment.
31. Plutarch, *Table Talk* 735bc: this is why dreams are unclear in autumn, when the winds disturb the flimsy films.
32. See Artemidorus ii.44; Harris 209, 155n thinks it may be spurious.
33. Ch. 9.
34. Van Lieshout 1980, 217ff.
35. A Mesopotamian dream about urination has a similar significance: Oppenheim 1956.
36. *De usu partium* ii.92–4; Oberhelman 1993, 139.
37. Harris 2009 (249 n. 117) rejects the view of Nutton, and thinks not.
38. Harris 2009, 275–7, with doxography.
39. Bottéro 1974, 82.
40. Lewis 1976, 88–97; others: Brackertz 1993.
41. Lawson 1901, 301.
42. *Myst.* iii.2–3.
43. Athanassiadi 1993a, 124–5.
44. Cf. Pl., *Rep.* 571, your dream is what you are: the more virtuous you are, the better will be your dream. Philostr. *VitApTy* ii.37. Antiochus *de insomniis* (*homily* 84, *PG* 89, 1687–92) enjoins prayer before sleep to ward off dangerous dreams. Cf. Harris 2009, 251, who cites Lycurgus, *Leocrates* 93: 'It would be terrible if the same divine signs appeared to the pious and the wicked.'
45. Eur. *IT* 1259ff. See ch. 2.
46. *De hominis opificio* 13.10, *PG* 44.169D.
47. Herodotus 4.172.3 mentions incubation among the Nasamones. It was also practised in China (Laufer 1931, d'Este 2008, 151); and Harrison 2000, 124–5, mentions a nineteenth-century instance.
48. Langdon 1914, 128–9, iv R 61.i.5–30. I use these translations for their sonorous biblical tone. Up-to-date versions in Parpola 1997. See in general Oppenheim 1956, and the masterly survey of Mesopotamian divination by Bottéro 1974.
49. Parpola 1997.
50. A similar dream at Oppenheim 1956, 249. Another fine epiphany of Ishtar is quoted in Dalley 2007, 74–5. More examples in Bottéro 1974, 76–7.

51. Oppenheim 1956, 251. But Nectanebo actively seeks a dream: ibid. 253, and n. 138 below.
52. Lichtheim 1980, 42–3.
53. Bottéro 1974, 95ff.
54. As suggested by Leick 2001, 235ff; F. Fales and G.B. Lanfranchi in Heintz 1997.
55. The medium is called a *muhhum* or (female) *muhhutum*: Dalley 1984, 127–33.
56. Here, too, it seems, Adad-Duri commissioned someone else to dream for her. Another example, Oppenheim 1956, 195: Dagon talks to Hur-Asdu in a temple (not a dream as such).
57. Gurney 1952, 132–3: 'a curious monument of misplaced ingenuity'.
58. Oppenheim 1956, 256–95; 282–3.
59. Bottéro 1974, 102–3.
60. Flower 2008, 226.
61. Leviticus 19:13.
62. Douglas 1999.
63. I Samuel 28:7.
64. Tambiah 1990, 7; cf. chap. 14 below.
65. The first verse of the books of Isaiah, Amos, Obadiah, Micah, Nahum and Habakkuk.
66. For the phrase cf. the opening verses of Haggai, Zechariah and Malachi.
67. Jos. *AJ* 11.327.
68. Jos. *AJ* 11.333–4.
69. II Maccabees 15.11–17.
70. A useful survey is still Hamilton 1906, which also covers saints' shrines.
71. Vincent Crapanzano describes the procedure for 'visiting Moulay Idriss', the saint: 'Pilgrims frequently sleep in the sanctuary in the hope of having a dream. . . . Further the saints resemble rather more the *jnun* than deceased human beings. There is belief in neither ghosts nor ancestral spirits in Morocco.' *Tuhami, Portrait of a Moroccan Village* (Chicago 1986), cited in Tambiah 1990, 106ff.
72. Harris 2009, 32.
73. Tr. Lewis 1976, modified.
74. Trophonius' oracle, as we have seen, is not exactly a dream oracle; that of Sarpedon in the Troad seems to be a mistake for Seleuceia in Cilicia, a healing oracle (p. 211 below); that of Hermione is mentioned nowhere else. That of Pasiphae is known from Pausanias 3.26.1 and an inscription (*IG* v.1.1317: C4/3), where the goddess prescribes to the ephor the restoration of the statue of another ephor. It may be that only ephors could consult it, and it certainly does not seem to have had healing functions. The only other indication of the content of Pasiphae's revelations is given by Plutarch in his life of Agis (9.1–4), who describes oracles regarding the fortunes of Sparta. He gives several identifications of the goddess, whose name means 'speaking to all', including Cassandra and Daphne. Pausanias (3.26.1) says the goddess is Ino, though there is a statue of Pasiphae there; while Cicero (*div.* 1.96) agrees with Tertullian in attributing it to Pasiphae herself. See Richer 1998, ch. 12.
75. Paus. 10.32.9. Contrast Hierapolis, Str. 13.4.14, where the fumes just kill you – and the oracles are given by dice.
76. Sineux 2007 is a masterly study of this hero-god.
77. Hyperides, *Eux.* 16; Davies, *APF* 5886; Sineux 2007, 104–5. Harris 2009, 157, points out that Amphiaraus is only being consulted on this matter because it concerns his own property.
78. Petrakos 329, *SEG* XV 293. The phraseology can be readily paralleled, e.g. Theon at Pergamum *SEG* XXXVII 1987.1019, Muller 1987, 194 1.6; Sineux 2007, 198.
79. Clement, *Strom.* 1.133, *Protr.* 2.11.1, Tert., *de anima* 46.11, Philo, *Emb to Gaius* 78.
80. A minimum of 9 obols, Sacred Law 69.
81. Cf. Philostr. *VitApTy* 2.37.2: no food for one day, no wine for three, 'in order that he may imbibe the oracles with his soul in a condition of utter transparence'.
82. Usually. Several reliefs depict consultants with rams, but there was a free choice of other animals. A fragment of Aristophanes' lost *Amphiaraus* (17 KA) says 'the cock kicked over the pot'. If this happened before the consultation, it may have been a bad omen.

83. Cf. Socrates' for Asclepius, *Phaedo* 118a.
84. *FGrH* 566 F 56, from a scholiast on Lycophron, 1050–1.
85. Sleeping on fleeces was also practised in the rites of Faunus to obtain an oracle from Faunus: V., *A.* 7.86–95, O., *Fast.* 4.651–73. Polemo on Διὸς κῳδιον.
86. Some other branches: Herzog 1931, W 33, 74–80.
87. The pleasure of the story defies scepticism. Parker 2005, 448 n. 210, notes that the snake's diet of eggs is now part of the myth. But see Connolly 1998 for a sceptical view of the whole story.
88. The life of this forgotten sanctuary is evoked in masterly fashion by Louis Robert 1973. See also the extended account of Apollonius of Tyana's stay there, *VitApTy* 1.7–13.
89. Riethmüller 2005, cf. Melfi 2007.
90. *Sons of Asclepius* 38.21.
91. Nissen 2001.
92. *VitApTy.* 1.13.
93. Cf. *Amph.* F24 KA: an old man who has taken a laxative prays the god for a stopper.
94. A snake appears to the patient in *Inscr. Cret.* XVII.21: see van Straten 1976, Dillon 1994.
95. LiDonnici 1995 is the most convenient collection; see also Edelstein 1945/1998. The original classic publication is Herzog 1931. Girone 1998 collects epigraphic testimonia excluding the four stelae of cures from Epidaurus. Guarducci 1978 discusses IAMATA inscriptions from Lebena (Crete) and the Asclepieum on the Tiber Island in Rome. The cures were written up by an official called the *aretalogos: SIG* 1133. See also Posidippus' epigrams 95–101, which are dedications following cures.
96. Herzog 1931, 154.
97. We are told that Hippocrates copied inscriptions there before the temple was destroyed by fire: Str. 14.2.19, Plin., *NH* 29.4. (The *Life* by Soranus says that Hippocrates burned the archives on Cos to make his own achievement seem the greater: Pinault 1992, 7.) Two rare exceptions are *Inscr. Cos.* 348, a dedication by one Hecataeus, 'according to a dream', and the incubation inscription of Daikrates, dedicated to the Graces. See van Straten 1976. Some records of cures by Sarapis include *IG* X 2.855 (Merkelbach 1973) and *IG* XI 4.1299, Maiistas' poem, see Powell 1925, 68–71.
98. Blacker in Loewe and Blacker 1981.
99. A count shows that 32 per cent of the Epidaurian inscriptions concern women, while the average elsewhere is 15 per cent; but Plato's *Laws* 909DE perhaps reflects a popular perception when he says that it is *mostly* women who establish shrines following dreams.
100. Isyllos' *Paean* (Powell 1925, 132ff.) is a song of gratitude to Asclepius for assistance in a military campaign.
101. Iamblichus, *Babyloniaka* 3 and 21; *Life of Aesop* 78, p. 97 Perry; cf. *Alexander Romance* I.32. Herzog 1931, 118–23, quotes modern parallels including a story of St Nicholas and one from Cervantes. In Washington Irving, *Tales of the Alhambra*, ch. 1, 'The Journey', a treasure is said to be hidden 'in the forehead of the bull'. Another treasure-dream (from Europe not China) is described in Laufer 1931, 215ff.
102. *Care for the dead* 13: see p. 106 above.
103. Weinreich 1931.
104. Philostr. *VitApTy* I.9: Asclepius at Aigeai fails to help someone *even* in a dream. The implication is that he usually comes in a waking vision. In our passage, the narrator has a vision, his mother a dream.
105. Lajtar 2006: Amenhotep's miraculous cure of Polyaratos, third century BC.
106. *c. Cels.* 3.5; 7.3: Dodds 1965, 125.
107. Herzog 1931 W 79, Edelstein 1945 I.247 (no. 432), Girone 1998 II.4.
108. Pearcy 1988.
109. Dodds 1965, 41.
110. In an inscription from Thera of the third century BC, Artemis promises ninety years to Artemidorus of Perge, and Providence adds 'three seasons'. See van Straten 1976.

111. Paradoxical prescriptions may be a guarantee of divine involvement. After all, they are things you would never do if a human doctor prescribed them, as Galen remarks, *Comm. Hipp. Epid.* VII.4, IV.8, XVIIb p. 137K: Walde 2001, 44. Cf. *I. Cret.* I.XVII.17 for another strange prescription.
112. Rostowtzev 1920; Lane Fox 1986, 124–50; on dreams 150–67.
113. Dion. Halic. 2.68.2.
114. Hdt. 2.141.3, Sethos' dream; Str. 4.1.4–5, a goddess in a dream commands the foundation of Massilia; Plut. *Pericles* 13.12–13, Athena in a dream offers a cure.
115. *IG* 2² 4326, Meneia makes a dedication after a vision of Athena.
116. Syll.³ 709.
117. Higbie 2003, esp. 273–83.
118. The repeated dream recalls that of Xerxes, Hdt. 7.12–18.
119. Libanius, *Antiochikos* 109. Dalley 2007, 139: Ishtar requests to be taken to Egypt.
120. *Vit. Soph.* 464, Loeb p. 391.
121. A couple of other examples in van Straten: Apollo Ptoos appears to Aristochos (*c*.4/3 BC); and another epiphany occurs at Manisa.
122. Fowden 1986, 162–4.
123. *PGM* IV 2441–2621: he is probably a real person, and the employer of the original Sorcerer's Apprentice: Ogden 2007, 248–55. Another spell, *PGM* VII 795–845, is entitled 'Pythagoras' request for a dream oracle and Demokritos' dream divination'.
124. Stoneman 2007, 534–7, 540–2, collects the bibliography; in general, Stambaugh 1972.
125. Arr. *Anab.* 6.2, Plut. *Alex.* 76.
126. Tac. *H.* 4.83–4, Plut. *IsOs.* 361F–362A. Clement, *Protr.* 4.48.1–3 says it was actually Ptolemy III. Stambaugh 1972, 6ff.
127. Koenen 1968.
128. On gematria see Lightfoot 2007, 388; Stoneman 2007, 545.
129. *Pap. Vogliano* 21: Merkelbach 1977, 198–200.
130. Stambaugh 1972, 11–12; Hölbl 2001, 99ff. Alexander is in fact said to have had a friend called Sarapion, a name that can only have existed when the god had come into being: Plut. 39.3; Welles 1962 takes this as genuine though Berve regards it as a mistake.
131. *UPZ* I, *PGM* xl. Several non-epiphanic dreams dreamt by Alexander the Great are recorded: they include his premonition of Clitus' death, his dream of the satyr at Tyre, which depends on wordplay for its interpretation; and his dream of a herb that would cure sickness in the army (Cic. *div.* 2.66.135, Diod. Sic. 17.103, Str. 15.2.7). Aristander, Alexander's seer, wrote a book about Alexander's dreams: Hughes 1984; Nice 2005, 94. Alexander seems to be exceptional among kings and rulers in receiving military guidance in dreams; but Ptolemy IV before the battle of Raphia had a vision of the gods: Harris 2009, 167.
132. Artemidorus III.44, Diog. Laert. V.76.
133. Stambaugh 47–52. *UPZ* 77–81 collects the testimonia; for example, 77.2: 'The dream that Ptolemaios saw at the Moon festival on Pachon 25th: I seem to see Thaues singing aloud in a rather sweet voice and in good spirits; and I see Taous laughing, and her foot is big and clean.' The dream is somewhat disorganized, but apparently symbolic rather than an epiphany.
134. *PSI* IV (1917), 435, *P. Edgar* (1918) 7 = *P. Cair. Zen.* I.59034; V. Longo, *Aretalogie nel mondo Greco* I (Genoa 1969) no. 62. See Rigsby 2001. Dreams often required the dreamer to found a new temple, not only in Egypt. A notable example is the fragmentary narrative of *The Dream of Nectanebo*. Similarly, Atargatis of Hierapolis ordered Stratonicea to build her a temple (Hajjar 1990, 2260), as did Isis to Seleucus: Libanius, *Or.* 11.114. In ancient Babylon the priest Gudea had a dream vision of Ningirsu who instructed him to build him a temple; King Nabonidus had a dream vision of Marduk.
135. *IG* IV.1299; Powell 1925, 68–9; Engelmann 1975.
136. Roussel 1915–16; Stambaugh 1972, 49 n. 1.
137. Page 1941, 96.
138. Ray in Loewe and Blacker 1981, 174ff. An imperial epigram on the wall of the Osiris temple at Abydos records how the priest Harpocrates 'often dreamt here, thanks to Bes'. See also Dunand 1997.

139. *Hist. Philos.* 9 Athanassiadi.
140. *PGM* v.447–58; cf. *PGM* v.1–53 for a method of producing 'an oracle of Sarapis by means of a boy, a lamp, a saucer and a bench': the conjurer then is not sleeping on this occasion.
141. Similar cases at 5.92 and 5.93.

CHAPTER 8 DICING FOR DESTINY

1. Green 2007, 142.
2. Paus. 7.22.3. He mentions that the same form of consultation was used at the oracle of Apis in Memphis, at Smyrna (9.11.5) and at Thebes (ibid.): ch. 5, end.
3. Lawson 1901, 304–6.
4. Wilhelm 1951; Shaughnessy 1996.
5. The major discussions are Horowitz and Hurowitz 1992, van Dam 1997 and van der Horst 1998.
6. Similar examples: I Samuel 30:8, I Samuel 2:1.
7. Cryer 1994, 325, thinks Urim and Thummim are 'a late catch-all invention symbolising divination'; but as they are in fact mentioned in the Old Testament, this will not do.
8. Hadas 1951, 139.
9. The bronze letters offer a curious parallel to a puzzling piece of evidence from Greek lot oracles, discussed by Heinevetter, 1912.
10. Cryer 1994, 225ff (summarizing Kammenhuber 1976) lists the five types of Hittite oracle: KIN, lots told by old women; MUŠEN, omens from the flight of birds; KUŠ, the omen sacrifice; HAL, observation of an animal before sacrifice; and MUŠ, the movements of a water-snake in a bowl. In none of these is there a suggestion that the gods are speaking directly.
11. Van Dam 1997 40–1; Horowitz and Hurowitz 1992.
12. Douglas 1999, 120–1.
13. Dalley 2007, 138, and 158–60.
14. Dalley 2007, 196.
15. Pi. *P.* 4.189–91.
16. Compare the Hittite procedure described by Taggar-Cohen 2002.
17. Kurke 1999, 293. In her discussion of dicing (283–95), Kurke argues for a distinction between *astragaloi*, used for gambling against fate, and *kuboi*, used for random chances, like battle; but the distinction seems a dubious one. In Artemidorus 3.1 both have a similar connotation. Cicero's *On Divination* 2.85 does not make such a distinction.
18. Cf. Pollux 9.99.
19. Coins of Samos, just over the strait from Ephesus, also show dicing children, presumably before Hera.
20. Milne 1941.
21. Nollé 1987 and esp. 2007; Graf 2005; Heinevetter 1912; Maltomini 1995; Larson 1995; Björck 1939.
22. Nollé 2007, 20ff.: Laodicea in Phrygia, Anabura, Ormeleis, Balbura, Takina/Kabalis; Prostanna in Pisidia, Sagalassos; Askeriye near Sagalassos; Yariköy near Sagalassos, Adada, Cremna, Termessos, Kitanaura, Attaleia, Perge, Incik, Coracesium/Hamaxia, Antioch.
23. Nollé 2007, 84–91.
24. Smith 1991, 1–2 and 236.
25. Palmer and Ramsay 2009.
26. Palmer and Ramsay 2009, 121–2.
27. Artemidorus 2.69 also regards this kind of divination as worthless, along with several other procedures including divination from cheese – which offers interesting possibilities for speculation.

28. This is the theme of Guillermo Martinez's 2008 novel, *The Book of Murder*.
29. See the discussion in Dennett 1995, 54; and on the ancient thinkers, Sedley 2007.
30. For the differences, see Dennett 1995, 512.
31. If proof were needed, there are some vivid pages in Fyodor Dostoyevsky's novel *The Gambler*, chapter 11. ' "To think that the accursed zero should have turned up now!" she sobbed. "The accursed, accursed thing! And it is all your fault," she added, rounding on me in a frenzy, "It was you who persuaded me to cease staking upon it." "But Madame, I only explained the game to you. How am I to answer for every mischance which may occur in it?" . . . "Very well. Stake another four thousand on the red." '
32. Dennett 1995, 52–4.
33. No. xlix in Graf's list, 2005, 82–97.
34. Hansen 1998, 286 citing Bolte 1903.
35. Adada/Sigirlik, Olympos (twice, one of them often falsely ascribed to Limyra: Nollé 2007, 240), Side, Aspendos, Kibyra, Pedelissos, Oenoanda; and a second group, with different verses, at Hierapolis (Troad; twice), Timbriada, Soloi on Cyprus.
36. *Iliad* I.72.
37. Lane Fox 1986, 210, 212.
38. Damascius, *Philosophical History*, F 138 Athanassiadi.
39. The bibliography is extensive and gathered by Nollé 2007, 255; for a text see West 1967. See also Parke 1985a, 180–3.
40. Damascius fr 87 Athanassiadi.
41. Burkert in Solomon 1994, 49–60.
42. Björck 1939.
43. Diogenes Laertius 1.2.
44. *PGM* 8.1.
45. Hansen 1998, 289.
46. Bolte 1903 assembles a number of other kinds of oracle book that insert successive stages of choice to increase the complexity of the randomization. E.g. pp. 305–6, a medieval Italian oracle table with a series of concentric circles, where successive choices lead you from the 20 kings to the 20 planets, each of which has 56 indications and 20 circles, each in 28 sectors. Next you reach the 20 prophets, each with a set of 56 ready-made answers. Another type of the same method is the Persian *Fal-nameh* or *Book of Fate*: see Farhad and Bağci 2010.
47. Apul. *Metam.* 9.8.
48. Zosimus 4.13; Amm. Marc. 29.1.27–32. Hajjar 1990, 2304.
49. A fragment of an object of this kind is illustrated in Donnay 1984.
50. Aristophanes, *Peace* 1089–94.
51. Dio. 79.8.6 and 40.3.
52. *Homer* 2.18.5.
53. *PGM* VII.112–19.
54. *SHA Hadrian* II.8, Alex. Sev. IV.6. Cf. *Clodius Albinus* V.3–4, *Claudius* X.2–6.
55. Van der Horst 1998; Drexl 1941.
56. Possibly also I Maccabees 3:48.
57. Jerome, *Ep. ad Paulinum Nola* 53.7; and church councils – van der Horst 1998, 157.
58. *Confessions* 4.3.5.
59. Matthew 19.21.
60. Romans 13.13–14.
61. Compare his scepticism about dreams: see ch. 5.
62. A lost divinatory text, condemned by the fifth-century AD councils: Klingshirn 2002.

CHAPTER 9 FOREKNOWLEDGE, FATE AND PHILOSOPHY

1. Cicero's dialogues *On Fate* and *On Divination* are our sources for much of this information. See the discussions of Guillaumont 2006, Schallenberg 2008 and Wardle 2006.
2. Cic. *div.* 1.64, 125ff.; Sandbach 1975, 81. Antipater and Diogenes of Babylon also wrote on divination.

3. Merkelbach remarks how the events of Heliodorus' *Ethiopica*, which look to the participants like a series of chances, are in fact directed by Fate, as is made clear, at least to the reader, by the frequent oracles and prophecies that keep the plot on track (see Morgan 1997, 299). At length the penny drops with the protagonists too, and they stop worrying, even when death by burning seems imminent.

4. *On Fate* XXXI. 203.1, a position from which Christian writers like Gregory of Nyssa were able to benefit: Gregory feels no need to discuss the myths of Oedipus and the rest in his discussion of fate in *Against Fate*.

5. Christian authors include Basil, *Hexameron* VI 5–7, Origen, *Philokalia* 23, Methodius of Olympus, *Banquet* VIII, Nemesius of Emesa, *de natura hominis* 35–8. See Motta 2009.

6. E.g. Iamblichus, *On Fate*, quoted in Stobaeus II.8.46.

7. *Republic* 617e, *Laws* 709e; Plut. *Q. Conv.* 9.740c.

8. *Letter to Menoeceus* 133.

9. *On divination in sleep* 463b28.

10. Anscombe 1956.

11. Diogenes Laertius 7.149. All Stoics accepted oracles except Panaetius, who thought there was room for doubt: Cic. *div.* 1.3.6.

12. Long and Sedley 1987, 263–6, 392–4, 463–7 are useful discussions. See also Sandbach 1975, 101–8. The fragments are collected in von Arnim 1923, II.264–98 (fate) and 343–8 (divination).

13. See also the fragments cited in the discussion of Dragoma-Monachou 1994, 4432.

14. Ps.-Plutarch, *On Fate*, 569c.

15. Kurt Vonnegut's novel *Timequake* explores a world in which time has abruptly reverted ten years; people simply repeat their actions of the previous ten years, like automata, only to be caught out when free will is restored without warning, and they fail, for example, to start steering their cars again.

16. Cicero, *On the Nature of the Gods* II.3: Balbus the Stoic is speaking.

17. In Dragoma-Monachou's formulation (4432): 'Providence is God's will and fate is the unimpeded fulfilment of this will.'

18. *Natural Questions* II.45.

19. 9.27 and *To Fronto* 4.

20. Cf. Dionysius of Halicarnassus 2.68, quoted in ch. 7 on epiphanies.

21. Sandbach 1975, 105. Similarly, for a modern Christian thinker, Richard Swinburne, God planned the Holocaust in order to increase the non-Jewish world's opportunities for compassion: Dawkins 2006, 89.

22. *Discourses* I.6, 11; II.16; III.17.

23. *On Fate* 30.

24. For Sophocles, it is Zeus who inflicts Oedipus' doom on him, whereas Apollo only predicts it.

25. Karen Owens, cited by Dawkins 2006, 101.

26. Cic. *div.* 6.12ff.

27. Gordon 1996, 110–11.

28. Diogenianus' arguments are excerpted and summarized by Eusebius, *PE* 4.3.137ff and especially 6.8.262ff. The same point is made by Lucian, *Jup. Confut.*, 12 and *Demonax* 37; Solon fr 31.

29. Guillaumont 2006, 339; he cites Lucilius' mockery of the position: 'If you don't know I don't know what I am asking, what can you tell me?' (342).

30. Long and Sedley 1987, 292–4.

31. Long and Sedley 1987, 463–7.

32. Compare the paradox of time travel. There may be three reasons why you cannot go back in time and kill your parents before your birth. (1) There is a natural law against it: this would be analogous to determinism. (2) Your free will in the past is limited to trivia: but how do you define these? (3) You can do this, but you will immediately generate a parallel universe, a garden of forking paths: this would be analogous to the idea that we have absolute free will, but God can foresee all the options. The Greeks

seem never to have developed the idea that the gods are outside time and see in a fourth dimension, like the aliens in Vonnegut's *Slaughterhouse Five*; as Salley Vickers puts it is *Where Three Roads Meet* (2007), 146: 'it is not that the timeless ones determine our universe, as some have falsely claimed; but that theirs is the vision of eternity, where time does not so much stand still as come full circle'.

33. *Letter to Menoeceus* 133.
34. Conversely, 'Fate annihilates Free Will': von Arnim 1923, II.947–1007.
35. DL 10.135. Plotinus II.1.3 puts it very clearly: 'Nothing will be ordered. . . . So there would be no foretelling or divination, neither that which comes from art . . . nor that which comes from divine possession and inspiration'.
36. E.g. Porphyry F 268–71.
37. Schallenberg 2008.
38. Even Epicureans could not escape the terminology, and regarded Epicurus as himself 'like an oracle': *Sententiae Vaticanae* 29 – quoted in Gordon 1996, 106, cf. Lucretius, 5.110–13.
39. Philostr. *VitApTy* 6.32.
40. Titus died from the bite of a poisonous fish.
41. Philostr. *VitApTy* 8.7.
42. Also in Pomponius Mela 2.83–4. Cf. also Jerome, *Ep.* 108.29.
43. Hdt. 6.77 with 19.
44. Piérart in Derow and Parker 2003. Many Latin omens exhibit this pattern.
45. Both Ps-Plutarch *On Fate* and Maximus of Tyre (13.3 and 29.7) make the same point. Cf. Hdt. 2.139.2: Sabacos will rule Egypt, but the oracle does not specify how this will come about.
46. Seneca, *On Providence* VI.1: the gods *externa contemnunt.* Cf. *Ep.* 95.50 the gods *qui universa vi sua temperant, qui humani generis tutelam gerunt interdum incuriosi singulorum.*
47. Diogenes of Oenoanda, the Epicurean, makes the same point – fr 54 = 32 Chilton, Gordon 1996, 108–9: if *mantike* is done away with, what proof is there of *heimarmene*?
48. Plato, *Laws* 12.966–7 had already rejected this criticism: 'No one who has contemplated all this [the movements of the universe] with a careful and expert eye has in fact ever degenerated into such ungodliness as to reach the position that most people would expect him to reach. They suppose that if a man goes in for such things as astronomy . . . and sees events apparently happening by necessity rather than because they are directed by the intention of a benevolent will, he'll turn into an atheist'.
49. *De libero arbitrio* and *Civitas Dei* 5.8–10, on Peter's denial of Jesus. Eusebius *PE* 6.11.40 uses the same example to argue the same case. See chapter 13. Knox 1957, 38ff., states clearly that the idea that Oedipus' fate should be predicted yet not predetermined is logically impossible.
50. Sharples 1983, 28.
51. F 339, Eus., *PE* 6.4.2. They were perhaps returning to a simpler time in the history of theology, when the Babylonian goddess Ishtar could simply override Fate: Dalley 2007, 196.
52. See Seneca, *On Providence* IV.11 quoted above.
53. Sandbach 1975, 103–4. Herodotus 6.135 says Yes.
54. Fr 30–1 Chilton.
55. See Schofield 1986.
56. *On the Laws* 2.32–4.
57. Guillaumont 2006; Wardle 2006. Harris 2009, 183, finds Cicero to be definitely sceptical about divination.
58. Schofield 1986, Beard 1986.
59. One might compare Cicero's 'failure of nerve' with David Hume's position in his *Dialogues on Natural Religion*: his speaker Philo, having produced arguments that demolish the Argument from Design, then 'caves in' and restates a theist position. His social circumstances, or his ingrained prejudices and beliefs, prevented him from following the argument to its real conclusion. See Dennett 1995, 32.

CHAPTER 10 SCEPTICS, FRAUDS AND FAKES

1. See also Cic. *div.* 1.3.5 = Xenophanes A 52 DK, and the discussion of Lesher 1978. Sophocles, *OT* 499–512 has a similar tendency.
2. Hammerstaedt 1988 and 1990; Parke 1985, 142–5. The ancient authorities differ as to his date but he is most probably to be located in the second century AD. Most of his examples concern oracles from Claros, which began to flourish soon after Plutarch wrote but was in eclipse by Porphyry's time. Furthermore, it seems that Oenomaus' book was also used by Clement of Alexandria (*c.* AD 150–220) in his attack on pagan religion.
3. Eus. *PE* v.22.
4. Eus. *PE* v.23. See p. 97 above.
5. Discussed in Shaughnessy 1996, 33. Another example, chosen more or less at random, from p. 53: 'Tied to a metal ladder; determination is auspicious. If you have someplace to go, you will see inauspiciousness; the emaciated piglet returns helter-skelter.'
6. Parke 1985, 142–5.
7. Berlin P 11517; Eitrem 1931.
8. *OT* 380–403, *Ant.* 1055; Flower 2008, 135–6.
9. Porph. F 341, quoted by Eus. *PE* vi. 5.2–4. See Busine 2005, 275.
10. This last example, Daphne, reappears in Tatian, *Or. ad Gr.* 8.4, as evidence of Apollo's failure of foreknowledge.
11. Antonius Diogenes' *Wonders beyond Thule* begins with a similar account of the discovery of the narrative: Photius 166.111b.
12. The Urim and Thummim thus naturalized themselves in America and in due course became the emblem on the arms of Yale University.
13. Mark Twain's comments on the origins of the Mormon religion in *Roughing It* are well worth reading; his tone is not unlike that of Lucian.
14. Hippolytus, *Refutation of all Heresies* 4.34.
15. Lajtar 2006. See also Ray in Loewe and Blacker 1981, on the bull-pedestal at Kom el-Wist.
16. Busine 2005, 174–8.
17. Robert 1980. Perdrizet 1903, 62–6 Lane Fox 1986, 241–50 inclines to believe that some of the details are invented or exaggerated, which may well be true. He is clear (246) that Alexander should not be judged simply as a hoax, but as a prophet among many. Lucian is 'one arriviste showing his contempt for another' (249).
18. Ogden 2007, 142–4.
19. Above, p. 69.
20. Jones 1920, 336.

CHAPTER 11 NEW QUESTIONS FOR THE ORACLES: PLATONISM AND THEOLOGY

1. *The E at Delphi; the oracles no longer given in verse; the decline (or obsolescence) of oracles. Mor.* 384–438, vol. V in the Loeb edition.
2. Shapiro 1990; Bowden 2003; Dillery 2005; Flower 2008.
3. *FGrH* 328.
4. *FGrH* 334, F50–53.
5. Henrichs 1978, 125–6.
6. F 130–41 Wehrli.
7. Other nuggets include the fact that the oracle of Apollo at Pagasae was founded by Trophonius; that Sarapis was identical with Pluto; and the oracle given to Alexander when founding Alexandria.
8. *FHG* 3.108–48.
9. Athen 6.234d is undecided as to his home city.
10. *AP* 14. 69, 76, 78–99, 112. Others known from elsewhere include 100 (papyrus), 69 (Diod. Sic.), 101 (Stobaeus), 66 and 150 (Plutarch), 65 (Pausanias), 40 and 64 (Athenaeus), 84 (Achilles Tatius) and 73 and 148 (Suda).

11. Cf. Fontenrose 1988, A7.
12. Robert 1968; Cameron 1993, 212–15.
13. Some of it is from Cephalas, most inserted by a redactor of the *Palatine Anthology*: Beckby 1958 ad loc.
14. Bowden 2005, 39, gives a brief doxography of 'decline'.
15. Bonnechère 1990 discusses fifteen, a high concentration in comparison with other regions. Arcadia, for example, had only three. See also Bonnechère 2003.
16. Eusebius, *PE* v.17.
17. Plato was not unusual here, for a similar doctrine appears in the almost contemporary Derveni Papyrus, col. 6: Betegh 2004, 76; see also Aristotle, *On divination in dreams* 463b12.
18. Eur. F 973 Nauck.
19. Cf. Apollonius of Tyana, the wise man foresees the future.
20. Strabo 7.7.9 had accounted Dodona 'virtually extinct' in the late first century BC.
21. Compare Hippolytus, *Refutation of all Heresies* IV. 30–1 on some other unpleasant tricks with ovines.
22. Betegh 2004, 353.
23. Cf. p. 58 above.
24. Betegh 2004, commenting on col. 7. See also ch. 3 on riddles.
25. Fontenrose 1988, no. 22.
26. See Robert 1960, 543–6.
27. *Divine Institutes* 7.13.6, Fontenrose 1988, 50; *de ira dei* 23, Fontenrose 1988, 51; *Divine Institutes* 4.13.11, Fontenrose 1988, 49 – 'quasi-historical'.
28. Fontenrose 1988, F33, Lact. *de mort pers.* 11.212–13. Eusebius (*vit Const.* 2.50) says that 'on this occasion it was Apollo who spoke from a cave and dark recess and not through a human agent . . . for his priestess, letting her locks flow down and driven by madness was lamenting this evil among men'. This sounds like literary embellishment.
29. Macrob. *Sat.* 1.18.19–21.
30. Such responses were not the sole prerogative of Claros, for Macrobius' *Saturnalia* 1.20.16 also describes how Nicocreon of Cyprus asked Sarapis who he is. The reply came, that his head is the firmament, his belly the sea, his feet the earth, and his ears are in the ether, while his eye is the sun.
31. Erbse 1995, no. 13; see Parke 1985, 165.
32. *Divine Institutes* 7.1.
33. Robert 1971; Hall 1978; Livrea 1998.
34. Other oracles attributed to, or definitely from, Claros, include one regarding Apollonius of Tyana, a henotheistic pronouncement that Zeus, Hades, Dionysus and the Sun are all one, and several known only from the *Theosophy* (but not therefore not genuine). See Oesterheld 2008 app. 4 = Philostratus, *VitApTy* 4.1.1, where Colophon praises the master as a sharer in its own knowledge; no. 28 = Macrobius, *Sat.* 1.18.18–21, from Labeo; app. 10 = Porphyry, *PO* F314–15; app. 11= Eus. *PE* 3.15.3, app. 13–17 = Erbse 1995, 15, 21, 35, 38, 44. See also the catalogue in Busine 2005.
35. Mitchell 1999, 128.
36. F 23, 26, 25 DK = Kirk and Raven nos 173–4. Compare also Plato's *Timaeus* 40a2, where God is fiery and spherical (i.e. like a heavenly body).
37. Elsewhere Malalas (II, 23; 40.17) cites an unidentified play of Sophocles (*adespota* 618) for a monotheistic thought: 'There is one God who created heaven and the broad earth, the swell of the gleaming blue sea and the force of the winds. But we mortals, being greatly deceived in our hearts, have established as solaces for our sufferings images of the gods made out of stone and wood or figures worked in gold or ivory. Performing sacrifices and empty festivals to them, we think we are pious.'
38. I paraphrase Athanassiadi 1999 (a superbly lucid study), 149. See also Athanassiadi 1992.
39. Fr. 1.1 = 6, heroically translated by Johnston 1990, 84.
40. Dodds 1961, 263.

41. Woodhouse 1986, 48–61, 319, 322.
42. Lewy 1978, 425. Iranian elements include the importance of the god Aion, who may be equivalent to the Iranian Zervan.
43. The oracle here issued several pronouncements in the reign of Septimius Severus and was still active in the late fourth century AD. Libanius, *Ep.* 1351 (AD 363): 'Apamea the beloved of Zeus, which continued to reverence Zeus when there were penalties for the worship of the gods.' See Balty 1981.
44. Cited by Dodds 1961, 268.
45. Fr. 149: Johnston 1990, 89.
46. Johnston 1990.
47. Cf. Plutarch, *On the face in the moon* 944c.
48. Wallis 1972, 106.
49. Athanassiadi 1992.
50. Athanassiadi 1993a.
51. Hekate says 'I have come, hearing your eloquent prayer . . .': *fr. dub.* 222; Johnston 1990, 86.
52. Marinus, *Life of Proclus*, 38.
53. Betegh 2004, 140.
54. Dodds 1961; Busine 2005, 196–206. Most notable is the importance of the goddess Hekate in both Porphyry and the *Chaldaean Oracles*, as the mystic link between gods and men. See *PO*, F308, 314–17, 319–20, 326, 327, 328, 329, 342, 345, 347.
55. Busine 2005, IV.
56. Clements 1996, 206.
57. Wolff 1856, 40.
58. Wolff 1856, 109 = F303 Smith.
59. Contrast his treatise *On Images*, with its allegorizing view of the benefits of statues of the gods, with the later *Letter to Anebo* where he is sceptical about the possibility of the gods being 'compelled': see Iamblichus, *On the Mysteries* 1.9.
60. Wolff 1856, 101–2, distinguishes genuine from fake.
61. Athanassiadi 1999, 178.
62. Tr. Edwards 2000, 40ff.
63. Busine 2005, 295ff. Cf. ch. 6 above, end.
64. See also F338.
65. Dalley 2007, 138–9.
66. And 330; cf. Plotinus, for whom the stars indicate but don't determine the future: Dodds 1961, 5. Origen ditto.
67. As in the Derveni Papyrus, *c.* 6; Betegh 2004, 76.
68. See Edwards 2006, 116.
69. F345a, cited by Augustine, *CD* XIX.23.43ff.
70. F323 = Eusebius, *PE* IX.10.1–2; a similar point in F324.
71. F343 = Augustine, *CD* XIX.23.1ff.
72. *CD* 19.23. 74ff.
73. O'Meara 1959.
74. This would be a main plank of the argument that *PO* also made use of the *Chaldaean Oracles*, since the extensive citations of *dra* by Augustine include plenty of quotations from the *Chaldaeans*. But if the two works were identical it would be very odd that Augustine should inveigh against it under one title in Book X of *The City of God* and under the other in Book XXIII. Perhaps *dra* was a reworking of some of the themes of *PO* with more material, composed later in life, and to be identified with the treatise that we know Porphyry devoted to the *Chaldaean Oracles*. See Edwards 2006, 117–18.
75. Busine 2005, 288, following Beatrice 1995, 414.
76. Lactantius *div. inst.* V.2. Johnson 2009 is sceptical.
77. De Palma Digeser 1998 argues that the structure of the *PO* is in fact reflected in that of Lactantius' *Divine Institutes*, and that the latter was written as a direct reply to it.

CHAPTER 12 'ECSTATIC PREDICTIONS OF WOE': *THE SIBYLLINE ORACLES*

1. Petronius, *Satyricon* 48.8.
2. DH 4.62, *Plin. NH* 13.27.88, Lact. *inst div.* I.6.10–11.
3. Wiseman 2008, 248. See Val. Max. 1.6.1 and Livy 1.39.1.
4. Lewis 1976, 114–31.
5. Phlegon of Tralles, *Book of Marvels* 10.
6. Wiseman 2008, 128.
7. Dio 39.15.1–4, 55.3, 56.4, 59.3, 60.4–61.4.
8. Lachmann 1848, 350–1; Feeney 2007, 146.
9. Ovid, *Fasti* 6.629–32; Wiseman 2008, 281.
10. Parke 1988, 142–3.
11. Wiseman 2008, 47.
12. See ch. 6.
13. Wiseman 2008, 43–4.
14. *De divinatione* 1.19. See also Plutarch, *Marius* 42.4, which lumps together 'Chaldaeans, sacrificers and interpreters of the Sibylline books'.
15. Parke 1988, 118–19.
16. Wiseman 2008, 55–6.
17. The major treatments are Collins 1987, Momigliano 1988, Parke 1988 appendix 2, Potter 1990 and 1994, Lightfoot 2007. See also Wood 2004, 114–20, for a brief summary. Translation in Charlesworth 1983, I.
18. Cassandra, too, spoke her own words, not those of the god; but her 'madness' was not a model of which Christians could approve: Lightfoot 2007, 19.
19. Cf. Dalley 2007, 128.
20. *BJ* 6.109; Barton 2007, 62.
21. *Div. inst.* 4.15.23. Contrast an otherwise similar text from a later age: the Icelandic *Voluspa*, in which a wise woman speaks when questioned, and foretells the end of the world.
22. Parke 1988, 152–3. See Osiek 1999, 1.2.2, 2.4.1. Cf. Erbse 1995, p. 8 (120ff.), where the oracle form is used for Christian purposes.
23. Eddy 1961, 290–4; Potter 1994, 194–203.
24. The prophecies of Isaiah are referred to as oracles at Is. 21, 23; otherwise the prophets usually describe 'visions': Is. 1.1, Amos. 1.1, Haggai 1.1, etc.
25. Agathias 2.23–5. Windisch 1929; De Jong 1997; Lightfoot 2007, 56–7, 80–2 (further references).
26. Lightfoot 2007.
27. Alexander 1967. It may have come to form Book III of the *Theosophy*, as Beatrice 2001 argues.
28. Alexander 1967, 127 and 143.
29. Lactantius, *div. inst.* 7.15.11 citing *Sib.* 3.316ff., 350ff. Fall of empires in kings' dreams: Cyrus in Cic. *div.* 1.23.46–7 (Magi – also on Alexander), Hdt. 1.209ff., Daniel 2.
30. See especially Collins 1987.
31. Potter 1990.
32. Collins in Charlesworth 1983 I.459.
33. Barton 2007, 226.
34. Lightfoot 2007, 65.
35. Potter 1990.
36. *Protrepticus* 4.50.1, citing *Sib.* 4.4–7.
37. Lightfoot 2007, 77–92.
38. *Div. inst.* 7.18.2 and 4.27.14.
39. Barton 2007, 227.

CHAPTER 13 SILENCING THE ORACLES

1. *Notes towards the Definition of Culture* (1948), 122.
2. Zosimus 4.3.3.

3. *Lives of the Sophists*, 476.
4. Counting from the earliest oracle stories in Herodotus' account of the sixth-century King Croesus.
5. Dodds 1965, 132.
6. *To the Greeks*, 18.
7. Cf. *c. Cels.* 1.68, 'sorcerers who. . . . Blow away diseases and invoke the souls of heroes'; Dodds 1965, 125. In August 2009 a man in Wisconsin who prayed to God when his daughter was mortally ill instead of calling the doctor was found guilty of 'reckless homicide': he took the view that 'If I go to the doctor, I am putting the doctor before God': *Guardian*, 3 August 2009.
8. Gregory 1983, supplemented by Markopoulos 1985.
9. Athanassiadi 1991.
10. Questions were even being put to the oracle of Castor and Pollux at Ostia in the third century AD: Lane Fox 1986, 189.
11. Amm. Marc. 22.13.15, Libanius, *Or.* 60, Julian, *Misopogon* 361bc, Philosotorgius, *HE* 7.8, Socrates, *HE* 3.18, Sozomen, *HE* 5.19.
12. Athanassiadi 1991.
13. Eusebius, *Life of Constantine* II.50; see ch. 11.
14. Thorough discussion by Busine 2005, 369–76.
15. E.g. the oracles to Diocletian complaining about the 'righteous on earth' interfering with Apolline transmission: see p. 180 above.
16. *Tübingen Theosophy* 16–18 are possible candidates.
17. Fowden 1986, 205 and 208; cf. 180ff. on Cyril's quotation of Hermes.
18. Malalas X.5. Also Suda s.v. Augustus 4412; Cedrenus 320.17–22.
19. Ellis Davidson in Loewe and Blacker 1981, 134.
20. Nonetheless it continued to function, at least until Constantius II: see Cameron and Hall's commentary on the passage.
21. The story is grippingly told by Herzog 1939.
22. Buresch 1889, 44.
23. See also Ammianus 19.12.14–17, Harris 2009, 221–2.
24. Ammianus 29.1.5–31, and 29.2.4 on his magic trials. See Downey 1961, 178; Potter 1994, 181ff.; also ch. 8 n. 49.
25. Wallace-Hadrill 1960.
26. Doxography in Johnson 2006, 13, 19.
27. Johnson 2006, 234–6.
28. In particular, he reproduces large portions of Oenomaus of Gadara's attack on the oracles as well as Porphyry's *Philosophy from Oracles*. He also gives us much of Porphyry's *Letter to Anebo* as well as writers on Fate including Diogenianus and Alexander of Aphrodisias (whose treatise is preserved independently).
29. No other Christian work attacks pagan theology so systematically. Gregory of Nyssa *On Fate* is a negative treatment but does not consider oracles at all. The same author's *De Pythonissa* is a discussion of the Witch of Endor; in it, he briefly rejects the idea of demonic possession (174b), and offers a list of types of divination in which he mentions oracles as one among many (103.258). Theodoret of Cyrrhus' discussion largely derives from Eusebius.
30. Johnson 2006, 160–2.
31. Johnson 2006, 168, speculates about the choice of this date.
32. *PO* II, F338 Smith: VI.3.1.
33. See also *in Hieroclem* XLII, where he attacks Apollonius of Tyana for believing in fate, on the grounds that this is destructive of morality. Wallace-Hadrill 1960, 145ff.
34. Compare the argument of Alexander of Aphrodisias: ch. 9. All Christian authors are, inevitably, anti-determinist: Motta 2008, 22.
35. Cf. ch. 9 (Q 7 section 2) and Augustine cited there.
36. 1.2.4.7, vol. I, p. 364, Everyman.
37. Gregory of Nyssa's *On Fate* argued that even astrology sometimes worked because the demons made it do so: Motta 2008, 165.

38. In the second century AD, Tatian in *oratio ad graecos* 8 had also attacked the demons for their evil doings.
39. As also for Antiochus, *On Dreams*: see ch. 5.
40. An interesting discussion in Wood 2003, 151–6.
41. Wood 2003, 144.
42. Nissen 2001; and on the cult of Thecla as such, Dagron 1978; Davis 2008. See also p. 103.
43. Zosimus 1.57.
44. Tertullian (*de anima* 46.11) may be referring to this place when he speaks of a dream oracle of Sarpedon in the Troad (if his geography was unsound). See p. 103.
45. Walde 2001, 49.
46. Frankfurter 1998, 145–97, esp. 193–7. Also Harris 2009, 75, and Herzog 1939 on the supplantation of Isis and Menuthis at Canopus by Christian saints.
47. Frankfurter 1998, 195.
48. These examples are all taken from Hamilton 1906.
49. According to Curnow 2004, 51, who cites no source.
50. Erbse 1995, p. 120 π^8; a shorter version at *Tübingen Theosophy* 16. Speyer 1970, 92–5, discusses 'Orakelfälschungen' in the Byzantine period, from the fourth century AD onwards; one example he cites is an oracle found in the grave of Constantine, which gives the initial letters of the words only, so that the reader has to deduce the complete text: George Scholarios, *PG* 160.767–73. Aesop used a similar device in the *Life of Aesop*, showing how the same series of letter could be interpreted in three different ways; and in the *Alexander Romance*, Alexander erects an inscription in Alexandria with the letters ΑΒΓΔΕ, meaning, 'Alexander the king, son of Zeus, built it'.
51. Jeffreys 1990, 194–5.
52. *Paradise Regained*, 460–4.
53. Erbse 1995, p. 123, μ.
54. Cf. VII.15, where Plato, mentioned in the same breath as the High Priest Jaddus, is said to have devised the theory of the triune God – The Good, Mind and Soul – which was then taken up by Cyril of Alexandria.
55. Bratke 1899: quoted text from pp. 5–9.
56. This story reappears in an eighth-century AD text attributed to John of Euboea, whence it is collected by Fontenrose 1988 among his quasi-historical responses of the Delphic oracle: Q268.
57. This prophecy of course really concerns Alexander the Great; it appears also at *Alexander Romance* 1.11, as the interpretation of an omen observed by Philip.
58. The word 'theosophy' seems to be of Neo-Platonic origin: Eus., *PE* IV.6.3, Beatrice 1995, 414. A version of the text (with material from elsewhere) was translated into Syriac by the end of the seventh century, and includes sayings of Thales and Orpheus as well as of Neo-Platonist thinkers and of Baba the god of Harran: Brock 1983.
59. Beatrice 2001.
60. Beatrice surmises that the Oracle of Baalbek is a fragment of Book III of the second part.
61. Brackertz 1993.
62. *PG* 107, 1122–68. See Mango 1960.
63. Brown 1971.
64. Athanassiadi 1992.
65. On which see Lightfoot 2007, 154–62.
66. Deisser 1990.
67. Mango 1960.

CHAPTER 14 CONCLUSION

1. Tambiah 1990, 45.
2. Tambiah 1990, 53.
3. Duffy 2001.

4. Thomas 1971, 301.
5. Tambiah 1990, 21.
6. Malinowski 1948, 87.
7. Wood 2003, 221.
8. Liebeschuetz 1979, 25–6.
9. Harrison 2000, 245: he is discussing how the failure of a Nuer prophet to achieve a predicted reconciliation with the British, ending in the prophet's death, showed only the failure of the prophet, not his god.
10. Parker 1985/2000, 103.
11. Dennett 1995, 54.
12. Dawkins 2006, 87–8, elegantly describes a scientifically conducted test on the efficacy of prayer. A total of 1,802 hospital patients were divided into three groups, the first of which was prayed for and didn't know it; the second received no prayers and didn't know it; the third received prayers and did know it. Those who were prayed for without knowing it showed no more improvement than the others, while those who knew they were being prayed for did slightly worse (perhaps because they assumed their case was so hopeless that no recourse remained but prayer). The end results were no different from those of chance.
13. Rhinehart 1998.
14. Wood 2003, 212. But it would not be correct to conclude that doctor's consultations are random procedures.
15. *Ode on the Morning of Christ's Nativity.*

Bibliography

Alexander, P.J. 1967. *The Oracle of Baalbek. The Tiburtine Sibyl in Greek Dress.* Washington, DC: Dumbarton Oaks Centre for Byzantine Studies.

Allen, T.W. and E.E. Sikes 1904. *The Homeric Hymns.* London: Macmillan.

Anscombe, G.E.M 1956. 'Aristotle and the Sea Battle', *Mind* 65, 1–15; revised in J.M.E. Moravcsik (ed.) 1968, *Aristotle: A Collection of Critical Essays* (London: Macmillan).

Arnott, W.G. 1989. 'Nechung: A Modern Parallel to the Delphic Oracle?', *Greece and Rome* 36, 152–7.

Athanassiadi P. 1991. 'The Fate of Oracles in late Antiquity', *Delt. Ch. AE* 15, 271–8.

Athanassiadi, Polymnia 1992. 'Philosophers and Oracles: Shifts of Authority in Late Paganism', *Byzantion* 62, 45–62.

Athanassiadi, P. 1993a. 'Dreams, Theurgy and Freelance Divination: The Testimony of Iamblichus', *JRS* 83, 115–30.

Athanassiadi, P. 1993b. 'Persecution and Response in Late Paganism: The Evidence of Damascius', *JHS* 113, 1–29.

Athanassiadi, Polymnia 1999. 'The Chaldaean Oracles: Theology and Theurgy' in Athanassiadi and Frede (eds) 1999.

Athanassiadi, Polymnia and Frede, Michael (eds) 1999. *Pagan Monotheism in Late Antiquity.* Oxford: Oxford University Press.

Aune, David E. 1983. *Prophecy in Early Christianity and in the Ancient Mediterranean World.* Grand Rapids, MI: W.B. Eerdmans.

Balty, J. 1981. 'L'oracle d'Apamée', *Ant. Class.* 50, 2–14 + pls I–II.

Barnett, R.D. 1953. 'Mopsos', *JHS* 73, 140–3.

Barton, John 2007. *Oracles of God* (2nd edn). London: Darton Longman & Todd.

Bartsch, Shadi 1989. *Decoding the Ancient Novel.* Princeton, NJ: Princeton University Press.

Bean, G. 1954. 'Notes and Inscriptions from Caunus', *JHS* 74, 85–110.

Bean, George E. 1962. 'Report on a Journey in Lycia 1980', *Anzeiger Wien* 2, 4–9.

Bean, G. 1978. *Lycian Turkey.* London: Benn.

Beard, Mary 1986. 'Cicero and Divination: The Formation of a Latin Discourse', *JRS* 76, 33–46.

Beatrice, P.F. 1995. 'Pagan Wisdom and Christian Theology according to the Tübingen Theosophy', *Journal of Early Christian Studies* 3, 203–18.

Beatrice, P.F. 2001. *Anonymi Monophysitae Theosophia: An Attempt at Reconstruction.* Leiden: Brill, *Vigiliae Christianae Suppl.* 56.

Beckby, H. 1958. *Anthologia Graeca.* Tusculum. Munich: Heimeran.

Betegh, Gabor 2004. *The Derveni Papyrus: Cosmology, Theology and Interpretation.* Cambridge: Cambridge University Press.

Bevan, E. 1938. *Sibyls and Seers.* London: George Allen & Unwin.

Bialik H.W. and Ravnitzky, Y.H. 1992. *The Book of Legends: Sefer ha-Aggadah.* New York: Schocken.

Björck, G.J. 1939. 'Heidnische und christliche Orakel mit fertigen Antworten', *Symb. Osl.* 19, 86–98.

Black Elk and John G. Neidhart 2000. *Black Elk Speaks*. Lincoln, NE: University of Nebraska Press (original edition 1932).

Bolte, J. 1903. *Zur Geschichte der Losbücher*. In G. Wickrams *Werke*, ed. J. Bolte, Bibliothek des litterarischen Vereins Stuttgart, vol. 230 (4.276–348) Tübingen.

Bonnechère, P. 1990. 'Les oracles de Béotie', *Kernos* 3, 53–65.

Bonnechère, P. 2003. *Trophonios de Lébadéé*. Leiden: Brill.

Bottéro, Jean 1974. 'Symptomes, signes, écritures en Mesopotamie ancienne', in Vernant (ed.) 1974.

Bouché-Leclerq, A. 1879–82. *Histoire de la divination dans l'antiquité*, 4 vols. Paris.

Bowden, H. 2003. 'Oracles for Sale', in Derow and Parker 2003.

Bowden, Hugh 2005. *Classical Athens and the Delphic Oracle*. Cambridge: Cambridge University Press.

Boyer, Pascal 2001. *Religion Explained*. London: Vintage.

Brackertz, Karl 1993. *Die Volks-traumbücher des byzantinischen Mittelalters*. Munich: dtv.

Branham, B. 1989. *Unruly Eloquence*. Cambridge, MA: Harvard University Press.

Bratke, Ed. 1899. *Das sogenannte Religionsgespräch am Hofe der Sasaniden*. Leipzig: Text u. Unters. der altchristl. Lit. ed. O. von Gebhardt u. A. Harnack XIX n.f. IV.

Bregman, Jay. 1982. *Synesius of Cyrene*. Berkeley, CA: University of California Press.

Bremmer, J.N. 1993. 'The Skins of Pherekydes and Epimenides', *Mnemosyne* IV.46, 234–6.

Bremmer, J.N. 2002. *The Rise and Fall of the Afterlife*. London: Routledge.

Bremmer, J.N. 2008. 'Balaam, Mopsus and Melampous: Tales of Travelling Seers', in *Greek Religion and Culture, the Bible and the Ancient Near East*. Leiden: Brill.

Brock, S.P., 1983. 'A Syriac Collection of Prophecies of the Pagan Philosophers', *Orientalia Lovanensia Periodica* XIV, Louvain, 203–46 = *Studies in Syriac Christianity*, Ashgate 1992, VII.

Brown, P. 1971. 'The Rise and Function of the Holy Man in Late Antiquity', *JRS* 61, 80–101; repr. in P. Brown 1982. *Society and the Holy in Late Antiquity* (Berkeley, CA: University of California Press), 103–52.

Buresch. K. 1889. *Klaros. Untersuchungen zum Orakelwesen des späteren Altertums*. Leipzig: Teubner.

Burkert, W. 1962. 'ΓΟΗΣ. Zum griechischen Schamanismus', *Rh. Mus* 105, 36–55.

Burkert, W. 1994. 'Olbia and Apollo of Didyma: A New Oracular Text', in Solomon 1994.

Busine, Aude 2002. 'La consultation d'Apollon dans le discourse de Jamblique', *Kernos* 15, 187–98.

Busine, Aude 2005. *Paroles d'Apollon. Pratiques et traditions oraculaires dans l'Antiquité tardive (IIe-VIe siècles)*. Leiden: Brill.

Calasso, Roberto 1993. *The Marriage of Cadmus and Harmony*. London: Vintage.

Cameron, Alan 1993. *The Greek Anthology*. Oxford: Oxford University Press.

Carney, E. 2006. *Olympias*. London: Routledge.

Carriker, Andrew 2003. *The Library of Eusebius of Caesarea*. Leiden: Brill.

Černy, Jaroslav 1962. 'Egyptian Oracles', in R.A. Parker, *A Saite Oracle Papyrus from Thebes* (Providence, RI: Brown University Press), 34–48.

Chadwick, Henry 1984. 'Oracles of the End in the Conflict of Paganism and Christianity in the Fourth Century', in E. Lucchesi and H.D. Saffrey (eds), *Mem. André Festugiére: Antiquité paienne et chrétienne = Cahiers d'Orientalisme*, 10, Geneva, 125–9.

Chandler, Richard 1971. *Travels in Asia Minor*, ed. Edith Clay. London: British Museum.

Charlesworth, J.H. 1983. *Old Testament Pseudepigrapha*. London: Darton Longman & Todd.

Clay, Diskin 2004. *Archilochos Heros*. Washington, DC: Center for Hellenic Studies.

Clements, Ronald E. 1996. 'Prophecy as Literature: A Reappraisal', in *Old Testament Prophecy: From Oracles to Canon*. Louisville, KY: Westminster John Knox Press.

Collins, J.J. 1987. 'Development of the Sibylline Tradition', *ANRW* II.20.i, 421–59.

Connelly, Joan Breton 2007. *Portrait of a Priestess*. Princeton, NJ: Princeton University Press.

Connolly, Andrew 1998. 'Was Sophocles Heroised as Dexion?', *JHS* 118, 1–21.

Cougny, E.D. 1871–90. *Oracula* in F. Dübner, *Epigrammatum. Anthologia Palatina* III. Paris.

Cryer, F. 1994. *Divination in Ancient Israel*. Sheffield: Sheffield University Press.

Cumont, F. 1912. *Astrology and Religion among the Greeks and Romans*. New York: Putnam's.

Curnow, Trevor 2004. *Oracles of the Ancient World*. London: Duckworth.

Dagron, G. 1978. *Vie et Miracles de Ste Thecle*. Brussels: Société des Bollandistes.

Dakaris, S. 1993. *The Nekyomenteion of the Acheron*. Athens: Ministry of Culture.

Dalley, Stephanie 1984. *Mari and Karana*. London: Longman.

Dalley, Stephanie 2007. *Esther's Revenge at Susa*. Oxford: Oxford University Press.

Davis, S.J. 2008. *The Cult of St Thecla*. Oxford: Oxford University Press.

Dawkins, Richard 2006. *The God Delusion*. London: Transworld.

Deisser, A. 1990. 'Les oracles de Léon le Sage, leurs origins et postérité', *Kernos* 3, 135–45.

De Jong, Albert 1997. *Traditions of the Magi*. Leiden: Brill.

Del Corno, D. 1969. *Graecorum de re oneirocritica scriptores*. Milan: Instituto editoriale Cisalpino.

Del Corno, D. 1978. 'I sogni e la loro interpretazione nell' età dell'impero', *ANRW* II.16.2, 1605–18.

Dennett, Daniel C. 1995. *Darwin's Dangerous Idea: Evolution and the Meanings of Life*. New York: Simon & Schuster (original edition).

De Palma Digeser, E. 1998. 'Lactantius, Porphyry and the Debate over Religious Toleration', *JRS* 88, 129–46.

Derow, Peter and Parker, Robert (eds) 2003. *Herodotus and his World*. Oxford: Oxford University Press.

Des Places, E. 2003. *Oracles chaldaiques*. Paris: Belles Lettres.

D'Este, Sorita (ed.) 2008. *Priestesses, Pythonesses, Sibyls: The Sacred Voices of Women who Speak with and for the Gods*. London: Avalonia.

Dietrich, B.C. 1990. 'Oracles and divine inspiration', *Kernos* 3, 157–74.

Dillery, John 2005. 'Chresmologues and *Manteis*: Independent Diviners and the Problem of Authority' in Johnston and Struck 2005.

Dillon, M. 1994. 'The Didactic Nature of the Epicurean *Iamata*', *ZPE* 101, 239–60.

Dodds E.R. 1951. *The Greeks and the Irrational*. Berkeley, CA: University of California Press.

Dodds, E.R. 1961. 'New Light on the *Chaldaean Oracles*', *Harvard Theological Review* 54, 263–73.

Dodds, E.R. 1965. *Pagan and Christian in an Age of Anxiety*. Cambridge: Cambridge University Press.

Donnay, Guy 1984. 'Instrument divinatoire d'époque romaine', *Colloque Apamée de Syrie* III, 1981. Brussels: Miscellanea 13, 203–10 + pl. LXV.1.

Douglas, Mary 1999. *Leviticus as Literature*. Oxford: Oxford University Press.

Downey, G. 1961. *A History of Antioch in Syria*. Princeton, NJ: Princeton University Press.

Dragoma-Monachou, M. 1994. 'Divine Providence', *ANRW* II.36.7, 4417–90.

Drexl, F. 1941. 'Ein griechisches Losbuch', *Byzantinische Zeitschrift* 41, 311–18.

Du Bois, Thomas A. 2009. *An Introduction to Shamanism*. Cambridge: Cambridge University Press.

Duffy, Eamon 2001. *The Voices of Morebath*. London: Yale University Press.

Dunand, F. 1997. 'La consultation oraculaire en Egypte tardive: l'oracle de Bes à Abydos', in Heintz 1997, 65–84.

Eddy S.J. 1961. *The King is Dead: Studies in the Near Eastern Resistance to Hellenism, 334–31 BC*. Lincoln, NE: Nebraska University Press.

Edelstein, E.J. and L. 1945/1998. *Asclepius: Collection and Interpretation of the Testimonies*. Baltimore, MD: Johns Hopkins University Press.

Edwards, Mark 2000. *Neoplatonic Saints: The lives of Plotinus and Proclus by their Students*. Liverpool: Liverpool University Press.

Edwards, Mark 2006. *Culture and Philosophy in the Age of Plotinus*. London: Duckworth.

Eidinow, Esther 2007. *Oracles, Curses and Risk among the Ancient Greeks*. Oxford: Oxford University Press.

Eitrem, S. 1931. 'Daulis in Delphoi und Apollons Strafe', *DRAGMA Nilsson*, 170–80.

Eliade, Mircea 1964. *Shamanism: Archaic Techniques of Ecstasy*. London: Routledge & Kegan Paul.

Ellis, Maria de Jong 1989. 'Observations on Mesopotamian Oracles and Prophetic Texts: Literary and Historiographical Considerations', *Journal of Cuneiform Studies* 41, 127–86.

Engelmann, H. 1975. *The Delian Aretalogy of Sarapis*. Leiden: Brill.

Erbse, H. 1995. *Thesophorum graecorum fragmenta*. Stuttgart and Leipzig: Teubner.

Evans, J.A.S. 1982. 'The Oracle of the "wooden walls"', *CJ* 78, 24–9 = *The Beginnings of History: Herodotus and the Persian Wars*. Campbellville: Edgar Kent, 215–24.

Evans, J.A.S. 1988, 'The "wooden wall" again, *Ancient History Bulletin* 2.2, 25–30 = *The Beginnings of History* (2006), 225–33.

Evans-Pritchard, E. E. 1976. *Witchcraft, Oracles and Magic among the Azande*. Oxford: Oxford University Press.

Fahd, Tawfic 1966/1987. *La Divination arabe*. Leiden: Brill.

Fahd, T. 1997. 'De l'oracle à la prophétie en Arabie', in Heintz 1997, 231–41.

Farhad, M. and Bağci, S. 2010. *Falnama: The Book of Omens*. London: Thames and Hudson.

Feeney, Denis 2007. *Caesar's Calendar: Ancient Time and the Beginnings of History*. Berkeley, CA: University of California Press.

Ferrary, J.-L. 2005. 'Les memoriaux de delegations du sanctuaire oraculaire de Claros et leur chronologie', *CRAI* 2005, 719–65.

Flower, Michael Attyah 2008. *The Seer in Ancient Greece*. Berkeley, CA: University of California Press.

Fontenelle, Bernard le Boyver de 1971. *Histoire des Oracles*, ed. L. Maigron. Paris: Didier (first published 1687).

Fontenrose, Joseph 1978. *The Delphic Oracle*. Berkeley, CA: University of California Press.

Fontenrose, Joseph 1988. *Didyma: Apollo's Oracle, Cult and Companions*. Berkeley, CA: University of California Press.

Forrest, W.G. 1982. *Cambridge Ancient History* III.2, 305–20.

Fowden, Garth 1986. *The Egyptian Hermes: A Historical Approach to the Late Pagan Mind*. Princeton, NJ: Princeton University Press.

Frankfurter, David 1998. *Religion in Roman Egypt*. Berkeley, CA: University of California Press.

Frankfurter, David 2005. 'Late Antique Egypt' in Johnston and Struck 2005.

Frei, Peter 1990. 'Die Götterkulte Lykiens in der Kaiserzeit', *ANRW*, II, 18.3, 1729–1864.

Gasparo, Giulia Sfameni 2002. *Oracoli profeti sibille. Rivelazione e salvezza nel mondo antico*. Rome: LAS.

Girone, Maria 1998. *IAMATA. Guarigioni miracolose di Asclepio in testi epigrafici*. Bari: Levante.

Goldhill, Simon 2009. 'Undoing in Sophoclean Drama: *Lusis* and the Analysis of Irony', *TAPA* 139, 21–52.

Golding, William 1995. *The Double Tongue*. London: Faber & Faber.

Gonzales, Matthew 2005. 'The Oracle and Cult of Ares in Asia Minor', *GRBS* 45, 261–83.

Gordon, P. 1996. *Epicurus in Lycia*. Ann Arbor, MI: University of Michigan Press.

Graf, Fritz 1992. 'An Oracle against Pestilence from a Western Anatolian Town', *ZPE* 92, 267–99.

Graf, Fritz 2005. 'Rolling the dice for an answer', in Johnston and Struck, 51–97.

Graf, Fritz 2007. 'The Oracle and the Image: Returning to Some Oracles from Claros', *ZPE* 161, 113–19.

Graf, Fritz 2009. *Apollo*. London: Routledge.

Green, Peter 2007. *Alexander the Great and the Hellenistic Age*. London: Phoenix.

Gregory, T. 1983. 'Julian and the Last Oracle at Delphi', *GRBS* 24, 355–66.

Guarducci, M. 1974. 'Nuove osservazioni sugli oracoli di Apollo Kareios a Ierapoli nella Frigia', *RFIC* 102, 197–202.

Guarducci, M. 1978. 'Guarigioni Miracolose (Sanationes)', *Epigrafia greca* 4, 143–66.

Guillaumont, François 2006. *Le de divinatione de Cicéron et les théories antiques de la divination*. Brussels: Coll Latomus 298.

Günther, W. 1971. *Das Orakel von Didyma in hellenistischer Zeit*. Istanbuler Mitteilingen Beiheft 4. Tübingen: Wasmuth.

Gurney, O.R. 1952. *The Hittites*. Harmondsworth: Penguin.

Gurney, O.R. 1955. 'The Cuthaean Legend of Naram-Sin', *Anatolian Studies* 5, 80ff.

Guthrie, W.K.C. 1952. *Orpheus and Greek Religion*. London: Methuen; repr. Princeton, NJ: Princeton University Press 1993.

Habicht, Christian 1985. *Pausanias' Guide to Ancient Greece*. Berkeley, CA: University of California Press.

Hadas, Moses 1951. *Aristeas to Philocrates*. New York: Harper.

Hajjar, Y. 1990. 'Divinités oraculaires et rites divinatoires en Syrie et en Phénicie a l'époque Greco-romaine'. *ANRW* II, 18.4, 2236–2320.

Hall, A.S. 1978. 'The Clarian Oracle at Oenoanda', *ZPE* 32, 263–8.

Hamilton, Mary 1906. *Incubation, or the Cure of Disease in Pagan Temples and Christian Churches*. London and St Andrews: W.C. Henderson University Press.

Hammerstaedt, J. 1988. *Die Orakelkritik des Kynikers Oinomaos*. Frankfurt: Beiträge zur klassischen Philologie.

Hammerstaedt, J. 1990. 'Der Kyniker Oinomaos von Gadara', *ANRW* II, 36.4, 2834–65.

Hansen, William 1998. *Anthology of Greek Popular Literature*. Bloomington, IN: Indiana University Press.

Harrison, Thomas 2000. *Divinity and History: The Religion of Herodotus*. Oxford: Oxford University Press.

Harris, William V. 2009. *Dreams and Experience in Classical Antiquity*. Berkeley, CA: University of California Press.

Heinevetter, Franz 1912. 'Würfel- und Buchstabenorakel in Griechenland und Kleinasien'. Diss. Breslau.

Heintz, J.-G. (ed.) 1997. *Oracles et propheties dans l'antiquité*. Paris: Actes du XIVéme Colloque Internationale 1995.

Henrichs, Albert 1978. 'Greek Maenadism from Olympias to Messalina', *HSCP* 82, 121–69.

Herzog, R. 1931. 'Die Wunderheilungen von Epidauros', *Philologus Supplementband* 22.3.

Herzog, R. 1939. 'Der Kampf um den Kult von Menuthis', in *Pisciculi F. Dölger angeboten*, 117–24.

Higbie, Carolyn 2003. *The Lindian Chronicle and the Greek Creation of their Past*. Oxford: Oxford University Press.

Hölbl, Günther 2001. *History of the Ptolemaic Empire*. London: Routledge.

Horowitz W. and Hurowitz V.A. 1992. 'Urim and Thummim in Light of a Psephomancy Ritual from Assur', *JANES* 21, 95–115.

Hughes, Donald J. 1984. 'The Dreams of Alexander the Great', *Journal of Psychohistory* 12, 168–92.

Huson, Paul 2004. *Mystical Origins of the Tarot*. Rochester, VT: Destiny Books.

Ivanov, S.A. 2006. *Holy Fools in Byzantium and Beyond*. Oxford: Oxford University Press.

Jaynes, Julian 1977. *The Origins of Consciousness in the Breakdown of the Bicameral Mind*. Boston: Houghton Mifflin.

Jeffrey, E. (ed.) 1990. *Studies in Malalas*. Sydney: Byzantina Australiensia 6.

Johnson, Aaron P. 2006. *Ethnicity and Argument in Eusebius' Praeparatio Evangelica*. Oxford: Oxford University Press.

Johnson, Aaron P. 2009. 'Arbiter of the Oracular: Reading Religion in Porphyry of Tyre', in A. Cain and N. Lenski (eds), *The Power of Religion in Late Antiquity* (Aldershot: Ashgate), 103–18.

Johnston, Sarah Iles 1990. *Hekate Soteira*. Atlanta, GA: Scholars Press.

Johnston, Sarah Iles 1999. *Restless Dead: Encounters between the Living and the Dead in Ancient Greece*. Berkeley, CA: University of California Press.

Johnston, Sarah Iles 2008. *Ancient Greek Divination*. Oxford: Wiley Blackwell.

Johnston, S.I. and Struck, P. 2005. *Mantike: Studies in Ancient Divination*. Leiden: Brill.

Jones, C.P. 1975. 'An Oracle given to Trajan', *Chiron* 5, 403–6.

Jones, C.P. 1986. *Culture and Society in Lucian*. Cambridge, MA: Harvard University Press.

Jones, C.P. 1998. 'Aelius Aristides and the Asklepieion', in H. Koester (ed.), *Pergamon: Citadel of the Gods*. (Valley Forge, PA: Trinity Press) 63–76.

Jones C.P. 2000. 'The Emperor and the Giant', *Classical Philology* 95, 476–81.

Jones, E.H. 1920. *The Road to En-Dor*. London: John Lane.

Kammenhuber, A. 1976. *Orakelpraxis, Träume und Vorzeichenschau bei den Hethitern*. Heidelberg: C. Winter.

Kapuscinski, Ryszard 2007. *Travels with Herodotus*. London: Penguin.

Keightley, David N. 1985. *Sources of Shang History: The Oracle Bone Inscriptions of Bronze Age China*. Berkeley, CA: University of California Press.

Kirchberg, Jutta 1965. *Die Funktion der Orakel im Werke Herodots*. Göttingen: Hypomnemata 11.

Klingshirn, William 2002. 'Defining the *Sortes Sanctorum*: Gibbon, Du Cange and Early Christian Lot Divination', *Journal of Early Christian Studies* 10, 77–130.

Knox, Bernard 1957. *Oedipus at Thebes*. New Haven, CT: Yale University Press.

Koenen, L. 1968. 'Die Prophezeiungen des Töpfers', *ZPE* 2, 178–200.

Kurke, Leslie 1999. *Coins, Bodies, Games and Gold: The Politics of Meaning in Archaic Greece*. Princeton, NJ: Princeton University Press.

Lachmann, K. 1848. *Die Schriften der römischen Feldmesser* I. Berlin: G. Reimer.

Lajtar, Adam 2006. 'Deir-el-Bahari in the Hellenistic and Roman periods', *Journal of Juristic Papyrology*, Supplement IV. Warsaw: Institute of Archaeology.

Lamoreaux, J. 2002. *The Early Muslim Tradition of Dream Interpretation*. Albany, NY: SUNY Press.

Lane Fox, Robin 1986. *Pagans and Christians*. London: Viking.

Langdon, S. 1914. *Tammuz and Ishtar . . . containing . . . all of the Arbela oracles*. Oxford: Oxford University Press.

Larrington, Carolyne 1996. *The Poetic Edda*, Oxford World's Classics. Oxford: Oxford University Press.

Larson, J. 1995. 'The Corycian Nymphs and the Bee Maidens of the Homeric *Hymn to Hermes*', *GRBS* 36, 341–57.

Larson, J. 2001. *Greek Nymphs: Myth, Cult, Lore*. Oxford: Oxford University Press.

Laufer, B. 1931. 'Inspirational Dreams in Eastern Asia', *Journal of American Folklore* 44, 208–16.

Lawson, J.C. 1910. *Modern Greek Folklore and Ancient Greek Religion*. Cambridge: Cambridge University Press.

Leick, Gwendolyn 2001. *Mesopotamia: The invention of the city*. London: Penguin.

Lesher, J.H. 1978. 'Xenophanes' Scepticism', *Phronesis* 23, 1–31.

Levi, Peter 1971. *Pausanias: Description of Greece*. Harmondsworth: Penguin.

Levin, S. 1989. 'The Old Greek Oracles in Decline', *ANRW* II.18.2, 1599–1649.

Lewis, Naphtali 1976. *The Interpretation of Dreams and Portents*. Toronto and Sarasota: S. Stevens.

Lewy, Hans. 1978. *Chaldaean Oracles and Theurgy*. Paris: Etudes augustiniennes.

Lichtheim, Miriam 1980. *Ancient Egyptian Literature Vol. III: The Late Period*. Berkeley, CA: University of California Press.

LiDonnici, Lynn 1995. *The Epidaurian Miracle Inscriptions*. Atlanta, GA: Scholars Press.

Liebeschuetz, W.H.G. 1979. *Continuity and Change in Roman Religion*. Oxford: Oxford University Press.

Lightfoot, Jane 2003. *Lucian, On the Syrian Goddess*. Oxford: Oxford University Press.

Lightfoot, Jane 2007. *The Sibylline Oracles*. Oxford: Oxford University Press.

Livrea, Enrico 1998. 'Sull' iscrizione teosofica di Enoanda', *ZPE* 122, 90–6.

Lloyd, G.E.R. 1978. *Hippocratic Writings*. Harmondsworth: Penguin.

Lloyd, G.E.R. 2002. *The Ambitions of Curiosity: Understanding the World in Ancient Greece and China*. Cambridge: Cambridge University Press.

Lloyd-Jones, H. 1966. 'Oracles for Apollo Kareios', *Maia* 18, 263–4.

Lloyd-Jones, Hugh 1976. 'The Delphic Oracle', *Greece and Rome* 23, 60–73.

Loewe, Michael and Blacker, Carmen 1981. *Divination and Oracles.* London: Allen & Unwin.

Long, A.A. and Sedley, D.N. 1987. *The Hellenistic Philosophers.* Cambridge: Cambridge University Press.

Lupu, Eran 2005. *Greek Sacred Law.* Leiden: Brill.

McCabe, Donald E. and Plunkett, Mark A. 1985. *Didyma Inscriptions: Text and List.* Princeton, NJ: Institute of Advanced Study.

Mackay, Theodora S. 1990. 'Major Sanctuaries of Pamphylia and Cilicia', *ANRW* II.18.3. 2045–2129.

McQueen, J.G. 1986. *The Hittites.* London: Thames and Hudson.

Malinowski, Bronislaw 1948. *Magic, Science and Religion and Other Essays.* New York: Anchor.

Maltomini, F. 1995. 'P.Lond. 121 (= *PGM* VII), 1–221: Homeromanteion', *ZPE* 106, 107–22.

Manetti, Giovanni 1993. *Theories of the Sign in Classical Antiquity.* Bloomington, IN: Indiana University Press.

Mango, Cyril 1960. 'The Legend of Leo the Wise', *Zbornik Radova Vizantološkog Instituta/Recueil des travaux de l'Institut d'Études Byzantines* 6, 59–93.

Markopoulos, A. 1985. 'Kedrenos, Ps-Symeon and the Last Oracle at Delphi', *GRBS* 26, 207–10; 1997, 155–218.

Mastronarde, Donald (ed.) 1994. *Euripides' Phoenissae.* Cambridge: Cambridge University Press.

Maurizio, Lisa 1995. 'Anthropology and Spirit Possession: A Reconsideration of the Pythia's Role at Delphi', *JHS* 105, 69–86.

Melfi, M. 2007. *I Santuari di Asclepio in Grecia* I. Rome: Bretschneider.

Merkelbach R. 1973. 'Zwei Texte aus dem Serapeum zu Thessalonike 2. Ein Missionswunder', *ZPE* 10, 49–54.

Merkelbach, R. 1975. 'Klarisches Orakel aus Nikomedeia', *ZPE* 18, 100.

Merkelbach, R. 1977. *Die Quellen des griechischen Alexanderroman* (2nd edition). Munich: Beck.

Merkelbach, Reinhold and Stauber, Josef 1996. 'Die Orakel des Apollon von Klaros. Epigraphica Anatolica' 27, 1–53 = Merkelbach, *Philologica: Ausgewählte Kleine Schriften.*

Merkelbach, Reinhold and Stauber, Josef. 1998. *Steinepigramme aus dem griechischen Osten.* Stuttgart and Leipzig: Teubner.

Metzler, D. 1990. 'Der Seher Mopsos auf den Münzen der Stadt Mallos', *Kernos* 3, 235–49.

Mikalson, Jon 1983. *Athenian Popular Religion.* Chapel Hill, NC: University of North Carolina Press.

Milne J.G. 1941. 'Kolophon and its Coinage'. New York: Numismatic Notes and Monographs.

Mitchell, Stephen 1999. 'The Cult of Theos Hypsistos between Pagans, Jews, and Christians', in Athanassiadi and Frede (eds) 1999, 81–148.

Mithen, Steven 1996. *The Prehistory of the Mind: A Search for the Origins of Religion, Art and Science.* London: Phoenix.

Momigliano, Arnaldo 1988. 'From the Pagan to the Christian Sibyl: Prophecy as History of Religion', in *Uses of Greek and Latin: Historical Essays,* ed. A.C. Dionisotti, A. Grafton and J. Kraye. London: Warburg Institute Surveys and Texts.

Moreau, A. 1990. 'Déjouer l'oracle ou la précaution inutile', *Kernos* 3, 261–79.

Morgan, Catherine 1990. *Athletes and Oracles.* Cambridge: Cambridge University Press.

Morgan, J.R. 1997. *Heliodorus, Ethiopian Story.* London: Everyman.

Motta, Beatrice 2008. *Il Contra Fatum di Gregorio di Nissa nel dibattito tardo-antico sul fatalismo e sul determinismo.* Pisa/Rome: Fabrizio Serra Editore.

Muller, H. 1987. 'Ein Heilungsbericht aus dem Asklepieion von Pergamon', *Chiron* 17, 193–233.

Needham, Joseph 1954. *Science and Religion in China.* Cambridge: Cambridge University Press.

Nesselrath, H.G. 1999. 'Dodona Siwa und Herodot', *Mus. Helv.* 56, 1–14.

Nice, A. 2005. 'The Reputation of the "Mantis" Aristander', *Acta Classica* 18, 87–102.

Nilsson, M.P. 1951. *Cults, Myths, Oracles and Politics in Ancient Greece*. London: Lund Humphries.

Nissen, Cécile 2001. 'Un oracle medical de Sarpédon à Séleucie du Calycadnos', *Kernos* 14, 111–31.

Nock, A.D. 1928. 'Oracles théologiques', *REA* 30, 280–90 = *Collected papers* I, 160–8.

Nock, A.D. 1934. 'A Vision of Mandulis Aion', *Harvard Theological Review* 27, 53–104 = *Collected Papers* I.357–400.

Nollé, J. 1987. 'Südkleinasiatische Losorakel in der römischen Kaiserzeit', *Antike Welt* 18.3, 41–9.

Nollé, J. 2001. *Side* II. Bonn: R. Habelt.

Nollé, J. 2007. *Kleinasiatische Losorakel*. Munich: Beck.

Oberhelman, S. 1991. *The Oneirocriticon of Achmet*. Lubbock, TX: Texas Tech University Press.

Oberhelman, S.M. 1993. 'Dreams in Greco-Roman Medicine', *ANRW* 37.1, 121–56.

Oesterheld, Christian 2008. *Göttliche Botschaften für zweifelnde Menschen. Pragmatik und Orientierungsleistung der Apollon-Orakel von Klaros und Didyma in hellenistisch-römischer Zeit*. Göttingen: Vandenhoeck & Ruprecht.

Ogden, Daniel 2001. *Greek and Roman Necromancy*. Princeton, NJ: Princeton University Press.

Ogden, Daniel 2007. *In Search of the Sorcerer's Apprentice*. Cardiff: Classical Press of Wales.

O'Meara, J. 1959. *Porphyry's Philosophy from Oracles in Augustine*. Paris: Etudes augustiniennes.

Oppenheim, Alan 1956. *The Interpretation of Dreams in the Ancient Near East: With a Translation of the Assyrian Dream Book*. Philadelphia, PA: Transactions of the American Philosophical Association.

Oppenheim, Alan 1964. *Ancient Mesopotamia*. Chicago: Chicago University Press.

Osiek, C. 1999. *The Shepherd of Hermas*. Minneapolis, MN: Fortress Press.

Page, D.L. 1941. *Select Papyri* III. Harvard, MA: Loeb Classical Library.

Palmer, Martin and Ramsay, Jay, with Man-Ho Kwok 2009. *The Kuan Yin Chronicles: The Myths and Prophecies of the Chinese Goddess of Compassion*. Charlottesville, VA: Hampton Roads.

Parke, H.W. and Wormell, R.O.W. 1956. *The Delphic Oracle*. Oxford: Oxford University Press.

Parke, H.W. 1967a. *The Oracles of Zeus*. Oxford: Blackwell.

Parke, H.W. 1967b. *Greek Oracles*. London: Hutchinson.

Parke, H.W. 1985a. *The Oracles of Apollo in Asia Minor*. London: Croom Helm.

Parke H.W. 1985b. 'The Massacre of the Branchidae', *JHS* 105, 59–68.

Parke, H.W. 1986. 'The Temple of Apollo at Didyma: The Building and its Function', *JHS* 106, 121–31.

Parke, H.W. 1988. *Sibyls and Sibylline Prophecy in Classical Antiquity*. London: Routledge.

Parker, Richard A. 1962. *A Saite Oracle Papyrus from Thebes*. Providence, RI: Brown University Press.

Parker, R.C.T. 1983. *Miasma: Pollution and Purification in Early Greek Religion*. Oxford: Oxford University Press.

Parker, R.C.T. 1985/2000. 'Greek States and Greek Oracles', in *CRUX*, 298–326; also in R. Buxton (ed.), *Oxford Readings in Greek Religion* (2000).

Parker, R.C.T. 1996. *Athenian Religion: A History*. Oxford: Oxford University Press.

Parker, R.C.T. 2005. *Polytheism and Society at Athens*. Oxford: Oxford University Press.

Parpola, S. 1997. *Assyrian Prophecies*. Helsinki: Helsinki University Press.

Parsons, Peter 2007. *City of the Sharp-Nosed Fish: Greek Lives in Roman Egypt*. London: Weidenfeld & Nicolson.

Patrides, C.A. 1965. 'The Cessation of the Oracles; The History of a Legend', *Modern Language Review* 60, 500–7.

Pearcy, Lee T. 1988. 'Theme, Dream and Narrative: Reading the *Sacred Tales* of Aelius Aristides', *TAPA* 118, 377–91.

Perdrizet, Paul 1903. 'Une inscription d'Anatolie qui reproduit un oracle d'Alexander d'Abonuteichos', *CRAI*, 62–6.

Phlegon of Tralles 1996. *Book of Marvels*, tr. William Hansen. Exeter: University of Exeter Press.

Piérart, Marcel 2003. 'The Common Oracle of the Milesians and the Argives', in Derow and Parker 2003, 275–96.

Pinault, Jodi Rubin 1992. *Hippocratic Lives and Legends*. Leiden: Brill.

Pollard, John 1982. *Virgil and the Sibyl*. Exeter: 14th Jackson Knight memorial lecture (1981).

Potter, D.S. 1990. *Prophecy and History in the Crisis of the Roman Empire*. Oxford: Oxford University Press.

Potter, D.S. 1990. 'The Sibyl in the Greek world', *JRA* 3, 471–83.

Potter, D.S. 1994. *Prophets and Emperors*. Cambridge, MA: Harvard University Press.

Powell, J.U. 1925. *Collectanea Alexandrina*. Oxford: Oxford University Press.

Propp, Vladimir 1968. *Morphology of the Folktale* (2nd edition). Austin, TX: University of Texas Press.

Propp, Vladimir 1975. *Edipo nella luce del folklore*. Milan: Einaudi.

Rehm, A. 1940. 'ΜΝΗΣΘΗ', *Philologus* 94, 1–30.

Rehm, A. and Harder, R. 1958. *Didyma II: die Inschriften*. Berlin: Mann.

Rhinehart, Luke 1998. *The Dice Man*. New York: Overlook Press (original edition 1971).

Richer, N. 1998. *Les ephores*. Paris: Sorbonne.

Riethmüller, J.W. 2005. *Asklepios: Heiligtümer und Kulte*. Heidelberg: Verlag Archäologie und Geschichte.

Rigsby, K.J. 2001. 'Founding a Sarapeum', *GRBS* 42, 117–24.

Roach, John. 2001. 'Delphic Oracle's Lips May Have Been Loosened by Gas Vapours', *National Geographic News*, 14 August 2001.

Robert, Louis 1936. 'Decrets de Kolophon: Études d'epigraphie grecque XLVI', *Revue philologique* 10, 158–68.

Robert, Louis 1937. *Etudes anatoliennes*. Paris: Institute français d'archéologie de Stamboul.

Robert, Louis 1948a. 'Sur l'oracle d'Apollon Koropaios', *Hellenica* 5, 16–28.

Robert, Louis 1948b. 'Inscriptions grecques de Lydie', *Hellenica* 6.

Robert, Louis 1960. 'Apparitions divins a Milet', *Hellenica* 11/12, 543–6.

Robert, Louis 1966. *Documents de l'Asie Mineure meridionale*. Geneva: Droz.

Robert, Louis 1968. 'Trois oracles de la Theosophie et un prophète', *CRAI*, 568–99 = *Opera Minora Selecta* v, 584–615.

Robert, Louis 1971. 'Un oracle gravé a Oinoanda', *CRAI*, 597–619 = *Opera Minora Selecta* v.617–39.

Robert, Louis 1973. 'De Cilicie à Messine et à Plymouth avec deux inscriptions grecques errantes', *Journal des savants*, 161–211.

Robert, Louis 1978. 'Sur un Apollon oraculaire a Chypre', *CRAI*, 338–44 = *Opera Minora Selecta* v.640–6.

Robert, Louis 1980. 'Lucien en son temps', *A travers l'Asie mineure*, 393–436.

Robert, Louis 1981. 'Le serpent Glycon d'Abonuteuichos à Athènes et Artemis d'Ephèse à Rome', *CRAI* 513–55 = *Opera Minora Selecta* v.747–69.

Rohmer, Sax 1914. *The Romance of Sorcery*. London: Methuen.

Rostowzev, M. 1920. 'Epiphaneiai', *Klio* 16, 17–20.

Roussel, P. 1915–16. *Cultes egyptiens à Delos: du IIIe au Ier siècle avant JC*. Paris:

Said, Suzanne 1997. 'Oracles et devins dans le roman grec', in Heintz 1997, 367–403.

Sandbach, F.H. 1975. *The Stoics*. London: Chatto & Windus.

Sasson, Jack 1983. 'Mari Dreams', *JAOS* 103, 283–93.

Schallenberg, Magnus 2008. *Freiheit und Determinismus. Ein philosophischer Kommentar zu Ciceros Schrift De fato*. Berlin: de Gruyter.

Schenke, H.M. 1963. 'Orakelwesen im alten Ägypten', *Das Altertum*, 9, 71ff.

Schofield, Malcolm 1986. 'Cicero for and against Divination', *JRS* 76, 47–65.

Sedley, David 2007. *Creationism and its Critics in Antiquity*. Berkeley, CA: University of California Press.

Shapiro, H.A. 1990. 'Oracle-mongers in Pisistratid Athens', *Kernos* 3, 335–45.

Sharples, R.W. 1983. *Alexander of Aphrodisias on Fate*. London: Duckworth.

Shaughnessy, Edward L. 1996. *I Ching. The Classic of Changes: The First English Translation of the Newly Discovered 2nd Century BC Mawangdui Texts*. New York: Ballantine.

Sineux, Pierre 2007. *Amphiaraos. Guerrier, devin et guerisseur*. Paris: Belles Lettres.

Sloterdijk, Peter 1985. *Der Zauberbaum*. Berlin: Suhrkamp.

Smith, Richard J. 1991. *Fortune-tellers and Philosophers: Divination in Traditional Chinese Society*. Boulder, CO: Westview Press.

Snell, Bruno 1948. *The Discovery of the Mind*. New York: Harper.

Solomon, Jon (ed.) 1994. *Apollo: Origins and Influences*. Tucson, AZ: University of Arizona Press.

Sourvinou-Inwood, C. 1987. 'Myth as History: The Previous Owners of the Delphic Oracle', in J. Bremmer (ed.), *The Interpretation of Greek Myths*. London: Croom Helm, 215–41.

Speyer, W. 1970. *Bücherfunde in der Glaubenswerdung der Antike*. Göttingen: Hypomnemata 24.

Stambaugh, J. 1972. *Sarapis under the Early Ptolemies*. Leiden: Brill.

Stark, Freya 1955. *Ionia: A quest*. London: John Murray.

Stoneman, Richard. 1992. 'Oriental Motifs in the Alexander Romance', *Antichthon* 26, 95–113.

Stoneman, Richard 1999. 'A Crazy Enterprise: German Translators of Sophocles, from Opitz to Boeckh', in Jasper Griffin (ed.), *Sophocles Revisited*. Oxford: Oxford University Press.

Stoneman, Richard 2007. *Il Romanzo di Alessandro*, vol. I. Milan: Fondazione Lorenzo Valla.

Stramaglia, Antonio 1992. 'Il leone e l'indovinello: *IG* IV² 1, 123, 8–21 e Giamblico, *Storie babilonesi* 3 e 21', *ZPE* 91, 53–9.

Struck, Peter 2005 in Johnston and Struck 2005.

Taggar-Cogen, A. 2002. 'The Casting of Lots among the Hittites in the Light of Ancient Near Eastern Parallels', *JANES* 29, 97–103.

Tambiah, S. 1990. *Magic, Science, Religion and the Scope of Rationality*. Cambridge: Cambridge University Press.

Thomas, Keith 1971. *Religion and the Decline of Magic*. Harmondsworth: Penguin.

Thomson, S. 1955–8. *Motif-Index of Folk Literature*. Copenhagen: Rosenlied & Bagger.

Ugolini, Gherardo 1995. *Untersuchungen zur Figur des Sehers Teiresias*. Tübingen: Narr.

Van Dale, Anton 1700. *De Oraculis veterum ethnicorum*. Amsterdam: Apud Henricum & Viduam Theodori Boom.

Van der Eijk, Philip 2005. *Medicine and Philosophy in Later Antiquity*. Cambridge: Cambridge University Press.

Van der Horst, P.W. 1998. 'Sortes: Sacred Books as Instant Oracles in Late Antiquity', in L.V. Rutgers et al. (eds), *The Use of Sacred Books in the Ancient World*. Louvain: Peeters, 143–73.

Van Lieshout 1980. *Greeks on Dreams*. Utrecht: HES.

Van Straten, F.T. 1976. 'Daikrates' Dream: A Votive Relief from Kos, and Some Other *kat'onar* Dedications', *Bulletin Antike Beschaving* 51, 3–18.

Vernant, J.P. 1974 (ed.). *Divination et Rationalité*. Paris: Sevil.

Von Arnim, J. 1923. *Stoicorum veterum fragmenta*. Leipzig and Berlin: Teubner.

Walde, Christine 2001. *Antike Traumdeutung und moderne Traumforschung*. Düsseldorf: Artemis & Winkler.

Wallace-Hadrill, D.S. 1960. *Eusebius of Caesarea*. London: Mowbray.

Wallis, R.T. 1972. *Neo-Platonism*. London: Duckworth.

Wardle, D. 2006. *Cicero: On Divination Book I*. Oxford: Clarendon Press.

Weinreich, Otto 1931. 'Imhotep-Asklepios und die Griechen: zu Pap Oxy 1381', *Aegyptus* 11, 17–22.

Weis, Bertold K. 1983. *Das Orakelheiligtum von Didyma*. Ludwigsburg: Karawane.

Weitzmann, Kurt 1974. 'Representations of Hellenistic Oracles in Byzantine MSS', *Mélanges Mansel*, 397–410.

Welles, C.B. 1962. 'The Discovery of Serapis and the Foundation of Alexandria', *Historia* 11, 271–98.

West, M.L. 1967. 'Oracles of Apollo Kareios', *ZPE* 1, 183–7.

West, M.L. 1993. *Greek Lyric Poetry*. Oxford: World's Classics.

Whittaker, C.R. 1965. 'The Delphic Oracle', *HThR* 58, 21–47.

Wickkiser, Bronwen L. 2008. *Asklepios, Medicine, and the Politics of Healing in Fifth-Century Greece*. Baltimore, MD: Johns Hopkins University Press.

Wilhelm, R. 1951. *I Ching*. London: Routledge & Kegan Paul.

Wilkinson, K. 2010. 'A Greek Ancestor of the Medieval *Sortes Sanctorum*', paper delivered at APA meeting, Anaheim, CA, January 2010.

Windisch, H. 1929. *Die Orakel des Hystaspes*. Amsterdam: Verhandelingen der Koninklijke Akademie der Wetenschappen, Afdeling Letterkunde n.r. d. 28 no.3.

Winkler, J.J. 1982. 'The Mendacity of Kalasiris', *YCS* 27, 93–158.

Wiseman T.P. 2008. *Unwritten Rome*. Exeter: University of Exeter Press.

Wolff, Gustav 1856. *Porphyrius de philosophia ex oraculis haurienda*. Berlin: J. Springer.

Wood, Michael 2004. *The Road to Delphi: The Life and Afterlife of Oracles*. London: Chatto & Windus.

Woodhouse, C.M. 1986. *Gemistos Plethon: The Last of the Hellenes*. Oxford: Clarendon Press.

Index